H. E. SAWYER

I AM THE
DARK TOURIST

TRAVELS TO THE DARKEST SITES ON EARTH

HEADPRESS

CONTENTS

Colour plates between pages 136 and 137

FOREWORD

by Dylan Harris

CEO and founder of Lupine Travel

ON MY FIRST VISIT TO AUSCHWITZ IN 2002, I WAS TAKEN ABACK even before I entered the gates. I was shocked but not in the way one expects to be, having travelled with the perhaps naïve expectation that the place would be a museum piece, remaining exactly as it was when liberated in 1945. The last thing I expected was a visitors centre, a cafeteria serving dinner options, and a noisy reception area pushing audio guides onto visitors. It felt crass and commercialised. This wasn't the way it should be.

So I thought.

But wandering around the site I became overwhelmed with grief. I saw the piles of personal belongings, the children's graffiti inside the Birkenau prisoner huts, the Death Wall, the cells, and the gas chambers. The magnitude of this grief hit home in a way I hadn't felt before, despite the many books I'd read and documentaries I'd watched on Auschwitz.

This was my first encounter with 'Dark Tourism', and, contrary to my impression on arrival, the importance of the site was clear to me. A visit to Auschwitz should be on the school curriculum, in order to educate children to the horrors of the past and thus possibly avoid them occurring again. What I'd initially perceived as commercialism, I now considered practical, in making the site accessible to as many people as possible.

I was to visit several other dark tourist sites. A trip to Chernobyl in 2006 put me on the path to setting up Lupine Travel, a tour provider that would, over time, focus partly on 'dark sites' and 'dark states' around the world.

In 2011 I was offered the chance to feature tours to Fukushima. I considered the possibility for several weeks before turning it down. The subject of dark tourism wasn't as cut and dried as I'd initially thought. While there can be an educational aspect to visiting a dark site, there are also moral and ethical considerations. For instance, what would be an acceptable timeframe between events that put a site on the map and the arrival of the first tourists? Could I justify sending in tour groups so soon after a catastrophe such as this, snapping photos of the destruction and sharing them on social media? In this instance I could not.

I felt it disingenuous to try to market trips to Fukushima as educational only

The gatehouse of Auschwitz II–Birkenau. Photo: Ron Porter

a few months after the nuclear disaster there. It was morbid. The wounds were still raw. People's lives had been devastated and they were still dealing with the pain and loss.

This was my first inkling of the huge dilemma of dark tourism, and the issues that face dark sites around the world. Each site had to be taken individually and evaluated on its own terms. Some of them I would feel to be an acceptable and worthy destination, others I wouldn't.

But then what gives me the authority to decide? Another realisation is that there are a multitude of reasons why any one person visits a particular site. Many people supported the reasoning behind my rejection of Fukushima while others are incredulous that I should have turned it down, convinced that there is no better time than immediately post-event for a true impression of a place. This juggling act, between moral reason and the individual's expectation, continues to this day.

I first encountered the author when he was looking to acquire permits to visit Chernobyl. On his return he produced an engaging article describing the trip and the background to the disaster. I took to his writing style immediately; the seamless mix of cultural and historical references transported me back to Chernobyl, and back in time.

We later travelled to Africa together, across Ethiopia and Somalia, including a riotous attempt to visit abandoned warships from the Somalian civil war.

The book is a testament to Aitch's knowledge and passion for this type of tourism. It covers every facet of the subject and gives a fascinating insight into its history, and what attracts people to these sites. It also provides contrast, from the 9/11 Memorial, with its exorbitant entry fees and tacky souvenirs, to Aberfan, where tourism is discouraged.

One of the most regular questions I am asked in my line of work is why people want to visit these types of places. There is no simple answer. The subject is too complicated for that. For anyone who asks in future, I'll point them in the direction of this book. There's no better way of gaining a deeper understanding of the subject.

In Memoriam

Through Light, Dark and Shade
In My Thoughts Every Step of the Way

Pam's Boy

18th June 2018

GOING DARKER

T HE BEGGAR IS FIRST TO ARRIVE, SPORTING A COOL BEANIE. HE retrieves the shabby grey scarf that staked his pitch, drapes it around his shoulders, and sits, cross-legged, empty Styrofoam cup in hand, to complete the look. Behind him, bathed in early evening sunlight, the Whitechapel art gallery, a KFC, and the Cashino amusement arcade. He catches my eye, and we exchange knowing smiles. His trap is set and about to be sprung.

Within moments he is lost in the melee of legs as the tourists congregate from all directions. Some look ready to tackle mountains, sporting North Face apparel and bulging day packs, but there are also middle-aged couples, learned fathers with their taller sons, a man in an Hawaiian shirt sporting a chinstrap

beard, and girlfriends in celebrity shades, who capture their first selfie of the evening. Then Phillip, our guide, arrives; baseball hat, cheeky cherubic smile, Dalmatian print shirt, and a pair of trainers that have weathered the relentless onslaught of the Whitechapel cobbles.

It's a Jack the Ripper walking tour of London's East End, hosted by a credible stand-in for the *League of Gentlemen*'s Legz Akimbo Theatre Company. What were you expecting: cape, top hat, and a surgical bag bristling with knives?

Phillip takes my tenner, and marks his register until we are all present and correct. A few stragglers have arrived on the speculative off chance of a place, however we are a full group of thirty. Our guide points them in the direction of a sombre figure under a bowler hat and overcoat, standing sentient across the road. This Kiss of Death is also running a Ripper tour, starting in five minutes time.

Now Phillip captures our attention with a high pitched screech, then conspiratorially beckons us in to set the scene. He informs us we will be crossing roads, that some of the streets and alleyways on this evening's adventure are narrow, so our consideration in leaving room for the locals to pass us by would be appreciated. Then we are off, an expectant schoolish gaggle, exchanging

Groups on the Jack the Ripper walking tour, Hanbury Street, Spitafields.

slightly embarrassed smiles, funnelling into the tiny passage that opens up into Gunthorpe Street, and the site of tonight's first victim, Martha Tabram, who was murdered on 7th August 1888.

We gather round an innocuous set of locked wire gates to a car park, and Phillip engages us with an anecdote about the man who lives up ahead, who occasionally ambushes the tour groups with shouted words of encouragement, the second inevitably being "Off!"

Using a laser pointer, Phillip focuses our gaze halfway up a wall, past the gates, where the body was found, on a landing inside a tenement block. We'll have to use our imagination, because that particular building has long since disappeared to London's eternal development. Our guide shares his painstaking research, producing laminated photographs from his courier bag, of both victim and crime scene, as they were at the time. The photos are offered face down, with a warning that the post-mortem image may be too graphic for some. We pass them round and naturally everyone has a good look, as Phillip continues to paint a vivid picture of Victorian Whitechapel, profiling the police and the prostitutes, and dispelling the seemingly endless myths of Ripper lore. The evening is already proving to be both educational and entertaining. Suddenly, without warning, it becomes revelatory;

"Because, let's face it, you've all come to see where the prostitutes were — MURRR — DAAARRRDDD!"

I cannot believe my luck. *Schadenfreude.* There's noticeable discomfort within the audience, a shuffling of feet and an unconvincing murmur of denial. Some look to their shoes, as if salvation lies upon the uppers, and I follow suit, in truth to mask my delight.

Phillip has ratcheted himself into full pantomime mode:

"OH! YES! — YOU! — HAAAAVE!'

To the jugular, with an incisive blade of insight, a posse of 'dark tourists', their ghoulish behaviour impaled, their ulterior motive exposed. Why are we here if not to see the actual spot where a bloated, stumpy, middle-aged streetwalker was repeatedly stabbed to death over a century ago?

THE EVOCATIVE TERM, 'DARK TOURISM', IS CREDITED TO DR JOHN Lennon and Professor Malcolm Foley of Glasgow's Caledonian University, with their 1996 academic paper, 'JFK and Dark Tourism: A Fascination with Assassination', and their subsequent book, *Dark Tourism: The Attraction of Death and Disaster*, published in 2000.

The phenomenon is also referred to as 'Thanatourism', derived from the Ancient Greek word 'Thanatos', the personification of death, articulated in Professor Tony Seaton's 1996 paper, 'Guided by the Dark: From Thanatopsis to Thanatourism', where the tourist is "motivated by the desire for actual or symbolic encounters with death."

Dr Philip Stone, Executive Director of the Institute for Dark Tourism

Research, described the term as, "the act of travel, whether intentional or otherwise, to sites of death, destruction or the seemingly macabre."

'Dark sites', the destination of the dark tourist, are diverse in nature and widespread in location, being found on every continent; one might consider the ill-fated Captain Scott's hut in Antarctica as a dark site. They are even found below the waves, in the form of shipwrecks.

Fortunately, as with this evening's excursion, many of them are very accessible, organised, and affordable. The Jack the Ripper tours run nightly, with tourists chaperoned through the very streets where the most notorious serial killer of all time stalked his prey.

Although the Ripper's manor was relatively small, and London-centric from the perspective of dark tourism providers, this has not deterred other companies, who provide something in a similar vein, such as ghost tours, which can be experienced in cities throughout the British Isles, including York, Edinburgh, Manchester, Liverpool, Chester, Dublin, Oxford, and Leicester.

One enterprise, based in Nottingham, offers overnighters in the now disused Towers Asylum, and weekend getaways to castles in Transylvania. Run by dedicated paranormal investigators and mediums, they employ no actors, but utilise state-of-the-art ghost hunting equipment, which can detect subtle variations in temperature, and sounds inaudible to the human ear. Their website warns potential customers that there is a strong behavioural policy; everyone attending will be doing so for the "right reason", although this reason remains undefined. However they will "evict anybody" who presumably messes about at the back, jeopardising the enjoyment of everyone else. This policy, they state, "is always enforced."

The seaside town of Whitby, North Yorkshire, has totally embraced its dark literary connections. The town was a setting for part of Bram Stoker's novel *Dracula*, and now hosts the biannual Whitby Goth Weekend, a festival that contributes over £1m to the local economy.

War and atrocity museums, former prisons, execution sites, battlefields, slavery heritage sites, and cemeteries are all likely destinations for both the committed and casual dark tourist.

Family-orientated dark adventures are also available, such as the Chamber of Horrors at Madame Tussauds, although it is suggested that the exhibits may not be suitable for young children, or pregnant women. After a renovation in the mid 1990s, the basement waxworks occasionally come to life, with actors playing the ghouls. This theatrical development may be in response to the rival flagship attraction from Merlin Entertainment, The London Dungeon, which has evolved from macabre museum to full-blown camp-it-up gore-fest, laden with gallows humour, special effects, rides, and audience participation. Merlin has eight dungeons throughout the UK, Germany, and The Netherlands, tapping into the public appetite for the macabre. The longevity of Tussauds' Chamber of Horrors, a London fixture since 1835, illustrates that this dark fascination appears constant, regardless of how times and attitudes have changed.

There are numerous dark exhibitions and museums, many housed within the very institutions where they gained their notoriety, such as the penitentiary of Alcatraz in San Francisco Bay, which can be toured day or night. As a tourist the only way you are escaping incarceration is through the gift shop, which is also available online. It sells everything from baseballs to stripy prison uniform oven mitts, and the obligatory American souvenir, the shot glass.

While such exploitative commercialism might seem inappropriate, given the draconian practices employed whilst a functioning prison (including sensory depravation for troublemakers, and enforced silence in the early years that reportedly drove several inmates insane), the tour itself is consistently reviewed as the best San Francisco has to offer. I didn't care for the personalised souvenir photograph, available to purchase at the conclusion of the tour, but was totally absorbed by the audio guide, where testimonies from former guards and inmates, supplemented by appropriate sound effects, brought incarceration on 'The Rock' to life.

For something slightly more macabre, there is anatomist Gunther von Hagens' travelling exhibition, 'Body Worlds,' where real corpses have been preserved through a technique known as plastination. The anatomy on display provides the general public with an insight into the human body usually reserved for the medical profession. Initially exhibited in Tokyo in 1995, it arrived in London in 2002, and ran for six months in the Old Truman Brewery on Brick Lane. Although controversial, over forty million worldwide have rolled up to view von Hagens' travelling cadavers. While this dark-show may blur the lines between education and entertainment, it affords objectivity, seeing what we all look like, stripped of skin and hair.

There are some destinations that cater for a niche market, for those looking for something more specific, and darker still.

Death and murder sites are a continual source of tourist footfall. Some are globally renowned, such as Dealey Plaza, site of the assassination of JFK. Originally devoid of specific tourist infrastructure, it was subsequently developed to accommodate those who came in large numbers, uninvited and unannounced. The Texas School Book Depository, now known as the Dallas County Administration Building, contains a museum, relating to the life, death, and legacy of President Kennedy, and the road outside is marked where the bullets struck their target whilst riding in his open top limousine. One can only suppose the authorities pinpointed the hit to prevent further fatalities, with assassination aficionados standing in the middle of a busy road, lining themselves up with the sixth floor window in question.

Fortunately since 1999, there has been a live camera feed from the sniper's nest, and indeed, while writing this, I have the live 'EarthCam' in-screen,

Former attic residence of serial killer Dennis Nilsen, Muswell Hill.

enabling me to watch tourists, waiting for a break in the traffic, so they can run into the road to be photographed standing on the requisite X marks the spot. This happens with metronomic regularity, day in day out, as if it were on a bucket list.

While tourists can be conveniently blamed for encouraging the authorities to facilitate and sanction their presence, as with Dealey Plaza, this is not always the case. There are those who visit sites where there are no facilities, provisions, or glossy publicity in place to encourage them.

Such an example would be 23 Cranley Gardens, a well-appointed three storey semi-detached house, internally divided into four flats, in leafy Muswell Hill, an extremely desirable suburb of north London. From the pavement the property appears unremarkable; white walls, decorative mock Tudor studwork, wheelie bins, and a spacious porch. The only thing that disappoints is the roof, where interlocking tiles have replaced the original slate that graces its neighbours. And the fact that serial killer Dennis Nilsen was arrested here, in his attic flat, with the dismembered body parts of some of his victims still in the wardrobe.

Nilsen had befriended and murdered at least twelve, possibly as many as fifteen men, mostly the homeless, between 1978 and his arrest in 1983. Although the majority of the killings took place at his previous address, 195 Melrose Avenue, Cricklewood, it is 23D Cranley Gardens that attracts the 'House of Horrors' tabloid tag. This may have something to do with the fact that Nilsen inhabited the attic, which implies 'sinister', rather than the ground floor flat he previously rented in Melrose Avenue. Or perhaps it is because it's impossible to capture a decent photograph of the property in Cricklewood, due to a tree on the pavement, which spoils the view.

Thoughtfully, at least two of the tabloids ran stories about the sale of 23D, in 2015, including photos of the interior, which has been extensively refurbished since Nilsen vacated to serve life imprisonment. One article highlighted the estate agent's request for prospective buyers to research the history of the property. It fetched the asking price of £300,000; an absolute steal given the location, with 25% off the market value due to its dark association.

So although there is no 'tour', the exteriors of both sites can be viewed, albeit surreptitiously, with a London Underground One Day Travelcard.

Whilst affluent residents may take umbrage at dark tourists indulging themselves with the stigma on their doorstep, some neighbourhoods are welcoming, as evidenced by the rise of the favela tour. Established in the slums of South America and the townships of South Africa, escorted tour groups are taken to see how the other half truly lives. Although considered voyeuristic, with the haves walking through the rustic doorways of the have nots, to witness poverty and deprivation before being returned to their luxurious hotels, these communities have aligned themselves with this developing brand of dark tourism.

I joined a tour in Peru, to visit Lima's Villa El Salvador, the second largest shanty town in South America, home to nearly half a million inhabitants and an unemployment rate estimated at 75%. The guide was raised there, and regularly returned with tourists in tow. The community benefits directly, with part of the tour fee funding their projects, and everyone on the bus contributed to buy practical gifts from the local market, such as chickens and the feed to rear them, that were distributed directly under the guide's supervision.

We were advised in advance to wear colourful clothing for the tour, as there existed genuine fear that 'outsiders' might try to steal children, and locals associated tourists in dark clothing with bad intentions. The tour company employed a policeman to accompany us for the duration, for the community's peace of mind as much as our own. We were also informed that, especially during the colder months, we might see bodies being removed. While the favela tour may have its critics, it does provide a means of direct contact between two diverse groups, and leaves an indelible imprint in the consciousness of the haves, and dollars that can be stretched a very long way in the hands of the have nots.

S WITH A WISH LIST ON SAFARI, THERE IS ALSO A 'BIG FIVE' within dark tourism.

The National September 11 Memorial and Museum in New York, commemorating the multiple terrorist attacks on the United States of America in 2001, and the six victims of the World Trade Center bombing of 1993. The site comprises two square waterfall pools where the Twin Towers stood, a memorial plaza, and a subterranean museum. In the first two years since the museum officially opened, in May 2014, over five million people have paid the $24 admission fee.

The exclusion zone surrounding the ruined nuclear power plant at Chernobyl, in the Ukraine, where 31 were killed in the world's worst nuclear accident in April 1986. The centrepiece of the experience is touring the ghost town of Pripyat, which reportedly receives ten thousand visitors annually.

Auschwitz-Birkenau. Arguably the cornerstone of dark tourism, the former concentration and extermination camp, located in Poland, saw an estimated 1.1 million deaths under the Nazi regime, predominantly Jews, but also Russian prisoners of war, political dissidents, homosexuals, Sinti, Roma, and Yeniche peoples. The Polish parliament declared it a state museum in July 1947. In 2016, over two million people visited the former camp.

The Killing Fields of Cambodia, where over two million people were killed in the state sponsored genocide under the rule of Pol Pot and the Khmer Rouge, during 1975–1979. Tourists visit the Tuol Sleng Genocide Museum, a former prison, torture, and detention facility, and the Choeung Ek Genocidal Center and 'Killing Fields', which opened in 1999. While many of the burial pits have been left undisturbed, there are thousands of human remains on display. Visitor numbers are increasing annually, with an attendance of 210,000 in 2014.

Hiroshima, Japan, the target of the first atomic bomb, dropped by the United States of America on the morning of 6th August 1945. The initial detonation killed an estimated 70,000, revised to some 90,000-166,000 by the end of that year, due to injuries sustained from the blast, and the subsequent effects of radiation. In 1955 the Hiroshima Peace Memorial Museum was opened in the Memorial Park, dominated by the Genbaku Dome, the only building to survive at 'Ground Zero'. It receives over one million visitors annually.

However, suicide spots remain the most likely destination for today's dark tourist to witness actual death. Despite closing the walkways at night, San Francisco's Golden Gate Bridge registers a jumper approximately every two days. The Nanjing Yangtze River Bridge currently has the dubious distinction of being the most popular site for suicide globally.

Visiting such sites can have unintended consequences, certainly in the UK, where genuine curiosity may result in a concerned, well-meaning local calling the police, in the mistaken belief that you yourself are contemplating suicide. This will inevitably result in a caution, and considerable embarrassment, when explaining to a thoroughly unimpressed police officer that you were merely 'just looking, to see how far down it was', and had no intention of delaying the approaching Intercity 125.

If you are considering taking a dive, then get the requisite training first. While academia references the *Titanic*, and the subsequent tourism industry the legendary sinking spawned, it has not recognised those dark tourists who took up scuba diving to explore shipwrecks and visit the underwater graveyards first hand.

Clearly, while a diversity of dark sites have been developed specifically for the purpose of tourism, others have not, yet independent dark tourists have chosen to visit them regardless.

THE INFLUENCE OF POPULAR CULTURE WITHIN DARK TOURISM should not be underestimated. Long before Dr John Lennon and Professor Malcolm Foley coined the term in 1996, The Sex Pistols had released their fourth single, Holidays In The Sun, back in October 1977, their perceptive unique take on the phenomenon.

"A cheap holiday in other people's misery!"

The song was inspired by their trip to the Channel Islands. The Pistols commented;

"We tried our holiday in the sun in the isle of Jersey and that didn't work. They threw us out."

Undeterred, the Pistols decamped to Berlin, where they hung around the Wall, in the rain. Coincidentally Lennon and Foley also covered Berlin in their book, focusing on the city's Third Reich sites, before a chapter entitled, 'Covering History: The Interpretation of the Channel Islands Occupation 1939–45'. Dark tourism academia apparently followed in the footsteps of the Sex Pistols.

The practice of leaving tributes at the site of a tragedy has become widespread, certainly since the contemporary watershed of public grief at the loss of Diana, Princess of Wales in 1997. While the UK had mourned its heroes on an epic scale in the past, such as Nelson and Churchill, Diana was a darling of the media age. Most mourners had never met her, but empathised nonetheless. Mass floral tributes were left at various sites associated with Diana in London, and at the scene of her death in Paris. Media commentators struggled to comprehend the abandonment of the stereotypical British stiff upper lip in favour of informal, spontaneous shrines, before suggesting the public were channelling their own personal losses through the 'Queen of People's Hearts'.

Subsequently it has become obligatory for the media to focus on mementoes left in remembrance at an appropriate site, which in turn fuels footfall to the shrine. Here people congregate with other members of their tribe, to pay their respects and leave messages, linking themselves to the tragedy or dead star, to be read by others attending.

This practice has become refined in the wake of terrorist attacks, where reporters use the publicly constructed shrine as their backdrop, to illustrate how people are 'coming together' and 'showing solidarity', coincidentally politically expedient for the Government of the day.

Media coverage, both mainstream and social, magnetises the shrine, drawing those willing to provide a suitable soundbite, and has led to the revival of

TV crew at London Bridge in the wake of the terrorist attack, June 2017.

the 'vigil'. Those who attend rarely maintain it through the night, as per the definition of vigil. This is left to illuminated landmarks, thematically lit, often by other countries to show solidarity, but, as with the vigils themselves, such displays appear politically motivated and strangely arbitrary.

Following the terrorist attacks on the offices of satirical French magazine *Charlie Hebdo* in January 2015, there was a vigil held in London's Trafalgar Square, although no British nationals were killed. This rite was repeated in the wake of the attacks of November 2015, again in Paris, where one Briton was killed, and in March 2016, after the attacks in Brussels, where again one Briton was killed. There was a huge gathering in London's Soho to support Orlando after the mass shooting in a gay club in June 2016, although again, there were no British casualties. Over a dozen buildings were lit in rainbow colours as far afield as the Sydney Harbour Bridge and the Eiffel Tower.

Curiously there was no reporting of the vigil held in Trafalgar Square after the attacks in Sousse, Tunisia, June 2015, where thirty of the thirty-eight victims were British. A gathering arranged on social media apparently attracted only nine participants, and no landmarks were lit in recognition, either here or abroad. Instead a minute's silence was observed in the UK at noon a week later, on Friday 3rd July, with the nation's flags flown at half-mast.

One can only assume this apparent lack of 'spontaneous' public mourning in the wake of Sousse was because the attacks happened to an older demographic, with most of the victims in Tunisia being aged fifty-plus, and that such vigils are predominantly attended by the young, for the young. Or maybe it was because the

Sousse victims were tourists, sunning themselves abroad when they were killed and the only people who could relate, or be bothered to react spontaneously, were other tourists in Tunisia, who did indeed light candles on the beaches at night.

Murals have also been used as a pictorial tribute to the fallen, notably on the house walls of Belfast during The Troubles. These huge artworks have now become tourist attractions in their own right. On the other side of the Atlantic, in Long Island City, New York, the graffiti mecca 5 Pointz, now sadly demolished, also carried pictorial tributes to lost cultural icons, as well as preserving the tags of fellow departed street artists.

The first 'ghost' bike, to commemorate a killed cyclist, appeared in St. Louis, Missouri, in 2003. At the time of writing there were 630 ghost bikes across 210 global locations. Painted white, and chained near the scene of the accident, they not only act as a memorial, but to remind passing motorists that they share the road with cyclists.

The iconography of shrines is also in evidence after a death in the world of sport, notably football, where fans drape scarves or replica shirts in memory of a former player, or manager, affiliated with their club. There's an obligatory minute's silence before the next game, where players, officials and fans unite in remembrance, although due to the tribal nature of football this has been abandoned in favour of applause, to drown out disrespectful cat calls by rival supporters and attention seekers.

Competitive mourning and ownership of grief is symbolised in the remembrance of Hollywood silent film star, Rudolph Valentino, who died from peritonitis at the height of his fame in 1926. Some 100,000 mourners lined the streets of New York, before Valentino's body was taken for interment in Beverly Hills. On the anniversary of his death a mysterious 'Lady in Black' visited his crypt, leaving a single red rose. Over the years this spawned many imitators, although it has been subsequently suggested that the original may have been a publicity stunt. The current incumbent of this ritual is motion picture historian and cemetery guide, Karie Bible.

The land and sycamore tree in Queen's Ride, Barnes, where singer-songwriter and Glam Rock pioneer Marc Bolan was killed in a car crash in 1977, was purchased by the T. Rex Action Group. The tree where the car came to rest has been preserved, and the steps providing access are lined with memorial plaques, recognising the passing of other band members. The shrine continues to draw fans from all over the world, and has been recognised by the English Tourist Board.

The plaque in Heddon Street, London, commemorating the site where the cover photograph of David Bowie's landmark album, *The Rise and Fall of Ziggy Stardust and the Spiders from Mars* was taken, became a focal point for mourning after Bowie's death in January 2016. Located between two functioning doorways, the shrine adopted the physical dimensions of a grave and headstone. There is also a mural on the wall of a department store, conveniently close to the tube station in Brixton, although Bowie was actually born in nearby Stansfield Road, died in New York and had his ashes reportedly scattered in Bali. Consequently these London shrines became natural, accessible places for his fans to publicly grieve.

Bowie's decision to leave no grave may have been to deter the fanatical, evidenced by the desecration of the Parisian cemetery, Père Lachaise, where tombs are indiscriminately scratch-sign-posted to direct pilgrims to the grave of American rock legend, poet, and leader of the Doors, Jim Morrison, who died from a suspected drug overdose in 1971.

Although Père Lachaise is the final resting place of many notable figures, such as Oscar Wilde, Chopin, Édith Piaf, and Marcel Proust, Morrison's iconic counterculture status dominates the necropolis. His grave had no official marker until French officials supplied a shield, which was subsequently stolen in 1973. In 1981, to mark the tenth anniversary of Morrison's death, sculptor Mladen Mikulin donated a bust of the icon, which was defaced, then subsequently stolen. In the early 1990s, Morrison's father had a flat stone, bearing a Greek inscription, 'True to Himself', placed on the grave.

I took my own pilgrimage to pay my respects to Jim in the summer of 2003. The grave was squashed and cramped; after 200 years of interment, the 110 acre site is bursting at the seams. As testimony to Morrison's enduring aura, his grave was attended by a uniformed guard, which, although necessary given the behaviour of the Lizard King's devotees, did make the experience somewhat anticlimactic, rather than reverential.

Walking away I encountered three fellow fans; a guy, a girl, and a Jim lookalike, resplendent in trademark black leather jeans and white shirt, carrying a ghetto blaster. Despite abundant directional graffiti they asked me where his grave was.

Minutes later I heard the Doors, and out of curiosity retraced my steps. There, under the shade of a venerable tree, a surreal tableau, reminiscent of Manet's, *Le Déjeuner sur l'herbe*. Jim's clone was stripped to the waist, gyrating, Morrison-esque, using an unrelated grave for a stage.

His friend was videoing the performance, with the girl, clearly embarrassed, in charge of the music. The grave acting as a makeshift stage was a curved shield, which may have contributed to the performer's lack of serpentine grace. That, or the boots he wore, because he swore and fell off.

What this anecdote illustrates is that while we go to pay our dutiful respects at dark sites, we, like the media, cannot resist the temptation to point the finger at others who do not conform to 'our' standards of acceptable behaviour in the presence of the dead. We may be dark tourists, but at least we are respectful, unlike everyone else.

Which brings us to the anti-shrine, extensively reported in the wake of the terrorist attack on the Promenade de Anglais in Nice, on Bastille Day, 2016. Stones and rubbish marked the spot where the truck driver, Mohamed

Lahouaiej-Bouhlel, was shot and killed by police. Passers by spat, and one man urinated on the pile, with no regard for the public works employee who would have to clean up the mess afterwards.

Public shrines have an indeterminate life span. Floral tributes are removed to become dedicated compost, with the mementoes offered to the relatives. In time a permanent memorial, less conspicuous, will be erected. While these memorials are visited, their function is not to accrue revenue. There is of course an exception: 'The King', Elvis Presley.

Elvis was, and still is, an industry. His home and burial plot at Graceland, Memphis, Tennessee is principally a commercial outlet with a shrine and grave attached. It receives around 600,000 visitors a year. The King resides in second place behind Michael Jackson on the list of top earning dead celebrities, according to Forbes, returning a steady $55m annually.

Among the notable visitors to Graceland are Prince William and Prince Harry, and in 2006 President George W. Bush took Japanese Prime Minister and die-hard Elvis fan, Junichiro Koizumi, for a tour of the mansion.

What truly sets Elvis apart is the commemorative merchandise. Consider this; Elvis died in 1977, yet there are eleven items in the '2016 Elvis Presley for President' range, from can coolie to golf balls, and the entire collection can be yours for $89.60 + p&p, if you are buying from the online store. If only they'd put Elvis on the ballot. There again, Clinton would have come third.

A S ILLUSTRATED THERE ARE A LARGE VARIETY OF SITES THAT FALL under the banner of dark tourism, although it's most commonly associated with sites of genocide, in particular the Nazi Holocaust of WWII.

Dark tourists usually visit a site where atrocities took place, such as a former concentration camp. However as noted by John Beech in *The Darker Side of Travel*, there are several museums at locations completely divorced from the events. An example would be the US Holocaust Museum in Washington, which opened in 1993. It now attracts nearly two million visitors per year, comparable with Auschwitz-Birkenau where atrocities actually took place.

During 1975–1979, the Khmer Rouge killed an estimated 2–2.2 million people, approximately one fifth of the population of Cambodia. There are two main sites for genocide tourism. The first, the Tuol Sleng Museum of Genocide, a former school requisitioned by the Khmer Rouge for torture and detention, has been mostly preserved in situ. The second site, Choeung Ek, which lies to the south of the capital Phnom Penh, is an example of the 'Killing Fields', where mass executions took place. The site is dominated by a large Buddhist stupa, filled with skulls.

Seattle, USA also has a memorial site, established by a survivor to honour the dead, and to remind those Cambodians who resettled in the city of their dark history.

The genocide in Rwanda took place between April and June of 1994. Some 800,000 Tutsi people were murdered by their Hutu rivals. The Kigali Memorial Centre is one of six major commemorative centres throughout the country. At this site alone, over 250,000 victims are buried. The former technical school at Murambi is also a genocide memorial centre. It is estimated some 45,000 were killed there. In a number of rooms, preserved bodies are laid out, including those of children and infants, the evidence of their violent and brutal ends apparent.

There is now a highly recommended day tour, 'Never Forget Srebrenica', referring to July 1995 when an enclave of Bosnian Muslims were surrounded by units of the Army of Republika Srpska. Over 8,000 men and boys were killed, the largest massacre in Europe since WWII.

The excursion takes in a cemetery, memorial, and museum housed in the former barracks of the UN peacekeepers, and also provides the opportunity to talk with a survivor of the genocide. Reviewers unanimously award the excursion five star ratings, commenting on how moving they found the experience, and saying that they now have a deeper understanding and knowledge of the events.

Some of these conflicts are relatively recent, so bizarrely perpetrators still share territory with their former victims, with reconciliation between the factions ongoing.

A LTHOUGH DARK TOURISM WAS ONLY CHRISTENED AS RECENTLY as 1996, the practice of travelling to encounter death and its representations has been around for centuries. Academia references those making a pilgrimage to a bone relic, and there was mass attendance for public hangings in the UK, before the practice was abolished in 1868. In France public executions by guillotine were carried out as recently as June 1939.[1] Authorities subsequently moved the blade behind closed doors in response to the behaviour of the spectators, including surreptitious filming of the execution.

The idea of taking a tour to one of the few domains that continue to practice public executions seems perverse, and tourists would likely be unwelcome. However there are independent travellers venturing into ongoing conflict zones, wannabe war correspondents who are likely to encounter death. Yet for the majority, dark tourism is perfectly safe and sanitised to draw large numbers to its sites.

Naturally dark tourism can only profit after a disaster or tragedy has occurred. Although the creation of two exclusion zones for visitors to explore

---

1) France continued to use the guillotine until 10th September 1977, when Hamida Djandoubi was the last to be executed by the device, having been convicted of rape, torture and murder. France abolished the death penalty in 1981.

in the wake of nuclear accidents at Chernobyl and Fukushima in the space of twenty-five years is impressive, the industry also relies on sites and experiences being created for them.

Rumours have circulated in media articles for several years over the potential development, for dark tourism purposes, of 'Jonestown', in the Guyanese jungle. Here over 900 people drank Kool-Aid laced with cyanide at the incitement of megalomaniac preacher, Jim Jones, founder of Peoples Temple, in 1978. There is currently no infrastructure, and the threadbare site has been reclaimed by jungle.

The Government of Guyana has a dichotomy: do they develop the site for dark tourism, or forgo the revenue and consign Jonestown to fading memory? It may be that speculative media articles are simply testing the waters, but if Guyana were to develop Jonestown, tourists would inevitably follow.

Dark tourism also profits from anniversaries. To mark the centenary of the loss of the *Titanic*, the *MS Balmoral* cruised the same route to the site of the sinking. Passengers dined over the wreck, enjoying the same menu, eating from replica china, serenaded by the same music. Many dressed in period costume to enhance their experience, and the tour company made every effort to achieve authenticity wherever possible, without hitting an iceberg with insufficient lifeboats, etc.

Yet despite the revenue that both packaged sites and celebrated anniversaries provide, there is a reluctance to be associated with the dark tag. Profit from dark tourism can be seen as exploiting the dead. Indeed it is difficult to see it from any other perspective.

In 2005, the Municipality of Phnom Penh agreed to lease the Choeung Ek Killing Fields to JC Royal Company, a Japanese consortium, for thirty years. They were allowed to develop the site and increase the entrance fee. It was estimated that the company would earn $18,000 a month, with any profit invested in a fund jointly owned by Cambodian government officials. Whether those officials include former members of the Khmer Rouge who perpetrated the atrocities is unclear.

This raises the question of who actually owns the memory of the dead. Is legacy merely a euphemism for commercial exploitation, utilised as a legitimizing, sanitising term by those who benefit? Within dark tourism, unlike real life, the status of the dead is not determined by those bereaved.

If the leasing of the Killing Fields seems strange, consider the National September 11 Memorial and Museum in New York. This was designed and constructed in the knowledge that it could not function without the tourist revenue that covers some 60–70% of its annual budget, which some estimates put at $72m. There is no state or federal funding, therefore the National September 11 Memorial and Museum depends on tourism.

This begs the question: why build a memorial that is literally "only possible because of your support", relying on perceived macabre curiosity, tourism, and patriotism? Staff salaries totalled a staggering $6.5m in 2010, an increase of 22% over the previous year, with the CEO reported to be on $378,288, and the National September 11 Memorial and Museum actively recruits volunteers to assist with its upkeep. The site has to keep tourists coming to survive. It has to promote itself.

Naturally the National September 11 Memorial and Museum has a Facebook page, where a daily drip feed of posts can fuel a chosen narrative, or counter any misconceptions that might deter the public from visiting. When the media suggested local people were avoiding the memorial, the story was subtlety negated by a slick video campaign, fronted by Robert de Niro, where New Yorkers were corralled to advocate the positive aspects of their visit. Both the National September 11 Memorial and Museum website and Facebook page now features, 'Our City Our Story', reaching out to Gothamites, appealing for their engagement.

In this battle for hearts, minds, and the tourist buck, the mainstream media plays an important role in promoting dark sites. For example, UK newspaper, the *Daily Mail*, have published articles on how Fukushima's dark tourism aids with "remembrance and healing"; how Chernobyl receives "TEN THOUSAND" tourists every year; that tourists visit the Killing Fields "in an effort to learn more about Cambodia's brutal history", and that "Auschwitz has become the world's most unlikely tourist hot spot".

Interestingly the *Daily Mail* has also featured articles on the Berlin Wall, and the former concentration camp on Jersey in the Channel Islands. Perhaps it too is following in the footsteps of the Sex Pistols.

THIS EVENING'S RIPPER EXPERIENCE RUSHES TOWARDS ITS conclusion like a Benny Hill posse. Pounding the pavement at the head of the gaggle, Phillip confides in me.
"I sometimes feel it's a bit of a circus."
When he started guiding Ripper walking tours thirteen years ago, he knew all the other guides on the Whitechapel beat. Not now, there are too many. I ask if it's a seasonal business. He dismisses this. Day of the week, month of the year,
"Makes no difference at all."
He tells me there can be half a dozen guides with their respective groups in Mitre Square, all vying for centre stage, shouting out over the heads of their audience. Business is booming and the competition is suitably cut throat.

Phillip has been obsessed with the macabre since childhood. He became an actor, touring the school circuit, raising 'issues' with the kids, "as you can probably tell," before becoming a renowned expert on Ripperology. He knows his brand of 'edutainment' isn't for everyone, but suggests it would be a very depressing couple of hours walking the streets of Whitechapel without a touch of gallows humour.

He recalls the couple that thanked him for his honesty, for not window-dressing the murders in mythology, but for giving it to them straight. Phillip spreads his arms open wide on the kerb at Duke's Place to prevent his charges pouring into the oncoming traffic.

"I took a lot of comfort from that," he adds.

We cross the road, enter the passage opposite, marching double-time, then our guide makes a dash over the last few yards to jump onto the coveted bench in Mitre Square, where he takes centre stage to tell us about the discovery of Catherine Eddowes. Phillip highlights the physical changes made to the pavement since the body was discovered by PC Edward Watkins, in the small hours of 30th September 1888, and naturally shows us the photographs to prove it. The only downside for our chaperone is that none of us are actually standing on the exact spot the corpse occupied.

"You're standing a couple of feet from where her head was, sir, to your right..."

He indicates with his laser pointer. The gentleman respectfully sidesteps away, giving the phantom cadaver more air. We collectively titter.

"And her feet would have been about there..."

And of course, we all look.

The square is filling up. The Kiss of Death guide with the bowler hat and overcoat has taken the bench behind us. Another, sporting a flat cap takes his group to one side. Then yet another group emerges from the passage, led by a character in a theatrical black cape.

The tour concludes as honestly as it began. Phillip can't tell us who Jack the Ripper was, because he admits he doesn't know. But he has debunked the myths and sensations of Ripper lore, and has shared his passion in his own inimitable style. It has been a thoroughly enjoyable experience, highly educational, and we have definitely had our money's worth. And of course we got to see where the prostitutes were murdered, which may, or may not, have been our primary reason for attending in the first place. There's a polite round of applause, then we disperse as quickly as we arrived. It will be dark soon.

It is incredible to think that Jack the Ripper, a legitimate historical figure, retains such infamy and pulling power after all this time. There were in excess of 100 tourists jammed into a tiny unremarkable square in the City of London at 9 p.m. on a summer's evening, who paid to see the scenes of his crimes, none of which remotely exist in their original settings. The suited City traders standing outside the wine bar down the street didn't know quite what to make of it.

Whoever the Ripper was, he could have had no idea his bloody exploits would create a thriving tourist industry over a century later. He evaded capture, and therefore through fortune or design, retained his anonymity. This in turn led to a guessing game, which fuelled his legend. His legacy would provide the living with a reliable source of income for generations to come.

Going Darker: Why This Book?

I FIRST DISCOVERED THE TERM 'DARK TOURISM' WHILE RESEARCHING a site I intended to visit in Japan in 2017. It soon became apparent that I'd visited a number of dark sites over the years. This made me uneasy. Naturally I didn't care for being pigeonholed, and felt disconnected. The implications the tag evoked were unsettling.

Then I remembered scuba diving. I couldn't possibly be a dark tourist! I'd learned to dive, and spent a decade travelling the world to exotic locations, diving... *shipwrecks.* Underwater graveyards, where the casualties of naval warfare lay, or those lost to storms and the reef. I'd written articles about them. Worse still, I'd even had one piece published in the UK, USA, and Australia, which focused on the *morality* of diving wrecks where souls were lost.

Interestingly, when confronted by the possibility of being a so-called dark tourist, my initial reaction was denial, recalling the underwater adventures like a drowning man clutching at straws. I dug out old holiday photograph albums and discovered a disproportionate number of images of graves. The well-thumbed South American phrasebook from '97 provided confirmation; in the pages for notes the only phrase I'd bothered to compose was, "*Estoy buscando el cementerio,*" "I am looking for the cemetery." Then there was my last annual holiday: a weekend trip to Chernobyl.

Having now seen the bigger picture, my wreck diving being the proverbial nail in the coffin, there was no escape from the fact that I was likely defined as a dark tourist, whatever that might actually mean. Inexplicably I'd reached my fifties, seemingly oblivious to who I was, or what I was. I'd been visiting dark sites for forty years with no inkling of the constant theme running through my chosen destinations, indulging myself in the luxury of total autonomy, with no checks, balances, or compromise as to where I went, why I went, or what I did when I got there. The lack of self-awareness was frightening.

While I accepted the label of 'Graveyard Rabbit', someone who toured cemeteries, that wasn't a problem. Twitchy nose, long floppy ears, cute; what's not to like about bunnies? The ridiculous thing was that the dark tourist tag alone was making me re-evaluate myself. It felt vampiric, feeding off grief.

The next morning saw me in the local bookshop, ordering academic publications relating to dark tourism. I dutifully read them as if they were self-help books, looking for answers as to why people might go on their travels searching for death, or representations of it, consciously, or otherwise. Essentially I was looking for a diagnosis.

As Nietzsche noted: "If you gaze long into the abyss, the abyss gazes also into you." I thought I'd just been having a look over the edge, out of curiosity; "How far down is it?" The reality was I'd been in serene, oblivious freefall for years.

Philip Stone, director of the Institute for Dark Tourism Research, maintains that, "There's no such thing as a dark tourist, only people interested in the world around them."

Yet reflecting on my travels, characterised by dark sites, and justifying this gravitation because I found such places 'interesting', seemed somewhat disingenuous.

The posters in the travel agent's windows sell the idyllic family escape poolside, the romantic fantasy, or exotic wildlife and adventure for the singleton. They are not pitching morbidity. Yet behind this glossy veneer, under the counter in the proverbial brown paper bag lay something darker that would cater for the likes of me, just as there had been when Thomas Cook, founder of the high street chain, offered tours to public hangings.

Perhaps I could apportion blame onto the authorities and the tourism industry. Both appeared to be colluding to make a buck. Remember Dealey Plaza; tourists came of their own volition and the authorities, recognising this, sanitised, legitimized, and capitalised. Increasing numbers were buying into this dark market that was expanding to cater for the demand. By visiting such sites I contributed to this industry. Furthermore, I was taking something positive from the experience that made me want to return, or seek other sites in a similar vein.

In truth, what had actually changed? A tag. A recognition and awareness of a behaviour pattern that now came with a pang of guilt. I couldn't un-visit all those places, or deny I'd ever been, and I wasn't about to stop visiting dark sites and sit beside a pool. Tourism wasn't turning my money away on the grounds of taste and decency, rather facilitating the likes of me. I didn't consider myself as particularly morbid, and cared enough to want to know why I'd been consistently visiting dark sites, although now the penny had dropped I'd inevitably see the destinations, those who presented them, the tourists who visited, and my own presence there, in a very different light.

Given the diversity of sites, the reasons for visiting them varies, from the simplistic, such as taking the kids to the Chamber of Horrors for entertainment, to the intensely personal, paying respects at a renowned suicide spot where a loved one found closure.

Yet there were individuals whom, knowingly or otherwise, visited a range of sites, as if compelled. I now only had to look in the mirror to see one. Certainly from the questionnaires drawn up by PhD students studying the subject, it's the key question: 'why do you go?' One might wryly reply, 'you first.'

Fortunately for the industry that caters for the increasing demand, why tourists are attracted to dark sites may be a moot point, just as long as they keep coming.

So I decided to revisit sites with fresh, honest eyes, and try to engage with those who administered them in order to further my understanding. I'd also visit that site in Japan I'd been researching when I first discovered the term. Now enlightened, my motives for going there were not only questionable, they could be considered morally indefensible. Then there was that dark place, much closer to home — the one that until now I'd never contemplated visiting, because going there wasn't just dark, but beyond the pale.

However, by writing this book, as John Lydon prophesied with Holidays In The Sun:

"Now I got a reason."

He was right.

"It's no real reason."

I suspected Lydon might be right about that too.

THIS BOOK FOCUSES PRIMARILY ON ESTABLISHED DARK SITES. SOME have better tourist infrastructure, (Auschwitz-Birkenau) than others (wreck of the *Salem Express*), and some (Aokigahara) have no specific dark tourism infrastructure at all. It also features a 'control' site that has, for fifty years, steadfastly rejected the very notion of tourism.

It does not include trips to so-called dark states, such as North Korea, or spontaneous travel in the immediate aftermath of a disaster, such as those who bought radios to track official search and recovery operations in the wake of the NASA Challenger space shuttle disaster in 1986.

9/11 INC.

September 11th, 2001, American Airlines Flight 11, Mohammed Atta at the controls, the North Tower of the World Trade Center rushing towards him. In a split second there will be a blinding flash, Atta will be vaporized, and, he trusts, on his way to paradise, free from earthly constraints, bequeathing only grief, war, suspicion, fear, and a sulky driving licence photo.

Yet in his wildest dreams he could never have envisaged what his actions would ultimately be employed for: an inappropriate quote stamped on souvenir stones sold to tourists at over thirty bucks a pop, from a hothouse gift shop sited atop the mass grave of his own design.

IT DAWNED A BEAUTIFUL TUESDAY, WITH 'SEVERE CLEAR' SKIES. Egyptian Mohamed Atta, thirty-three, the son of a Cairo lawyer, boarded a Boeing 767 at Boston's Logan airport, destined for Los Angeles. Atta, his travel companion, Saudi Abdulaziz al-Omari, and three other conspirators, carrying concealed knives, took their respective seats. American Airlines Flight 11 took off at 8:00 a.m., with ninety-two on board.

Approximately fifteen minutes into the flight, when the fasten seat belts sign was switched off, Atta's accomplices hijacked the plane, and he swapped seats, upgrading from 8D to the one at the controls, where he turned the Boeing north, away from its southerly flight path. Air traffic control tried to raise Flight 11, but there was no response from the man with the commercial pilot's licence, now ensconced in the cockpit. Communication came instead from a flight attendant, who informed American Airlines that two of her colleagues had been stabbed, and a passenger had had his throat cut.

Listening to the conversation, with the benefit of hindsight, is excruciating; the 'i's and 't's laboriously dotted and crossed, right up to the point where the call abruptly terminated, when Flight 11 disappeared from the radar screen over Lower Manhattan, ploughing into the northern face of the North Tower of the World Trade Center at 8:45 a.m., at a speed of nearly 400 mph.

The plane vanished in a fireball, leaving just black smoke pouring from a grotesque, cartoon-like imprint in floors ninety-four to ninety-nine. Everyone above the point of impact was trapped. Some would choose to jump.

From the Fire Department New York Emergency Center Phone Log:

09:09 a.m., "male caller states that people are jumping out of a huge hole in the side of the building — probably no one catching them."

They were still jumping nearly three quarters of an hour later.

At 8:43 a.m., two minutes before Mohamed Atta hit the North Tower, a second Boeing 767, also out of Boston, United Airlines Flight 175, was taken. With Marwan al-Shehhi, twenty-three, a student from the UAE at the controls, the plane also changed course, heading towards New York and the Twin Towers.

With the North Tower now on fire, and with a second plane no longer responding, two F-15 fighter jets were scrambled from Cape Cod at 8:52 a.m. They would be too late.

At 9:02 a.m., Flight 175, with sixty-five aboard, hit the South Tower, on a diagonal trajectory around the eighty-fifth floor, knifing through the southeastern face, exploding out the opposite corner. The angle of the strike left one stairwell intact, which afforded an escape route. This is why some occupants on floors above the impaction point in the South Tower survived, and those above in the North Tower did not.

A third hijacking was already underway. American Airlines Flight 77, a Boeing 757 with sixty-four on board, took off after a slight delay from Washington Dulles International airport at 8:20 a.m., heading for Los Angeles, with Hani Hanjour, twenty-nine, from Saudi Arabia, and his team, aboard. They took control of the plane sometime between 8:51 a.m. and 8:54 a.m., when the plane changed course, heading south towards Washington D.C.

The Boeing dived and accelerated to maximum speed, sheared trees and street lights, then crashed into the west wall of the Pentagon in Arlington County, Virginia at 9:38 a.m., where 125 were killed in addition to everyone on board the aircraft.

The fourth plane to be commandeered that morning was United Airlines Flight 93, a Boeing 757. It was due to depart from Newark for San Francisco at 8:00 a.m., but took off forty-two minutes late, with forty-four on board.

By 9:30 a.m., Ziad Jarrah, 27, Lebanese, popular, from a good family, and a natural pilot, had command. He deviated from the flight path, hooping the plane back towards the east. His intended target was unknown, but is assumed to be the Capitol Building in Washington D.C. Unlike the three previous flights, hijacked with five-men teams, Flight 93 only had four.

The delayed departure of Flight 93 meant that the other three attacks had already occurred, and this information filtered through to the hijacked passengers in phone calls with their loved ones on the ground. Just before 10:00 a.m., resigned to their fate, they attempted to storm the cockpit, and Jarrah flew Flight 93 into a field in Shanksville, Pennsylvania. Eyewitnesses saw the plane go in upside down. The rest of the world was totally oblivious, transfixed by what had just happened in New York.

At 9:59 a.m., the South Tower imploded and collapsed. Although this skyscraper was the second to be hit, Flight 175 had impacted lower down the South Tower, than Flight 11 had on its sister, therefore there were more floors, and weight, bearing down on the damaged section. At 10:28 a.m., the North

Tower followed suit. There was a beautiful, horrendous symmetry. Twin smoking steel chimneys, collapsing at freefall speed, like a concertina, back into its box, spewing out billowing tentacles of debris, which impacted on the ground, and pursued terrified runners through the grid of Lower Manhattan, like monsters from their childhood nightmares.

Ash grey dust and paper covered everything. Both towers were gone, and so were those who'd been trapped inside, as well as those who'd gone in to rescue them.

World Trade Center 7, evacuated, but weakened by fires started from the North Tower, collapsed at 5:21 p.m.

America had never known a day like it. Four planes had been co-ordinately hijacked, specifically for kamikaze-style attacks. Three had hit their intended targets, the Twin Towers of New York's World Trade Center, and the Pentagon. The remaining flight had self destructed after its passengers had staged a counterattack. As a result of the terrorist attacks, the World Trade Center site lay in ruins, and the Pentagon had four sides.

By staggering their attacks in New York, in the cradle of the global mass media, the terrorists had ensured the world was watching TV in time to see the second plane hit. They could never have imagined the towers would have disintegrated so swiftly afterwards, and in such spectacular fashion.

And perhaps, subconsciously, one of the reasons why so many compared the events of 9/11 to a movie, was because the running time from the hijack of Flight 11, at 8:15 a.m., to the North Tower being reduced to a cloud at 10:28 a.m., was just 133 minutes. America, which had long fed the world a diet of disaster movies, now reaped the reality of its own imagination. But there was no flawed action hero to save the day; indeed, their real life heroes, the passengers on Flight 93, and the first responders on the ground, had perished in their efforts to save others.

The United States, the dominant global superpower, had been brought to its knees, not in some foreign field, but in its own back yard, in a spectacle staged by a group of seemingly unremarkable men between the ages of twenty and thirty-three, while the whole world just stood and watched in stunned disbelief.

Before the toxic dust that covered Lower Manhattan had been swept away, there was the inevitable rise of the conspiracy theory.

The shouting about an 'Inside Job' became so persistent that the State Department created a web page to debunk the criticism and scepticism of the NIST (National Institute of Standards & Technology) report, which had produced the official version of how three steel towers collapsed at virtually freefall speed within hours, disintegrating in a manner 'Truthers' associated with controlled demolition.

What is of interest to dark tourists, in the wake of the attacks of 11th September 2001, is not what *may* have been done that resulted in the deaths of nearly 3,000 people, but rather what *has* actually been done *after* the deaths of nearly 3,000 people. Because within days of 9/11, amidst the debris of what was once the World Trade Center, artefacts were being set aside for the creation of the Greatest Dark Tourism Site the world has ever seen.

Fuck, yeah.

I'M RIDICULOUSLY EARLY. THEY'RE STILL WET-VACCING THE MEMORIAL Plaza, although the snail trail dries in no time. 7:30 a.m., and the heat is already breaking through. I circumnavigate both memorial pools at a respectful distance, with a measured gait, then take a last cigarette on the kerb before tagging on the back of the queue for the 'Early Access' Museum Tour, scheduled for 8:15 a.m., currently Thursdays and Saturdays only, price $65.

Yes, that's right; $65. Plus a $2 'service fee'. $67. I booked months ago, and printed off my ticket at home, so I've absolutely no idea why there is a $2 service fee, and I'm sure no one else has either. Back in the UK, I assume any charge levied for printing out my own ticket is simply a con.

General admission is $24, Sunday to Thursday, 9:00 a.m.–8:00 p.m., and Friday to Saturday, 9:00 a.m.–9:00 p.m. With a guided tour it's $44. A forty-five-minute tour, explaining the symbolism of the Memorial Plaza and pools, is $39. For those seeking free admission, there are first-come first-served tickets on a Tuesday, from 4:00 p.m.

We enter the striking rhomboid pavilion through the mandatory security screening. Amongst the many criticisms levelled at the National September 11 Memorial and Museum, there's only passing reference to its 'airport-style' security. It's so airport-style as to be a facsimile. One assumes it's described as 'airport-style' because everyone understands the irony of entering a museum, dedicated to the events perpetrated by hijacked planes, through airport security.

Perhaps the greatest twist is that the X-ray machines at Boston, Washington, and Newark were all working that day; civil aviation regulations at that time did not restrict knives with short blades in carry-on.

Consider that in the 1970s, the hey-day of the airline hijacker, terrorists would seize a plane by secreting guns and explosive on board, take the passengers as hostages, and issue demands for their release. But in contemporary times, with the advent of improved screening and the rise of martyrdom, all that's required is a pilot willing to make the sacrifice. Atta and Co. were not concerned by airport security X-ray machines because their weapon was already waiting for them at the gate. Over time airport security merely encouraged terrorist thinking outside the box.

Whilst some form of screening at the museum is to be expected, it's regrettable that it mirrors the passage of those aboard the planes who lost their lives, and gave the memorial its *raison d'être*. This is not 'interactivity'; we are

Entrance pavilion, National September 11 Museum.

not intended to 'experience what it must have been like for the unsuspecting passengers on that fateful day'. It's security. Unfortunately it's comparable with presenting freezing temperatures at a *Titanic* exhibit, or using a Jewish 'ID card', corresponding to a real person, as a ticket for admission to a Holocaust museum.

When entering the 9/11 memorial, please note bags should be no more than 8″ x 17″ x 19″. For the record, both United and American Airlines requirements for carry-on cabin baggage are 9″ x 14″ x 22″. I checked to see if the museum had perversely followed US civil airlines specifications.

The 9/11 Foundation spends $12m annually on security for the museum and memorial, due to concerns over terrorism. That is either a fifth of its annual budget, if reported at $60m, or a sixth of its annual budget, if reported at $72m. I have asked the media contact for clarification, but they have declined to answer my questions. Basically they spend so much on security they believe the government should support the cost. The then Foundation President and CEO, Joseph Daniels, told the *Daily Mail*:

"The fact of the matter is that this was a place that was attacked twice."

Which is true. However the "fact of the matter" is that the most recent attack involved two commercial airliners that flew directly into it, at high speed. The security to prevent such a thing that day were two military jets, the spearhead of a multibillion dollar defence and intelligence industry, that arrived too late.

The 9/11 Museum now places its faith in the same system the hijackers by-passed so effectively. The screening feels like its function is to provide emotional security and reassurance to visitors, to enhance the aura of the site as 'sacred ground', to prevent any tourist blood being spilt on the 'sacred ground', and to control the influx of visitors during peak times. Incidentally, the same level of security does not appear to operate at the memorial for Flight 93 in Shanksville; surely that site is 'sacred ground' too.

We loiter in the airy ground floor lobby, waiting for our guide, facing a wall inscribed with the names of the great and the good, Walt Disney, Coca-Cola and the New York baseball teams amongst them, who have all made contributions to the National September 11 Memorial and Museum. Then follows the names of the members of the board, which includes movie stars Robert de Niro and Billy Crystal. Yet the name that catches my eye on that list is towards the bottom: Monika Iken, who lost her husband of less than a year, Michael Patrick Iken, in the South Tower. Monika Iken wanted the site to be rebuilt as a memorial, but had expressed reservations that it might end up as 'Disneyland', which makes Walt's subsequent contribution rather surreal. For the record, the Walt Disney Company Foundation donated at what is referred to as the '$5m level'.

The cynic within me wonders if this holding pattern is merely a tourist trap, to allow our eyes to wander down the list of the contributors, in the hope that we will look upon them with favour; a subtle form of product placement. Worth noting that on the official National September 11 Memorial and Museum website there was one anonymous donation at the $500,000–$999,999 level, four anonymous donations at the $250,000–$499,99 level (sic), and seventeen anonymous donations at the $10,000–$99,000 level. Not everyone who contributed felt the need to have their name up in lights.

I TAKE A HEADCOUNT TO PASS THE TIME. THERE ARE TWENTY-NINE IN pastel polo shirts, khaki cargo pants, sandals and trainers, plus one Kiss of Death, suited and booted in black. I thought it was appropriate attire given the surroundings, but in retrospect may have overdone it, given today is 9/8, not 9/11. Still, everyone affords me plenty of space, as if black, or whatever it represents, is contagious.

Our guide, Meredith, arrives, cradling a drink. She's so young she must've been about twelve when 9/11 happened, but I suspected that this tour would be scripted, rather than interpretive, which is why I've booked another across the road with the 'rival' 9/11 experience at the Tribute Center tomorrow. She leads us down the escalators, past the recovered twin steel tridents, to the lower lobby, where atmospheric gloom prevails. We're issued with our headsets, tuned in, then set off downhill, the corridor lined with staggered audio visual display units, designed in proportion to the towers.

As usual I'm dawdling at the back. However, as when entering any final resting place since adopting my 'Golden Rule of Self Preservation '97', I habitually cast a glance over my shoulder. The security guard does his best to project a coincidental presence, immediately statuesque, surveying the ceiling for signs of damp, but fails, and I'm tailed at a discreet distance, to the balcony overlooking the cavernous expanse of Foundation Hall and the final steel girder cut from the site, smothered with graffiti from the recovery workers. Everyone takes photos. If there's a Kodak moment to be had America has always found the perfect place to capture it from, and designed easy access accordingly.

Our route is a switchback, taking in the vast undersides of one of the memorial pools above, which hangs down from the ceiling, clad in silver. It's a structure reminiscent of Andy Warhol meets Frank Lloyd Wright. We pass two large photos of the Manhattan skyline; one taken in 1995, the other during the attacks. This will transpire to be a selfie stick pinch point later in the day, as a backdrop for souvenir photos. Interestingly everyone poses in front of the scenic 1995 skyline, and no one goes for the 'sick shot'. Everyone stays within safe, self-imposed, tasteful boarders.

We reach the 'Survivors' Staircase', which was the last remaining structure above ground on the site, used by hundreds evacuating WTC5, adjacent to the Twin Towers. The pockmark stairs are also referred to as, 'The Path to Freedom', and I wondered if there were two rival factions, vying for their chosen moniker to be officially adopted. 'Path to Freedom' does seem a touch Nelson Mandela, and in fairness, it is a staircase. The security guard is proving a distraction, but only because I can't stop swivelling to see if he's dutifully keeping up his surveillance. He is. Poor guy doesn't know where to look now.

We arrive at bedrock, some seventy feet below ground, to look up at that last steel girder, thirty feet of totem, and the repository wall, covered in blue tiles, every hue unique and hand painted by the artist Spencer Finch, a striking composition aptly entitled 'Trying To Remember the Color of the Sky on That September Morning'.

What is perhaps not so apt, and what troubled the classicists, was the steel quote insert, forged from the tower remnants by New Mexico blacksmith, Tom Joyce. Some reported that the text, 'No day shall erase you from the memory of time', from Virgil's *Aeneid*, referenced two Trojan warriors, Nisus and Euryalus, complete with classical homoerotic connotations, who slaughtered their enemy as they slept. The Trojan assassins were killed in turn, their heads stuck on spears. The quote, the classicists noted, on what is effectively a mass tombstone, seemed more appropriate for the terrorists, rather than the victims. As Caroline Alexander, writing in the *New York Times* pithily observed:

"There is an easy mechanism, also time-hallowed, for winnowing out what may be right from what is clearly wrong: it's called reading."

The repository, which holds the remains of those yet to be identified, is naturally off limits. The work relentlessly continues as science advances, and in 2015, remains of an individual were named and returned to their mother. As a dark tourist you can't help wondering what she was given to bury, and how the final dignity of laying the remains of her child to rest was accomplished.

The tourists seem unconcerned with the semantics of Virgil's quote, or the likely size of any remains behind the wall, awaiting matchbox coffins, and snap away, before being led to a section of the North Tower antenna, and a partially crushed fire truck from Ladder 3. The security guard is still with us, but there's also a smattering of other visitors, the museum now officially open for the day. Stewards in their $50 trident ties and $68 silk scarves are now on station.

Meredith reminds us that the events of 9/11 happened in the space of 102 minutes; however that is the time elapsed from when the North Tower was hit, to its collapse, not from when Flight 11 was hijacked, when the bloodletting and terror actually began. Besides, my 133 minutes fits in better with the movie analogy. Part of me wants to ask why this official narrative, with a timeline of 102 minutes, excludes the attacks on the crew and passengers of Flight 11, one of whom had their throat cut. However the guide's not engaging us by asking any questions, to see if we're paying attention, so I let it go unchallenged, like a compliant tourist, rather than a dark, unwelcomed one.

As Meredith focuses on the obligatory memorial quilt, I'm drawn to a glass case containing the camouflage jacket of one of the Navy SEALs who stormed the compound and killed al-Qaeda founder, Osama bin Laden. And there's a brick, recovered by a journalist, who saw the hideout being demolished. This exhibit, prominently positioned for all to see, perhaps provides a sense of justice, given the actual perpetrators of the attacks are beyond reach.

And then the guide delivers the cornerstone of the tour, the 'Core Mission Statement' of The National September 11 Memorial and Museum at the World Trade Center Foundation, Inc. The mission statement requests that we:

"Remember and honour the thousands of innocent men, women, and children murdered by terrorists in the horrific attacks of February 26, 1993 and September 11, 2001."

There's the sense that this is repeated, verbatim, by every guide on every tour. It feels as if the Foundation is trying to convince itself of the reason it exists, perhaps in the hope that tourists will take the message and regurgitate it beyond the confines of the museum. However there's no way of knowing if the tourists, of which there have now been seven million since the museum opened in May 2014, share those aims, or are spreading the word. It feels as if the object of the Core Mission Statement is to play down the fact that this is now a major New York tourist attraction. The proclamation of a Core Mission Statement is counter-productive, because it focuses thoughts on what it might be trying to divert attention away from. It's corporate speak after all.

If the foundation was primarily established to 'remember and honour' the victims in the minds of the casual tourist, then unfortunately it's failed. There are simply too many people photographing themselves, or having their picture taken. It is unlikely they are doing this to provide a sense of scale.

They are taking photos to remember and honour themselves for being there.

If honouring the victims were indeed the principal aim, then the institution would change the 'No day shall erase you from the memory of time' quotation, to something more appropriate. That the museum has been intransigent regarding this, to the point of using it on merchandise to reinforce it, suggests the primary concern is protecting the reputations of those who approved the quote, rather than 'honouring' those who died and are now indelibly linked to it forever.

Meredith closes by thanking us for being part of it, especially for being there "at this time", which presumably refers to the imminent anniversary. While the bereaved must perpetually dread the 11th, the Foundation must be longing for it, the annual shot in the arm to inject media interest and focus attention on itself and its activities. Similarly I wonder if our tour group decided to visit early in term time, to avoid the parties of schoolchildren who will be descending on Greenwich Street by the busload in the weeks to come.

She asks if there are any questions. There's none. In fairness the tour has incorporated how the buildings fell, the calls for another inquiry, and the subsequent health issues that affected the recovery workers and residents, thereby deflecting any questions pertaining to the more controversial aspects of 9/11 and its aftermath. In all honesty the early tour wasn't worth $67, other than for avoiding the queue and having an empty museum in which to wander. And our very own security guard, but now even he's melted away.

I return my headset and set off to find the cafeteria for a coffee. Perhaps I should have asked Meredith why she really thinks tourists are coming here, but she's not going to tell me. There is a media department who are paid to deflect any awkward questions. Besides, it would be disingenuous to ask. I've already concluded that the vast majority are coming for a day out, to tick the box and 'do' 9/11, the tourist attraction where nearly 3,000 people died. And despite wearing black, and writing this book, I'm no different. Because I was here in 2013, before the museum opened, to see the memorial pools, doing exactly that.

T HE ATTENDANTS AT THE FOOT OF THE STAIRS LEADING TO THE atrium are wearing caramel blazers, which implies seniority over the museum steward's blue. They politely steer me towards the lift, as there's an official gathering at the top of the stairs, with the American flag originally mounted atop the last steel girder, now being presented to the museum in time for the fifteenth anniversary, this year's media event. The lift advertising suggests I 'take a moment' in the café. I intend to. Blinking into the light, I find the café blissfully deserted, although it can cater for 165. Airy, funnel-shaped, a suitably neutral stage, it provides a view of sorts and a break from the subterranean world.

The fare consists of salted caramel, Danish pastries, boxed salad and fruit etc. A ham and cheese (gruyère) croissant, and a cappuccino cost $9. The café, by Danny Meyer, CEO of something called the 'Union Square Hospitality Group', initially attracted criticism over plans to serve alcohol and gourmet 'comfort food', and responded by withdrawing them from the menu to quell the rumblings. The reality is I'm a captive audience and there's no re-admittance, not even with my $67 ticket.

In practical terms the café contributes to the running costs of the museum, in the same way the motorized juice cart stationed outside London's Highgate Cemetery makes a donation, commendably voluntarily. Even my local cemetery and crematorium has a tearoom, albeit one that provides food and drink at sensible prices, served with crockery and metal cutlery, and has the enlightened policy of employing people with learning difficulties. However what is of interest is how I *know* Danny Meyer is CEO of the 'Union Square Hospitality Group', and that he's responsible for the National September 11 Museum catering. There's a café at Auschwitz-Birkenau, but I have no idea who runs it, and furthermore I don't care, although subsequently it occurs to me that perhaps I should.

As I relentlessly try to stir sugar into my cappuccino with the stick Mr Meyer has thoughtlessly provided, I reflect that, despite the Core Mission Statement, the name that sticks the most from this morning is Walt Disney. Disneyland was what the relatives wanted to avoid. Yet there his name was, front and centre, just to remind everyone that Walt helped to make this institution possible. Why not put the contributors and board members by the exit, *after* those we're supposedly here to remember and honour? We, the living, collectively follow the coffin, rather than precede it.

Through the glass, past the foliage of the swamp oaks, the plaza is starting to fill, and the admission queue is lengthening. At the opposite end of the floor the presentation pauses for a token round of applause at the end of one speech, before another suit starts his response, and the standing audience shift their collective weight. Breakfast done, I ride back into the depths to consider the two exhibitions; one memorial, one historic, set behind glass walls underneath the pools. The museum tour doesn't cover the two permanent exhibitions, just the general public area.

The 'In Memoriam' exhibition features a room within a room. The inner sanctum plays audio tributes to the people who died. I stick my head in and withdraw just as quickly. The room was empty, but the womb-like surroundings infer that this is a place where people come to grieve. The outer room is described by the museum as a "Wall of Faces" — although I'd call it a Facebook wall, because that is what it is — composed of profile pictures of the victims from the February 26th 1993 and 11th September 2001 attacks. There are only a few portraits missing, where the swamp oak leaf logo, which cleverly denotes the deceased throughout the museum, takes their place. My eye is drawn to Igor Zukelman, who sits alone at the end, courtesy of the alphabet.

There are several glass cases where relatives have donated personal items from the deceased — interests in baseball, music, the church — and this, together with the touch screen desktops, allows the visitor to pull up information and photos of those lost. There's a page on the website asking for contributions to the Memorial Exhibitions, for artefacts, photos, video, and audio, so that the museum can convey a sense of who the victims were, and what they were in the middle of doing on the day they died, in terms of work or travel.

But it feels very much as if this is the place within the museum for those who lost friends and family, and I can't help but feel the lack of visitors in this section reflects that. It feels intrusive being in here. I look in three times during the day, but there's never more than a handful of people, where by contrast the historic exhibition of the events of 9/11 is constantly rammed. We don't seem to have an issue with confronting mass death, until an individual's face and personality are highlighted.

The historical section has everything, from the prequel to 9/11, the events of the day itself, and the aftermath. Artefacts range from the Xeroxed plea posters for the missing, to a church pew used by the rescue workers to snatch some sleep; a section of fuselage with a window from one of the planes, to the wooden steps and viewing gallery constructed over the site, so the bereaved could come together and pay their respects. And of course three pairs of shoes, including a pair of high heels that survived and walked miles in the mass exodus from Lower Manhattan.

There are newspapers from the day, with absolutely no inkling of what was about to happen, the last editions in a pre-9/11 USA, video loops of breakfast TV as the disaster broke, and a superb timeline map, showing the flight paths of the planes, and the reconnaissance the terrorists undertook in the months preceding their mission. And there, set alone on a short bevel wall, illuminated with barely enough light to attract a moth, the photos of the nineteen hijackers. Bizarrely, they are set so low that if you want to look the terrorists in the eye, you'll need to get down on your knees.

BUSINESS IS BRISK BACK AT THE CAFÉ, NOW IT'S LUNCHTIME. There's even a queue. I wasn't overly impressed with the breakfast croissant, so it's just a cappuccino with a resplendent stick to stir, perched on a stool at a side bar, now all the tables are occupied. This morning's presentation has finished, although not that long ago, judging by the media dribs and drabs still packing up.

The day beyond the glass wall of the café looks tempting, but I've more to see in the historical section. The storytellers have done a comprehensive job filling in the 110,000 square feet available, and I feel obliged to give their efforts due diligence. How they expect visitors to 'do' the museum in the recommended two hours is beyond me. The queue in the cafeteria is lengthening. I relinquish my space to an elderly couple with a tray. They'd prefer table and chairs, but given the circumstances look relieved to have any seat at all.

The darkest section of the museum is the smallest, screened from cursory view, behind a wall, with a notice warning that the images beyond may be distressing. Looped footage shows the jumpers in freefall.

There are two quotes juxtaposed on the wall, both from Lower Manhattan residents, and although the sentiments are contrasting, they don't conflict.

"She had a business suit on, her hair was all askew... This woman stood there for what seemed like minutes, then she held down her skirt and stepped off the ledge ... I thought, how human, how modest, to hold down her skirt before she jumped. I couldn't look anymore."

"You felt compelled to watch out of respect to them. They were ending their life without a choice and to turn away from them would have been wrong."

The woman next to me in the dark is crying quietly, scrunching a tissue. She's the first person I've seen visibly upset. I refocus on the jumpers. Some fall in groups of twos and threes. It is estimated there were about 200 who fell in total. It's advocated that no one 'jumped', because that would imply they weren't murdered (as if burning alive would have been preferable), or that a conscious decision to jump implies a slap in the face of God.

Watching those who jumped, or fell, repeatedly, recalls a review of the Washington Holocaust Memorial Museum by political scientist Philip Gourevitch, where an execution by firing squad was also looped. Gourevitch reminds us that those who died suffered enough the first time their lives were taken, without being perpetually screened for our consumption, even if set within the confines of an educational memorial. This is now the fate of those who jumped, or fell, to their deaths on 9/11, repeated eleven hours a day, twelve on Fridays and Saturdays.

Gourevitch is right. If I watch for long enough it will become digital wallpaper, desensitizing me to the horrendous predicament these people faced, collectively and individually. However I still watch the loop through twice to make sure I haven't missed any of them tumbling to their death, then head for the gift shop.

The National September 11 Museum opened amidst a blaze of controversy in May 2014, and in preparation for my trip I'd read numerous articles from both the UK and US press, where criticism abounded; the overall cost, the annual running cost, the salary of the CEO, the admission fee, and the anger of the bereaved over the thousands of unidentified remains in the repository, their consternation fanned by a VIP drinks reception within the museum for invited donors and sponsors.

"You enjoy dinner & drinks on top of my brothers grave last night douchebags?" (Tweeted by the sister of one of the victims.)

Yet it was the gift shop that took a disproportionate amount of flak. There was a cheese plate, subsequently withdrawn, in the shape of the US, with hearts marking the sites of the attacks. The Foundation said it carefully selected items for sale as memorable keepsakes, but would in future seek approval from those family members of the victims who sat on the board.

The harsh fact is the memorial and museum needs to generate revenue. It's estimated to have cost in the region of $700m to construct, but there are also reports the total bill was $1.3 billion. Initial estimates for the annual running costs were set at $60m. The actual annual running costs now appear to be $72m. According to the *Wall Street Journal*, the revenue generated through ticket sales, tours, donations, and merchandising in 2015 came to just shy of $60m, the shortfall being offset by private donations. National September 11 Memorial and Museum chairman, and former Mayor of New York, Michael Bloomberg, gave a low interest loan to the museum of $15m, to help with the cash flow.

Clearly there is going to have to be a federal bailout in the future. Even with a discount in the Foundation's utility rate, and unpaid volunteers on the ground, there's a reason why there are calls for the $12m annual security budget to be offloaded elsewhere. The current level of expenditure appears unsustainable, and the institution seems destined to go the way of RMS Titanic Inc. Only this particular memorial simply cannot be allowed to sink, so the money to bridge the gap is going to have to be found from somewhere. The question is: why spend so much to 'honour' the memory of the dead in the first place? The answer to that may lie with your local undertaker; go and ask why people spend excessive amounts on a funeral and memorial for their dearly departed. Mine said "guilt".

In contrast to the prevailing gloom of the lower lobby, the shop, situated at the foot of the escalator, is saturated with light. A volunteer 'Retail Greeter' smiles and we exchange perfunctory enquiries after each other's wellbeing before he leaves me in peace to browse for a 'meaningful keepsake'. It is a veritable Aladdin's Cave for the dark tourist, and I have to concede that, in terms of the sheer range of souvenirs, 9/11 has left no stone unturned; in fact they're even selling them. There's a basket of flat grey cobbles, bearing the "No Day Shall Erase" quote. The stones aren't available through the online store. I heft one in my hand. Probably not the best idea sending rocks through the post. I replace it, carefully. It costs $32.

Books and DVDs on every aspect of 9/11, bar 'inside jobs', run down the right hand side, along with 'inspired' silk scarves and — "A-ha!" — the Men's Trident necktie! I'd been coveting this design classic, created by someone called Josh Bach, for months, deterred by the online shipping costs. Now I'm here it's going straight in the basket. The pattern depicts the ribs and steel tridents that formed the external skeleton of the towers. It will look splendid against the black shirt I'm currently sporting. Now if only I can find a tie clip, featuring a Boeing 767, I will be able to sartorially recreate 9/11... That's wrong and twisted, but as soon as I saw the tie online it was too late, the thought ambushed me. The joke is as crass as it is thin, and as the tie retails at $50, is actually on me.

Moving swiftly on there's the usual paraphernalia associated with any souvenir shop at a major tourist attraction: kitchenware featuring the New York skyline, fridge magnets, bookmarks, jewellery, 'apparel', including some cold weather headgear with furry earflaps, which seems a bit premature, given it's probably still a balmy September day outside.

There are no shot glasses, but if you're feeling thirsty there are five different water bottles; the cheapest plastic model retails for $20.95, or there's the top of the range metal pair at $38.95 each; one white, '9/11 Memorial Honor & Remember', or

Trident pin souvenir.

military green, branded with 'They' Witnessed–Volunteered–Sacrificed–Responded'. The metal flask reminds me of the WWII German stick grenade. Further research reveals this comparison is not without foundation, as it transpires to be a collaborative piece between the 9/11 Memorial and 'Fashion Has Heart', a non-profit collective that annually selects 'five wounded heroes' from across the US armed services to work with artists to design merchandise.

There are also a number of products featuring the cadaver dogs, who searched the smoking ruins of the WTC, known as 'The Pile', for remains, and boosted the morale of rescue and recovery workers The canines are well represented in store: 9/11 memorial dog collar/leash/jacket (Fire Department and Police Department logo-ed), bandanas, (also FDNY and NYPD logo-ed), a book, badges, a mug, a tray, the pooches are even plasticised as decorations to hang on your Christmas tree, price $17.95.

I admire the framed 9/11 Flag of Honor, mounted on the wall ($32, Fifteenth Anniversary Edition), the Stars and Stripes, where the stripes have been composed with the names of the 'Heroes & Victims' in red and navy blue. It's the same price if you buy the standard edition, but then you won't get the silver dollar sticker on the pack that tells you it's specifically for the fifteenth anniversary. Created by John Michelotti, so the museum informs me, it's five-foot by three-foot, with grommets, is 100% American made (materials and labour), and when framed in red, white and blue trim, as illustrated in store, looks very impressive. I decide to buy it, in part to make amends for my guilt over the Men's Trident necktie.

Then I find the paper cranes. They're presented in clear acrylic boxes, and cost $16.95. Although initially puzzled by the presence of the dog-themed gifts, (until I recalled their role in the recovery programme), the presence of origami cranes for sale has me flummoxed, and I have a needling curiosity, because there's a packet of origami paper in my bag specifically for folding paper cranes. Fortunately the gift shop has provided an explanatory script.

Japanese tradition says that anyone who folds 1,000 origami cranes gets a wish. In contemporary culture the paper crane denotes peace, epitomised by the story of Sadako Sasaki, who was two years old when the first atomic bomb was dropped on Hiroshima. Sadako was diagnosed with leukaemia at the age of eleven as a result of her exposure, and while hospitalised, she began folding cranes, before she passed away, aged twelve. In 1958 a memorial statue of her holding a golden crane was established in Hiroshima Peace Park.

I knew all that. I also knew the paper crane is known in Japan as *'orizuru'*, that the discipline of folding 1,000 cranes is known as *'Senbazuru'*, and that the USA dropped the atomic bomb on Hiroshima, which the text neglected to mention. What I didn't know was:

"Children around the world adopted the gesture after 9/11 and sent paper cranes to the rescue and recovery workers and 9/11 families."

That's a nice touch, I think. Then I think again. When the museum says, "Children around the world", what exactly does it mean? It conjures the image of numerous contributing countries, spread across continents, with thousands of school kids folding cranes for America under tutorial supervision. Thoughts turn inevitably to home, and England. Would our kids really fold origami cranes to send for comfort? Surely they'd use their dexterity to send a text: "Sosz 4 u r loss. Bummer 😞 "

In addition, the National September 11 Memorial Museum has 1,000 origami cranes folded by Japanese schoolchildren. I assume the one for sale that I'm holding ($16.95!) was not one of those folded and sent by the schoolchildren of Japan, or anywhere else. Naturally this leads me to wonder exactly who *did* fold the one in the box, how much they get paid, what the mark-up might be, and, having appropriated a symbol of peace that originated from Japan for sale in its New York gift shop, whether the National September 11 Memorial Museum sends a donation to Japan in return? The boxed crane goes back on the shelf. I can fold my own. I turn and discover paper crane earrings, price $26.

The heat inside the shop from the lights is becoming oppressive, although this may be exasperated by my confusion over the merits of the merchandise available. On a whim I decide to collect commemorative 9/11 pins, so stalk the store like a magpie until I've one of each, before joining the short queue. The first gentleman to be served is asked if he would like to make a donation in addition to his purchases? He would. The gentleman in front steps forward, and is also asked if he too would like to make a donation in addition to his purchases? He declines. At the beckoning smile I step forward, drawing the

Early Access Museum Tour ticket from inside my jacket.

"It says here, on my ticket, that I have a 10% discount off my purchases in store..."

The girl dutifully registers the contents of my basket, includes my discount, adds the tax, and asks me for $96.19, and would I like — a free Recycle Tote bag? I would indeed, as they're $4.95. As the transaction is processed, I imagine she's wondering what on earth I've been doing in the museum for nearly nine hours, while I wait for her to ask if I would like to make a donation, but she doesn't. Clearly there's a 'They have Honored, Remembered, and Spent Enough Already' cut off point, or perhaps because I'm from overseas my donation wouldn't be tax deductible.

The media controversy over the gift shop has blown itself out. Some of the items might not be everyone's idea of a 'memorable keepsake', but it's perfect if you are of a certain age and looking to spoil grandchildren.

It is worth noting that the USS *Arizona* memorial in Pearl Harbor was financed in part from a concert by Elvis Presley, and from the sales of a model kit of the USS *Arizona*, produced by Revell. According to Lennon and Foley in *Dark Tourism: The Attraction of Death and Disaster*, the memorial is accessed by a boat shuttle service, taking suitably attired visitors, (no beach wear permitted), for a designated period, before returning them to shore before the next group are ferried across. Thus the USS *Arizona* is arguably the most revered memorial in the United States, yet was funded, in part, by a pop concert and sales of a toy, which in no way detracts from the memorial's solemnity.

Beyond the bright lights of the store there's still the promise of exclusive video footage of former New York Mayor, Rudy Giuliani, President George W. Bush, and Tony Blair, in the series '9/11 Decisions', being screened in the auditorium. Blair struggled to fake sincerity at the best of times, and is now considered toxic by the British public. The thought of his sycophantic rictus, pledging allegiance that will ultimately culminate in yet more death, after a day spent focusing on so much actual death, is untenable. Up above, outside, there are still a couple of hours of sunshine left to enjoy.

Before leaving I visit the restroom. It is well appointed in light grey tiles, a row of stalls across the far end, urinals, basins and side-lit mirrors along the walls. Overall the National September 11 Museum is very impressive. They have covered 9/11 in comprehensive detail. Nor have they missed a trick at the box office. Whether it cost $700m, or $1.3 billion, no expense has been spared, other than on crockery and cutlery in the cafeteria. And, it transpires, on the doors of the toilet stalls. They're brushed steel, and very much in keeping with the grey aesthetic, but why are they so short.

It's a rogue's gallery of sneakers, socks, trousers, underwear and shins, an unedifying spectacle below the saloon style cubicle doors. There is more privacy to be had amongst the trees and bushes at Chernobyl. Fact. Later research establishes that although short stall doors are indeed cheaper, they also allow air to circulate, assist with ease of cleaning, permit anyone locked inside to escape beneath, and deter inappropriate behaviour, such as 'cottaging', or drug taking. This is 'sacred ground' after all. However I've explored numerous cemeteries worldwide, including those in London where rent boys roam, yet never recall the toilet stall doors being this short. Therefore toilet cubicles (at dark sites) is something I will now look into.

It's a relief to finally step outside into the sunshine, the site still heaving with people surrounding the memorial pools, sitting on benches, or grabbing shade on the trim lawns under the oaks. A group of lads are crossing the plaza, one carrying a very cheap, very pink, blow up doll. A security guard intervenes and sends them back the way they came.

There's a uniformed cop on the corner. He sports insignia on his shirt that designates him as a member of the 'Counter-Terrorism Squad', and a protruding forearm covered in snaking tribal ink, which turns out to be a conversation piece. I ask him if this is his regular beat, and if it's a bit boring, patrolling tourists.

"It's fine — so long as there's not a terrorist attack!"

But yeah, the plaza is his permanent beat, where he gets to meet lots of people, and he's paid his dues.

"Compared to the boroughs, this is a country club."

I wonder if that's how the borough fire crews regarded Ten House, the World Trade Center's very own fire station, before 9/11.

IT'S ANOTHER GLORIOUS SEPTEMBER MORNING IN NEW YORK. I'M booked on the 11:00 a.m. walking tour from the 9/11 Tribute Center, just off the Memorial Plaza in Liberty Street, and, yet again, I'm ridiculously early. Obviously I apologise for this. The 'Greeter' is the genuine article, and having signed in (my name is ticked off a list) I'm overwhelmed by the hospitality extended:

"Do you need to use our restroom?"

"No, I'm good, thank you."

I will be checking it out later though. I'm now genuinely curious about the length of dark site toilet stall doors.

"As you are early, would you like to have some breakfast first?"

"I've had breakfast, thanks."

A number three set, with bacon and a cappuccino at the 'Essex World Café', next door but one. Plastic cutlery, but at least there was a 'teaspoon'.

"Would you like to join the earlier 10:30 a.m. tour?"

"Honestly, I'm fine waiting for 11 o'clock, thanks."

The 10:30 a.m. looks busy, and includes a few hard-core trekkers, although I assume we're only going to the memorial pools and back. The 'Greeter' and I are getting on like the proverbial house on fire, but that's okay, because the Ten House fire station is next door.

"Would you like to see our museum now?"

"I think I'll wait until after the tour."
I may be inside for some time.
"Where do you come from?
"London."

Finally we're exhausted and I excuse myself to pop into the adjacent New York souvenir shop. It's one of those generic affairs found in cities the world over, selling every conceivable kind of memento. Naturally I'm looking for anything related to 9/11, in particular snow globes featuring the Twin Towers within the plastic skyline. Shaking one evokes the memory of the fluttering paper and debris after the planes hit. The snow globe skylines of New York have all been remodelled post 9/11, and not one features the Twin Towers; such collectibles are now found on eBay. I settle for a pair of suitably tall and proportionate shot glasses, bearing the legend, "We Will Never Forget," with the date '9–11–01' immediately below, so you won't, and 'Bravery Sacrifice Honor' beneath the Lower Manhattan skyline, where the Twin Towers are replaced by columns of light. There's a choice of blue or red, so I buy one of each, at $6.99.

Back on the pavement our group has assembled, and we're introduced to Barry, a sprightly sixty-something with a kindly face. The Tribute Center is a non-profit, organised by the families of the victims of 9/11, and was functioning long before the National September 11 Museum.

Here's a question: why are there two institutions, separated by less than 500 yards, one charging $24 for admission, the other $25, both devoted to the same tragedy? I asked the Tribute Center, because the National September 11 Memorial and Museum informed me that they wouldn't be answering my questions. To be fair the media contact at the Tribute Center wasn't replying to my emails either, so I posted the question on their Facebook page, repeatedly every day until they replied:

"That is a great question — but we can only speak with authority about the 9/11 Tribute Center which is a 501c3 nonprofit organisation opened in 2006 to serve the 9/11 community who were directly impacted by the events — family members who lost loved ones, survivors, first responders, rescue and recovery workers, civilian volunteers, and Lower Manhattan workers and residents. We are now a community of over 800 volunteers who share their personal stories with visitors and by doing so provide an understanding of the loss and impact of 9/11 while demonstrating the resilience and recovery of New York City.

"The National September 11 Memorial Museum opened in 2014 as the historical museum of the events of 9/11 They are also a 501c3 nonprofit organisation and honouring the lives of those who were lost is at the heart of their mission. They tell the story of 9/11 through multimedia displays, archives, narratives and a collection of monumental and authentic artefacts which is different than Tribute's focus on personal stories. [sic]

"Both welcome visitors and remember our loved ones who were lost. Thanks for helping us clarify to all of our followers. Hope you will visit us soon."

So essentially the National September 11 Museum is there for the historical perspective, although they have a permanent 'In Memoriam' exhibition, devoted to the people lost. Clearly there is enough tourism to support both institutions.

The Tribute Center volunteers who conduct the walking tours are comprised of those who survived, responded, witnessed, or who were bereaved. Barry could be a former fireman, he's got the physique, but behind his sunglasses there's a sense that this is first and foremost a man who lost someone. I was aware of the possibility of taking a tour led by one of the bereaved, so I've toned down today's black with jeans.

We're issued with headsets, and then we're off round the corner of Ten House, the WTC's very own fire station. Mounted on the flank wall is a bronze bas-relief memorial plaque, fifty-six feet long by six feet high, recording the efforts of the fire fighters on 9/11, with the central panel depicting the burning towers, and the names of the 343 fire fighters who died listed alphabetically below. It is beautiful, and beyond that it carries the most powerful sentiment:

"Dedicated to those who fell and to those who carry on."

It is the public acknowledgement of those who carry on that resonates, and it is all the more touching because this scripted nod to the bereaved is

not echoed elsewhere. The firefighters have managed to capture the essence of the disaster and its aftermath in less than a dozen words. And they didn't need Virgil to do it for them.

The tour group who arrived just ahead of us have already taken their photos and moved on. Barry is in our ears:

"See how long that group gave it?"

He tells us how the memorial was created in a partnership between the New York Fire Department and the Holland & Knight law firm, who lost one of their partners, Glenn J. Winuk, a volunteer fireman, who left his desk to respond and never returned. Apparently all the firemen depicted in the relief have the same face, symbolising 'everyman'. There is, I discover on closer examination later, one face that is unmistakably African-American. But the sentiment is what is really important here. All ranks, brothers together.

We cross the road towards the Memorial Plaza where Barry informs us that the gleaming skyscraper, One World Trade Center, is the tallest building in the northern hemisphere by dint of its decorative pinnacle, which extends the structure to 1,776 feet, echoing 1776, the year the United States Declaration of Independence was signed. He points out the eight faces of the structure,

Firefighter's Memorial. Ten House, New York

Memorial pool, on the 15th anniversary of 9/11.

which mirror the two original four-sided towers, the security features at the base, the use of the trident motif, and the heat reflected by the glass, before walking us onto the Memorial Plaza itself.

"Does anyone notice anything about this light post?"

"It's in proportion to the Twin Towers."

That was an educated guess, based on simply looking at it, and noticing the reminiscent vertical ribbing, but it turns out to be correct. Barry draws our attention to the stone floor, where the blocks are also cut in the same proportion, and the entrance pavilion to the museum, which resembles a fallen building. Symbolism is everywhere. The tree line surrounding the pools, and not the pools themselves, denote where the outer walls of the Twin Towers once stood.

"Does anyone know what these trees are?"

"Swamp oaks."

They are indeed. They took swamp white oaks, indigenous to the three sites attacked, New York, Pennsylvania and Washington, and planted them here. Barry describes them as "the most pampered trees in all of America". There are underground cisterns that collect the surface water, a drip feed irrigation system, and aeration pipes, to supply air to the roots, which are braced, so they don't buckle the hard standing. Each tree has its own monitoring system that sends reports on the tree's health and growth.

"So if they need water — they get it!"

This is great. Barry is entertaining and informative. We walk to the twin pools, or voids, entitled 'Reflecting Absence', the winning design by New York architect, Michael Arad. They are enormous, simple, fitting, and beautiful. Water cascades down the sides in rivulets, reflecting the individuals, before pooling, or forming a community, and running into a second sunken pool, which acts as an abyss, where the bottom is never seen. The falling water muffles the noise of the city, but it could also suggest the sound of implosion, in the way the cascade lends itself to the image of the towers in perpetual, eternal freefall. The names, cut into bronze plates, are ranged in meaningful connections around the sides, and include those lost in the initial WTC attack in 1993. Flowers are placed among the names of the victims on their birthdays.

Essentially the memorials are sunken squares within sunken squares[1], and during my time in New York I spend hours gazing at them. The perimeter and positioning allows people to freely move around, reading the names that catch their eye, and the size and uniformity of each side allows people to be lost in thought amongst bystanders without the sense of intrusion. This is an absolutely brilliant piece of memorial design, stunning from every angle, truly fitting, symbolic, and empathetic to the disaster.

Barry gathers us together.

"Now does anyone know what this tree is?"

"It's a pear."

"That's right. It's a Callery pear."

I'm on fire. I *knew* it was a *Callery* pear, but I don't want anyone in the group to think I'm a 9/11 geek. Barry tells the story of how the tree was recovered from the rubble in October 2001, with snapped roots, burnt and broken. Yet someone had faith, and gave the pear to the New York City Department of Parks and Recreation, who replanted it. The tree produced new growth, before it was subsequently blown over and uprooted. Back it came again. Even when hurricane Sandy tried to flood it, the tree simply refused to die.

"Someone finally figured out that perhaps this tree is trying to tell us something."

Now it occupies pride of place in the plaza, aptly named 'The Survivor Tree'. Barry indicates the new growth, post 9/11, which is rather magical. It seems fitting that the new WTC is being built around this stubborn individual that steadfastly refuses to quit. Barry smiles:

---

1) In five months time a letter will arrive from Stuttgart, Germany bearing two identical 45¢ stamps, depicting an aerial view of a structure, again essentially a sunken square within a square. The similarity of the design with the New York memorial is striking.

The building on the stamp is the 'Topographie des Terrors', the award winning design from architect Ursula Wilms of Berlin architects Heinle, Wischer and Partner, and landscape architect Heinz W. Hallmann from Aachen. It is an indoor/outdoor history museum, detailing repression under the Nazis. Opened in May 2010, at a cost of €20m, it resides on the site of what was the headquarters of the Geheime Staatspolizei and the Schutzstaffel: the Gestapo and the SS.

"Don't even think of touching it…"

He leads us round to the North Pool and hands me his bag to hold, reward for answering his questions I like to think. He pulls out a black and white photo that he took in the early 1970s. It was taken from the roof of the North Tower, looking across at the top of the lower South Tower, captured rising up towards the lens, still under construction. He explains that he was in healthcare, and in his spare time, with a family to support, he took a second job, as an on-site medic at the WTC, to tend to any injuries the construction workers sustained.

He was taken up by lift to treat a worker, but afterwards had to walk down, all 110 storeys, and even as a young man it took time. So when his daughter-in-law called on the morning of 9/11 to tell him a plane had hit the North Tower, and he turned on the TV and saw the pictures, he was desperately trying to remember if the stairs he'd descended all those years ago were in the corners, or at the core. Because his son, Josh, worked in the offices of Cantor Fitzgerald.

That's the problem with research: sometimes you know what's coming next. Cantor Fitzgerald is synonymous with 9/11. The financial services firm occupied floors 101–105 of the North Tower. No employee in those offices survived. The firm lost 658 of the 960 staff members employed in New York.

Barry stoops and wets his hand in the moat that flows beneath the memorial plates, and then washes his son's name.

"So when I realised… then I knew…."

Behind his tinted glasses Barry has a twinkle in the bottom corner of his eye. No one knows what to say, there's just a murmur of condolence. A guy in the group puts his hand on our guide's shoulder. Everyone takes a collective moment, but Barry is like that Callery pear. He talks about his son and shows us a photograph of Josh. You think of his wife, beaming from the photo, who lost her husband. Then Barry shows us the name of Josh's father-in-law, close by, who also worked for Cantor Fitzgerald.

He closes the tour by saying that he's happy with the compromise between the memorial and the rebuilding of the World Trade Center complex. He's particularly satisfied that The Sphere, the metal sculpture that originally stood in the middle of the WTC plaza, which has resided in Battery Park for the past fourteen years after being recovered from the debris, is going to be returned to the site.

"Finally someone's listened about that one…"

The tour ends with our thanks. Barry collects the headsets before we disperse. I return to the Tribute Center with him, and ask if he'll be attending the memorial ceremony for the families on Sunday, the fifteenth anniversary.

He tells me he won't. He only comes up from his home in Washington one Friday every month, to takes two tours. He smiles.

"That's enough for me."

THERE IS A $15 ENTRY FEE TO THE MUSEUM AT THE TRIBUTE CENTER, but free if you book a tour, which is $25, and well worth it. The walking tour lasts approximately an hour and a quarter, and the museum could be covered in three quarters of an hour, at a push, either before or after the tour.

The Tribute Center tells the story of 9/11 on a much smaller scale than the National September 11 Museum. There are fewer pairs of shoes on display. However there is plenty to draw the attention in terms of artefacts, audio, and video loops, which includes footage of Cantor Fitzgerald CEO and chairman, Howard Lutnick, who lost his brother, as well as so many of his employees. Mr Lutnick was late for work on 9/11, because he took his son to his first day at kindergarten. It's a hard yet compelling watch of a man utterly consumed with grief, almost to the point of disintegration, and it epitomises what so many of the bereaved endure in private.

The Tribute Center also features paper crane chains, hanging in curtains from the ceiling, and one of Sadako's actual cranes, miniscule, made of foil, donated in person by her brother when he visited New York. Having folded a few in my time there's wonderment and envy at her dexterity. Sadako's story is presented with an accompanying portrait photograph.

There is a small gift shop at the entry/exit, selling much of the same merchandise available in the National September 11 Museum, although the Tribute Center don't appear to be selling any cranes. They do however have their own shot glasses. Here we're invited to "Take your experience home", and I spend $50.79 on more commemorative pins.

Yet it is in the presentation of the photographs of the victims where the Tribute Center has really excelled. Mounted behind glass on three sides, with a viewing bench and a convenient box of tissues to hand, the pictures plaster the walls. There's no formal arrangement, and it is this seemingly slap-dash presentation that brings the subjects to life, as much as the photographs themselves; at work, at play, with families, on holidays, graduations, parties, and candidly captured, the personalities leap out. Indeed in some photos it is difficult to work out who was actually lost, yet this is why it works; they have become real people, glue in the lives of others. The arrangement strikes a chord because it's how we would curate our own lives, rather than having them displayed by someone who had no idea of who we actually were.

The overall effect is to draw the viewer in, and engage. As a result I spend far more time looking at the people in the photographs than I did yesterday, where I was simply looking at formally presented individuals without really seeing who they were. Yesterday they were islands. Today there's not a chink between them. In the Tribute Center those lost aren't presented as victims, but as people given the freedom to escape a mounted statistical fate. It's far more personal, as if you've been invited into someone's home, and seen the photographs of those they love.

Photo shrine, 9/11 Tribute Center.

Randomly scattered throughout the photographic display are personal items: caps, shirts, mugs, patches, belts, books, a bird nesting box, a Fisher-Price model racing car, sport trophies, a pair of spectacles, even a Spider-Man figurine. It does add a certain shrine-like quality, and makes the montage a piece of art in its own right.

In the basement there is a small presentation area, where volunteers periodically share their experiences of the disaster, and a table where visitors are encouraged to write their reflections on cards. A selection of these are presented on the wall, so you can read their thoughts, with translations provided for those cards written in other languages. It is also possible to download the card from their website, so you can write at home and mail it in:

*"**Please share your thoughts with us**. Share your September 11th story. How have you been changed by the events of September 11th, or what action can you take in the spirit of Tribute to help or educate another?"*

The wall is changed periodically, with cards taken from the archive, which means there is a very good cross section to read, including comments from younger visitors, those who were children in 2001, or born post 9/11.

("I was only three months old when it happened and I can't believe that all of this chaos happened and so many lives were lost. But I am overall devastated but happy that all the people were dead but people care about them instead of ignoring it like other causes in the world.")

The Tribute Center and the National September 11 Museum have different attributes. I spent less money and less time at the Tribute Center than in the

National September 11 Museum, yet valued the experience with the Tribute Center more. The reason for spending more time in the National September 11 Museum is because there's more to see, and it was taxing. The Tribute Center is not 9/11 'lite', especially given Howard Lutnick's gut-wrenching testimony, but the atmosphere is considerably more at ease with itself. This may be due to the oppressive confines of the subterranean National September 11 Museum and its use of sombre lighting, and that the Tribute Center comes from the bereaved, thus from the heart, rather than being stage-managed solemnity.

The Tribute Center also succeeds because it retains a tangible connection with the events through its large pool of volunteers, who bring their diverse, uniquely personal experiences, and crucially, their *personalities* to the audience, which we can relate to. It is character and personality that the National September 11 Museum lacks. The Tribute Center is also helping those who suffered from the events of 9/11 in a therapeutic way. Barry, and those who carry on, can tell others about their loved ones, and the bereaved take comfort that as long as those who've passed are remembered, they're never really gone.

The Tribute Center has now moved to a new, expanded location nearby on Greenwich Street, adopting an additional role to promote voluntary service, and changed its name to the 9/11 Tribute Museum. Hopefully it will retain what it has so successfully encapsulated from 9/11.

On reflection, the National September 11 Museum already feels stagnated, looking back on the events of 9/11 as if they were 100 years ago, rather than fifteen, a disconnect all the more remarkable given the museum has only been open since 2014. It feels like a time capsule, literally buried. The

Visitor message displayed at the 9/11 Tribute Center.

dislocation seemed to reference Victorian times, when undertakers employed professional mourners to swell the cortège for the deceased, to add prestige. Essentially I think that is what the National September 11 Museum is: a professional mourner.

Between May 2014, when it opened, and May 2016, the National September 11 Museum received 5.7 million visitors, but only 20% came from New York, New Jersey, and Connecticut; international visitors accounted for 30%. In the week the museum opened, the *New York Times* ran a poll asking readers if they would attend. The majority of those who responded said they would not.

They saw the museum as being "filled with gawking, ghoulish out-of-towners", and that they "did not need a public exhibition to remind them of a personal tragedy that they could not forget".

The museum and memorial countered with promotional advertising on the subway and local cable, and the vox pop 'Our City. Our Story' to entice locals, and provided annual membership packages, ranging from 'Individual' ($74), 'Dual' ($108), 'Family' ($250), through to 'Patron's Circle' ($2,000), designed to create regular visitors with a range of packages to suit every pocket.

Post-Traumatic Stress Disorder (PTSD) in the wake of 9/11, especially within

New York, has been recognised. The effects can last for years, in some cases a lifetime. There is a display in the National September 11 Museum relating to PTSD, although you have to descend seven floors to the substratum to see it, which may be testing for a populace who've been chased through their streets by a pair of skyscrapers, and might be experiencing PTSD as a result.

The museum needs to get everyone through their doors, including New Yorkers. There's a price on 'Remembering and Honoring', which is currently $24, and someone's got to pay. The National September 11 Memorial and Museum needs tourists, even dark ones. Alice Greenwald, current CEO of the Greatest Dark Tourism Site on Earth, may well have her fingers crossed, hoping there's enough of us, and that we keep coming.

SUNDAY MORNING, THE FIFTEENTH ANNIVERSARY OF 9/11, AND I've had a lie in, so I'm late. Not that I'm getting anywhere near the memorial. There's a ring of steel across Liberty Street as I emerge from the shade of Zuccotti Park. Both Presidential hopefuls are in attendance for the reading of the names. I have no idea if Hillary has fallen over yet, but I will if I don't have some breakfast. The Essex World Café sits, tantalizing, just

St. Paul's Chapel, on the 15th anniversary of 9/11.

yards inside the cordon. I explain to the cop on duty in perfect Estuary English that 'The Essex' is my regular. He feigns kindly suspicion, but the chirp has won him over, and he lets me through. After all, this is America; "it's the economy, stupid."

The café appears empty. It's Sunday, so there's no footfall from the construction site that is the WTC. I take the tray round the corner into the dining area at the rear, past the framed photo of the café smothered with dust in the immediate fallout from 9/11, only to discover I've walked straight into the commode scene from Tarantino's *Reservoir Dogs*. Thirty fold. New York's Finest, resplendent in their parade dress black, look up. I smile weakly, nod in acknowledgement, and take a seat in the corner, under a framed 'Never Forget' Twin Towers skyscape, keeping my hands visible at all times. They're already done with me, so I furtively take in the scene over the rim of the cappuccino. There are several senior firefighters towards the rear, and a smattering of beautiful wives and girlfriends in black, tapping manicured nails on their phones.

I make short work of breakfast, exit through the rear, and peer in through the window of O'Hara's classic Irish pub opposite. The TV screen above the bar shows an immaculately dressed young couple, wearing white and pale blue lapel ribbons, the 9/11 badge of bereavement. Behind them stands a first responder of senior rank, as they read out the names. The subtitles tell me they're into the 'K's'. Igor Zukelman is a long way off. The service takes about four hours. The memorial won't be open to the public until mid afternoon, so I turn my attention elsewhere.

Hooping round the ring of steel I arrive at St. Paul's Chapel, The Parish of Trinity Church Wall Street, on the corner of Broadway and Vesey Street. They are offering silver ribbons, marked September 11, 2016, for people to write messages on before tying them to the black railings of the church. They're everywhere and the effect is beautiful. I take one and pull up a kerb, pen in hand, but absolutely nothing will come. There are names I remember from the past few days, and some that have been in my head for months, but feel that it's inappropriate for me to add them. I didn't know them, I'm disconnected from this tragedy, and every sentiment feels incredibly trite.

Resigned I carefully wind the ribbon round my fingers and slip it in my bag. Another souvenir. Across Vesey Street the annex National September 11 Memorial Museum Store is open. I find two more pins for my expanding collection and lose the receipt.

Down on the corner at Church Street there are a couple of 'Truthers'. A TV crew are interviewing a supporter of 'InfoWars', the website created by Texan radio show host and conspiracy theorist, Alex Jones. The activist is handing out newspapers called *The Patriot*. TV asks him if he receives abuse from the families and relatives of the victims.

"Very little, really," replies the stalwart, his baseball cap on back to front.

This wasn't the answer TV was hoping for, judging by his next line:

"I see you've got a Trump patch on there..."

I walk on past a man holding a sign asking for the Twin Towers to be rebuilt, and another claiming WTC7 is the 'smoking gun', but in the afternoon sunshine the mood is benign. Passers-by cast a cursory glance at most. Indeed the rallying cry is more about patriotism and truth, rather than suggesting the Twin Towers were raised by controlled demolition. This is reflected in the price of the '9/11 was an Inside Job' t-shirts, available through the InfoWars online store, which are now discounted by five bucks.

By 3:00 p.m. the Memorial Plaza is opened to the public. It is a picture with so many of the names now bearing tributes left by the bereaved; flags, poems, photos, sprays of forget-me-knots, there are flowers everywhere. Tourists are taking selfies like never before. Today elevates the site from being a tourist attraction, to a specific, recognised, moment in time, perfect for the essential 'And I was there' capture. An Asian lady brandishes her selfie stick, smiling broadly, standing next to her husband, who conversely hides, arms folded across his chest, sulky, and fish-lipped. His demeanour does not improve, because she's not satisfied with the result. She makes three attempts until she's finally satisfied, although his posture and face remains the same throughout.

I return to Ten House, the bas-relief memorial now flanked by uniformed firemen, a large floral tribute on a stand in the centre, the kerb lined by a phalanx of Stars and Stripes. Behind the crowd that have gathered, Harry John Roland, known as the 'World Trade Center Man', paces up and down his pitch;

"History!... Don't let it be a mystery!'

He turns up every afternoon, and has been doing so for years, an unofficial guide who sees it as his self appointed duty to inform anyone who will listen that three buildings fell that day, not just the Twin Towers. When he's not shouting out his catchphrase he busies himself buffing the bronze memorial, but not today. Someone senior from the station calls time on him, so that they can change the honour guard, which Harry acknowledges and complies with immediately. Now you could hear a pin drop. It is perfect.

And when the names had been read, the parades marched, and all the memories churned, darkness fell like a warm blanket over New York, and the Twin Towers illuminated the night sky once again.

Then the men in uniform undid their top buttons, and together with their brothers and with their girls, retired round the corner to O' Hara's bar for a bloody good drink.

WORLD'S END

The sapling's claw is persistent.

"Will you let GO of me!"

Yesterday's grasping branches were an amusing distraction, but today that's all changed. Perhaps prolonged exposure to abnormal levels of radiation fuels paranoia, because the snags now feel intended, and in the past hour I've become convinced I'm being followed.

But the trail over my shoulder lies empty, save for a solitary leaf that cartwheels, pirouettes and innocently curtsies to the floor at my heels as the breeze dies. The others have gone. There's no sound of them. There again, there's no sound at all. I'm in a corridor of thicket between deserted apartment blocks that stare down through square, soulless eyes. A face at a window now and I'll be a gibbering wreck. This abandoned town of Pripyat, in northern Ukraine, once home to the workers of the Chernobyl nuclear power plant, is without doubt the most surreal environment for a 'holiday'.

IN THE SMALL HOURS OF SATURDAY 26TH APRIL 1986, THE STAFF OF Block 4 at the Vladimir Ilyich Lenin nuclear power plant initiated a test on the reactor to see if they could save energy. Instead they released it. There was a series of explosions, the lid of the reactor flipped like a coin, and a rainbow column of fire shot 1,000 metres into the night sky. Some of the inhabitants of Pripyat watched the pyrotechnics from a railway bridge on the outskirts of town, to get a better view. They spoke of the beauty of the flames, composed of burning graphite, oblivious to the fact that as they watched they were simultaneously receiving a lethal dose of radiation. None would survive. Their vantage point is now known as the 'Bridge of Death'.

The firemen sent to fight the blaze had never fought anything like it. They tried to extinguish it with water, whilst wearing no specialist protection. Although they managed to subdue the secondary fires, they had no means to fight the one inside the reactor. Two of them died from exposure to lethal levels of radiation that night, others succumbed during the months that followed.

Lieutenant Vladimir Pravik was one such casualty. One of the first firemen at the scene, he died of acute radiation sickness on 11th May, just days before his twenty-fourth birthday. He was laid to rest in a sealed zinc coffin, posthumously decorated with the Order of Lenin, and made a Hero of the Soviet Union.

The official death toll in the aftermath of the accident was set at 31.

Three kilometres away from the plant, the inhabitants of Pripyat dealt in rumour, as soldiers and police arrived on their streets. By that evening readings taken by the plant showed the radiation was 600,000 times above normal levels. Soldiers questioned whether their machines were working properly, but they could all sense the metallic taste in their mouths. If they didn't act, the residents of Pripyat would be dead in four days.

On the morning of Sunday 27th over 1,000 buses arrived from Kiev to evacuate the townspeople, who were given two hours to pack essentials for what they were told would be a three day trip. The atomic refugees, all 43,000 of them, were evacuated within hours, except one elderly man who decided to remain behind. His body was discovered a few weeks later. By evening, the only people left were the military, and the scientists, who'd been sent to discover the extent of what would become the world's worst nuclear accident; an accident the world, as yet, didn't even know had happened.

Monday morning, 28th April, and during a routine check at the Forsmark nuclear power plant in Sweden, the soles of the shoes worn by a safety engineer registered radioactive. Additional checks established radioactivity wasn't emanating from Forsmark, which meant they had no idea what the source was. Military jets were sent into the clouds to take readings, and the Swedish authorities contacted Hans Blix, director of the International Atomic Energy Agency, (IAEA), in Vienna, to ask if they knew where the radioactivity detected in Sweden was coming from.

Speaking twenty years after the events on the Discovery Channel documentary, *The Battle of Chernobyl*, former leader of the Soviet Union, Mikhail Gorbachev, said that Sweden effectively told Russia the scale of the problem. Gorbachev had been advised that the 'accident' and 'fire' at the plant amounted to 'a kettle on Moscow's Red Square'. He directed the KGB to put the experts sent to Chernobyl under surveillance, so the Politburo would know what was really going on. By now American and European satellites had images of the ruined plant, and the news broke to the rest of the world. Chernobyl, a place that until then no one had heard of, was now on the map. It would now be a place no one would ever forget, not least because it had the potential to make the map redundant.

I WAS LIVING IN 'EAST GERMANY' AT THE TIME — THAT'S NOT A FAIR description of Romford, the market town of urban Essex, more commonly associated with the stereotypical 'Essex girl' jokes prevalent during the 1980s and 1990s. However East Germany is an extremely apt description of the rented first floor 'flat' I occupied in '*Kreuzungon Straße*', on the edge of town. A cold, unwelcoming room in milky green, furnished with mismatched and unloved pieces from the fifties, including a steampunked sofa bed that concertinaed like a mantrap, and a cankerous gas fire best condemned. I spent my waking hours in the parallel corridor that served as a galley kitchen, despite the draught whistling through the hole in the window, where an extractor fan had once whirred. I could never entirely shake the suspicion that the odious gas fire and the hole in the window might somehow be connected.

The house belonged to an elderly lady, who dwelt below, her presence only evident when you entered the rickety porch, when her door would surreptitiously open a chink so she could spy. Her son-in-law, a policeman, was in charge. He slept in the adjoining first floor bedsit during the week, when his audio curfew from 10 p.m. was strictly enforced, inevitably whilst I was busy bashing away like a dissident on my portable typewriter.

With no television or telephone, and only the resident Stasi for company, the radio had become my umbilical cord to the outside world, and the drip feed of news coming from the Ukraine. Up until that point my biggest concern had been the fitness of Bryan 'Captain Marvel' Robson for the impending FIFA World Cup Finals in Mexico. Chernobyl changed that. The combination of 'accident' and 'nuclear power plant' monopolised my attention. I was a child of the Cold War, and it had been less than a year since I'd sat in the shadow of Hiroshima's skeletal Genbaku Dome with the local schoolchildren, folding origami cranes for peace. Although I was no scientist, I knew something of the

potential dangers. The fact that this had happened behind the Iron Curtain, but was now being reported by the BBC, indicated the severity of the incident.

Some sort of radioactive fallout was inevitable, and although this Chernobyl might be 1,000 miles away to the east of Romford, that meant nothing to the wind. There was no point trying to run and hide. I plugged the missing glass in the kitchen with several layers of cardboard and tape, before going to work covered from head to toe, making a mental note to buy extra tinned peaches and powdered milk on the way home.

Sure enough, the officials and experts were soon all over the news in an attempt to soothe and placate, which in itself meant there was likely some cause for concern. The cloud of contamination spread. Having dusted much of Scandinavia, it split and touched Bavaria, Northern Italy, and France, where its presence was notably downplayed by the authorities, before moving on to Corsica, then Greece, and before long rains brought Chernobyl onto UK soil. The British government imposed a ban on the sale and movement of sheep that grazed on the infected upland pastures in Wales, Cumbria, and Scotland. Restrictions would remain in place on the affected farms in the regions, not for the predicted few weeks, or possibly months at worst, but for a quarter of a century.

Abandoned apartment blocks, Pripyat.

During those first few days of awareness I would examine the backs of my hands as though they were strangers, over-soap in the shower, and exacerbate the mildest irritations. But after a week or two, as is always the case, the headlines moved on, the disaster in the Ukraine dropped down the pecking order, and I became distracted once again by the footie in Mexico, and a curious young waif from Manchester, known only as Morrissey. No doubt at some point in the future the world would wonder whatever happened to ~~Morrissey~~ Chernobyl, but that would most likely be when an anniversary came around, by which time everything would've been sorted, by someone else.

Russia mobilised half a million men and women to tackle the catastrophe over the next seven months. They were fighting an omnipresent yet invisible enemy. Eighty helicopters took to the air to carry the fight to the stricken reactor, with pilots recalled from the conflict in Afghanistan to hover over the breach so sand, lead, and boron could be thrown onto the fire. Dosimeters were off the scale, and flying at the low altitude required to dump meant even exposure for thirty minutes could prove fatal. Pilots lined their seats with lead. Some flew over thirty sorties a day. Six thousand tonnes of 'neutron absorbers' were dropped from the air in a forlorn attempt to form a plug, yet virtually none of this bombardment ever reached the core.

Radiation casualties from the emergency workforce continued to arrive at Moscow's Hospital No. 6, where bone marrow transplants were conducted on an unprecedented scale with the help of specialists from the USA. The victims were young, fit men, but they died quickly having been directly exposed to massive doses of radiation at the plant. For the next fifteen years, only the first victims were acknowledged. The Soviet news agency, TASS, carried a government report on Wednesday 30th April, contradicting the mass casualties reported in the western media. TASS claimed that only two had died during the initial incident, and that a further 197 had been hospitalised, but that the level of radiation was now decreasing.

Thursday 1st, and the annual May Day parade in Kiev took place as usual, to project a state of normality. However the wind had changed direction, and was now blowing fallout towards the city. While bureaucrats had removed their own children from the area immediately after the accident, other schoolchildren were invited to join the parade. Photographer Igor Kostin, who'd flown over the plant and taken the first radioactively exposed images before his equipment jammed, described the May Day festivities as the 'Parade of Death'. Film of the event has apparently been withdrawn from the Ukrainian archives.

Back at the site, scientists were fearful of a second, potentially far more devastating explosion. The graphite and other components had reached a temperature of 1200°c, and were burning through the reactor floor as corium, radioactive lava. Below lay a reservoir, now flooded with water from the initial firefighting, and ruptured pipes. The fear was that if the corium came into contact with the water, there could be a subsequent steam explosion that would eject even more radioactive material from the reactor into the atmosphere. The exact consequences of such an event were unknown, but having initially underestimated the extent of the problem, there was now a fear that large tracts of Europe could become desolate wastelands.

Three engineers volunteered to open valves to drain the water and succeeded in their task, to the relief of their colleagues. The three later died from radiation sickness. To reduce the chance of the corium reaching the water table, it was decided to dig a room beneath the stricken reactor and fill it with concrete, and 10,000 miners and Metro construction workers were drafted in for this purpose. Before the room could be made, a tunnel had to be dug to its location. This took a month, with thirty miners taking three-hourly shifts around the clock. What little personal protection workers had they abandoned, due to the excessive heat, and although the subterranean environment afforded them some sanctuary from the radioactivity, they still had to run to and fro at the tunnel entrance. Miners drank water from open bottles and ingested radioactive particles. It is estimated that a quarter of these men died before they reached their fortieth birthday.

On the surface the situation was equally fraught. A week after the explosion, the ten kilometre exclusion zone was expanded into an evacuation zone; civilians from the villages in a thirty kilometre radius around the plant, approximately 68,000 people, many already contaminated, were evacuated. Further detection of isolated radioactive hot spots outside this thirty kilometre zone brought the total number of permanent evacuees to 135,000.

Over the course of the first year, personnel known as Liquidators tackled the immense clean up. Hunters shot contaminated cats and dogs; houses were cleaned one by one; some villages were razed and buried under the earth, and everything was sprayed with a PVA-based solution known as 'bourda', to stick and seal the dust. Teams felled and buried the most radioactive part of the adjacent 'Red Forest', so-called because the radiation had scorched the trees to rust.

All of these jobs involved exposure to the radioactive atmosphere. However the task that will linger in the collective memory is that of the 'bio-robots'. The explosion had scattered highly radioactive graphite onto the roof of the plant, and this had to be cleared. Initially robot machines were used, both Soviet and Western, but these snagged on the debris, or broke down within days, as the radiation fried their circuits; one even committed 'suicide', propelling itself into the breach.

So reservists were used; men replaced machines. Aged between twenty to thirty years old, they made improvised lead suits the night before, so had to work carrying up to thirty kilos on their bodies, running out onto the roof in relays, eight soldiers and an officer, for two–three minutes, sometimes for only forty seconds if the levels were too high, to shovel graphite off the roof. Three and a half thousand men were deployed in this work. Some went up as many as five times. At the end they couldn't make a fist with their fingers, their eyes hurt, and they couldn't feel their own teeth. Soldiers would wash up, eat, and then vomit. They received a certificate of recognition, $100, and a dose far greater than the one stated on their records.

Designs for a gigantic sarcophagus to encase the reactor had begun in May. It was prefabricated before being brought to the site for assembly. The unique structure was built from over 7,300 tons of metal framework and 300,000 tons of concrete. Nothing like this had ever been constructed, and because of the high levels of radiation, robots were again used where possible. The cabs of the cranes and vehicles were lead-lined to minimise the risk to the operatives, or to allow them to work for longer in the danger zone. It took sixty people to do one hour's worth of work.

By mid-December 1986, the roof of the sarcophagus was in place. When snow fell and settled it was hailed as a sign that the containment worked. A flag was erected as a symbolic gesture to show the triumph over radioactivity, and the workers added their graffiti to the tomb.

It was estimated that the whole operation had cost the Soviet Union eighteen million roubles, and at the time the rouble was pegged to the US dollar. The human cost of Chernobyl has never been adequately defined. Thousands, tens of thousands, no one knows for sure.

THE FLOOR CRUNCHES UNDERFOOT, SMOTHERED WITH SHARDS OF coloured glass mosaic that has fallen from the windows of Pripyat's iconic atomic café. Many of the panes remain in situ. Some have slipped. Women, messengers of the gods, with flowing hair and robes, extol the virtues of the nuclear age. It must have been the coolest place to take a drink when the sun shone. Below the tableau, I peer out through the missing glass, past the scrub and saplings, towards the dormant apartment blocks in the distance. No one is ever coming back, and if they do, only as tourists or scientists. Picking a way out through the debris across the glass and ripple floor, it seems ludicrous now to think that Chernobyl would simply fade away, like a footnote into history. The enormous financial cost of temporary containment may have hastened the dissolution of the Soviet Union, but the result of the accident is evident. These lands are unfit for human habitation, and the lease back to nature, free of charge, will run for approximately 20,000 years.

As well as the recorded deaths there has been the steady depressing demise of the Liquidators, and the documented increase in thyroid cancers in children across Belarus, Ukraine, and Russia. The IAEA's post-mortem on Chernobyl apparently took place behind closed doors, with no journalists present. Initial studies that predicted mass casualties as a result of the increased levels of radioactivity were radically reduced, from a projected model of 40,000 to a more acceptable 4,000.

FIVE YEARS AFTER THE DISASTER I'D ACQUIRED A PORTABLE BLACK and white television, so was glued to the BBC Horizon documentary, *Inside Chernobyl's Sarcophagus*, where Soviet scientists gave a tour to the first western film crew to be granted access to the interior. The Soviet scientists all looked suitably mad, an impression reinforced by them taping their overalls into their boots and breathing through respirators ordinarily used when doing some DIY. The western film crew went in with far more protection, and divided their exposure between two teams, thus minimising the risk. The scientists were credited with some of the footage, indicating that they'd ventured into areas the film crews had not.

Off duty the scientists smoked cigarettes, drank vodka, and spoke pragmatically about their work: the problems with their technology, the stifling bureaucracy, shortage of funding, even the lack of socks. Victor Popov, owl-like glasses and face of a bloodhound, was reduced to tears, speaking of the colleagues they'd lost, whose photographs now adorned the memorial wall in their living quarters. Popov said he could never have imagined working in areas registering 200 roentgens prior to the accident, yet now it was common practice.

What was terrifying was the condition of the sarcophagus itself. It was never designed as a permanent form of containment, just something to last twenty to thirty years. Built in haste, at great risk, and onto an existing

Mural, Chernobyl. Photo: Igor Bodnarchuk

structure that was unsound, birds were now nesting inside, and the scientists revealed there were holes large enough to drive a car through. Again, the scientists, who knew far more about the dangers, seemed pragmatic, rather than panicked. When Horizon returned five years later, in 1996, ten years after the accident, much had changed.

Victor Popov was no longer working at Chernobyl and was waiting for surgery to fit a lens to his eye, having already had one replaced. Some of the scientists who'd been filmed five years ago had subsequently died, and although patchy maintenance had been undertaken, the sarcophagus containing over 100 tonnes of corium, radioactive dust, uranium, and plutonium, was fundamentally doomed. Some form of new containment was required, one that would last longer than the original.

The media were reviving interest in Chernobyl for selected anniversaries, and with their chosen narrative. That monopoly would be eroded as their audience began to drift online. Whilst casually 'surfing' on a computer more suited to weighing down a body, I stumbled across Elena Filatova's blog site. Armed with a Geiger counter, camera, and motorcycle, she was entering the exclusion zone and posting incredible photographs, showing what happened after humans abandoned their world for twenty years. More to the point, the first pioneers had penetrated 'The Zone of Alienation'. It was only a matter of time until packaged tourists followed. In February 2011, Ukraine's Emergencies Ministry began licensing tourist trips. There were teething troubles, essentially with bureaucracy objecting to the excessive unaccounted profits, as tourists flocked to the zone, paying $100 per person for entry, but eventually common sense prevailed. It was Chernobyl after all; it wasn't going anywhere. In January 2013, Pripyat was re-opened for business; the cost of entry now $130 per person.

I T'S CRACK OF DAWN EARLY. NINE OF US BOARD THE MINI BUS OUTSIDE the Kozatskiy Hotel on Kiev's Independence Square. There are a number of Chernobyl tours starting from here, so there's a bit of shuffling between the day-packers, and some tentative introductions to work out who is with which group.

I'm having a year where real life is going to impinge on any dark travel plans, and this weekend to Chernobyl will serve as my annual holiday, so I'm most definitely going dark site specific. Irritatingly my commitments are such that I won't even have time to see Kiev's Chernobyl museum before I fly home. It's got excellent reviews and you can find it at 1 Khoryva Lane, open Monday to Saturday, 10 a.m. to 6 p.m., closed on Sundays and the last Monday of the month.

Our group is an all male affair; two from Texas, and the rest from around the UK, a group of four, two other Chernobyl singletons and yours truly. One assumes the ladies opt for a day trip, rather than this Full-Blown Geek Weekender. Whether that's because ladies choose to avoid geeks, or because

Town sign, Pripyat.

there's a lack of facilities within the exclusion zone, I'm unsure. I'd guess it is the former. As for the latter, we'll be using the bushes when required.

Before we get underway, Igor, our driver, guide, and radiologist conveniently all rolled into one, presents his Geiger counter, registering 0.13 microsieverts, which he assures us is lower than the reading inside his apartment in Kiev. This positive reading isn't due to the fallout from 1986. Background radiation is everywhere, from kitchens with granite surfaces, to the interior of New York's Grand Central station. In the UK, 0.15 microsieverts is considered an acceptable level, but we're aware we're going well beyond that on this trip. In 1986 it was roentgens, now they have been usurped by sieverts. I don't pretend to understand the need to switch measurements, or indeed the conversion rate, but I'm working on the principle that anything and everything on this tour will be 'hot'.

Once we're clear of the city, heading north, we're entertained during the journey by the documentary, *The Battle of Chernobyl*. I'd seen it before, several times. In fact I'd watched it the evening before catching my flight to Kiev as a refresher course on the salient facts, but I watch it again anyway. It serves as a reminder as to how many people were affected by the disaster, and how many sacrificed their lives to prevent the tragedy escalating. As we approach our destination the landscape changes, the roadside markets and the traffic thin, then disappear altogether to leave an empty road and endless trees.

It's a beautiful sky blue day by the time we pull up at the military checkpoint on the border to the exclusion zone, where we disembark, resisting the temptation to take any photographs of the installation or personnel, while Igor has our paperwork processed. There's another mini bus waiting to complete the formalities, and the only reason that's noteworthy is because there's a *girl* in their party. Peroxide crop, black vest, tattoos, combats, and boots. She looks effortlessly cool. I take another look at our group, this time from a sartorial perspective. We do not look cool, far from it; we look like a tapestry of tablecloths in our checked shirts. With trees dominating Chernobyl we have subconsciously adopted the lumberjack look.

Once back on the bus we head deeper into the zone, parking at the end of an overgrown track leading to an abandoned village, hidden in the undergrowth. Igor shows us a reading of 2.8 over the soil. It's lower over sealed surfaces, such as the road.

Fanning out we enthusiastically explore, weaving between the saplings into desolate cottages, ravaged by weather and time, creeping over spongy floors littered with debris and glass. This was once someone's home. Now only their ghosts remain, disturbed by us bloody foreigners granted tourist legitimacy to trespass, motivated to see what the end of civilisation will look like.

Further down the track, past dense thicket, the imposing architecture of the cultural centre, once upon a time the life and soul of the community. The steps leading up to the imposing double doors are cracked and broken. Inside decorative plaster reliefs are in the inexorable process of falling from the walls, and the stage lies forlorn. But what captivates my attention is the poster in the foyer, in faded Ukrainian yellow and blue. I can't understand a word, so cannot read the text, but this is one poster where that's not an issue. I recognise the pictograms only too well. Expressionless people, constructing a DIY fallout shelter, then sitting and waiting for the 'All Clear'. It's the Eastern Bloc's version of 'Protect and Survive'.

We wander back to the bus and stamp our feet a couple of times to remove the dust. Our principal contact with contamination will be the soles of our shoes, and clearly we don't want to be traipsing any radioactivity back inside the bus with us.

"If your shoes are radioactive when you are leaving the zone, either you wash them, or you go home with no shoes." Igor informs us with a pragmatic shrug. Chernobyl village is surreal. We crawl along the main street past dilapidated cottages with ragged fences, then are suddenly confronted by a picture postcard perfect clapboard, lovingly maintained with curtains and smoke curling leisurely from a stovepipe chimney. Some of the elders returned, unable or unwilling to make the transition to a new life away from the place they called home. The authorities became resigned to their intransigence, and they are now informally allowed to stay.

There is one functioning Eastern Orthodox Christian church, St. Elijah, which is chocolate box beautiful, both inside and out, and is notable for having extremely low levels of radiation. This abnormality has naturally been

afforded miraculous status, which led to some Liquidators renouncing their atheist beliefs and turning to God. Why nuclear reactors aren't built inside churches in the first place remains a mystery.

There are a number of memorials dotted around Chernobyl, but none could be described as ostentatious. The most emotive is the one to the firefighters. The plaque translates as 'For Those Who Saved The World', and was built by the surviving firefighters in memory of their fallen comrades. It is constructed out of cement, so has to be regularly maintained and repaired, and is done so with considerable artistry, given the intricacy of the caged chimney stack centrepiece, the life sized protagonists, and their equipment. Someone has left fresh flowers.

Our hotel is a two-storey prefabricated construction, situated in its own compound on the corner of the village. There is a small neat memorial to the victims of Fukushima in the car park, a salient reminder that nuclear accidents keep happening. Igor organises our accommodation, and as the other singletons have decided to pay the supplement to have their own rooms... "So, no one wants to share with you!" says Igor, smiling as he hands me the key, and I have my own room by default. It's basic, but more than adequate, with spotless shared bathroom facilities down the hall.

Lunch is served in the dining area downstairs. Our food is apparently imported from 'outside' the zone. No one says where it has come from, and no one asks. Any contamination from Chernobyl that coated the topsoil was subsequently absorbed into the earth, and after thirty years scientists calculate it will have sunk about a foot. There are still some eight million living on contaminated lands outside the exclusion zone, so locals are likely eating root crop from their own kitchen gardens, and fruit from their orchards, and they look fine on it. Whatever, I'm famished, the food is delicious, everyone clears their plate, some even come back for seconds, and the only metallic taste in my mouth comes from licking the spoon for my borscht to bits. Delicious. They must have a secret ingredient.

Adopting the pragmatism of the bio-robots, I resolve to drink copious amounts of vodka and smoke cigarettes, regardless of the Russian First Deputy Health Minister, circa May 1986, who dashed the popular belief that consumption of vodka (and red wine) is a cure for exposure to radiation. Besides, I'm the oldest of our party, so rationalise that I have less left to live for.

Ready for an afternoon's exploration we file outside, past a glass cabinet in the hall offering a selection of souvenirs. They are sadly underwhelming, some very cheap looking atomic button badges and a t-shirt, predominantly yellow to match the radiation markers, and a baseball cap bearing the 'S.T.A.L.K.E.R' legend. I have absolutely no idea what this signifies, but it transpires to be a first person shoot 'em up video game, set in Chernobyl. To be honest I'd already done an online search for souvenirs before my trip, and those I found were predominantly glow-in-the-dark products, the sort of merchandise associated with fans of flying saucers. I'll pass.

We clear a second inner checkpoint and enter the ghost town of Pripyat itself, to view the sites made famous online. Our minibus pootles through deserted streets, fenced in by dense stick undergrowth. Spring and autumn trips are ideal times to visit, because when the trees are in leaf the view of the ruins behind them is severely restricted.

Officially guidelines dictate that entry into the buildings is prohibited, and with good reason. As we follow Igor on foot he shows us what is left of a four-storey school; the sides of the building have collapsed and sheared away, creating a giant doll's house, with a landslip of rubble at the base. We can look up directly into open floors at pictures hanging on the wall, including Lenin, and a smattering of desks and chairs now eternally vacant. However there are no guards patrolling the streets, so we are free to enter buildings at our own risk. Inside the town's theatre Igor points out the lighting rig, once suspended high above our heads, now smashed on the floor at our feet. You wouldn't have wanted to be under it when it fell.

Over the years the roofs have developed leaks. With no one to patch them the wooden floors below are now soft and spongy with moss and rot. So 'eyes everywhere' is common sense, especially before walking through doorways. I cannot resist stepping down through the auditorium to the stage, and the solitary grand piano below. In truth it's a minefield of sagging boards, detritus from the walls and ceilings scattered everywhere, and I pick my way, aiming for the edges of the steps where I theorise there will be more support. When

I finally make land on the island stage, and skirt the piano to focus on the missing ivories, I notice no one else has followed me down, preferring to remain in a tight, chummy cluster, just inside the doorway.

Having captured my trophy photo, it soon becomes apparent that pianos in Pripyat are hardly rare. Igor tells us that although some residents did return to take more possessions after their lightning evacuation, many did not have transportation to remove larger items of furniture, such as pianos. Liquidators took axes to them in an effort to deter looters.

Whilst disappointed by the selection of Chernobyl souvenirs, I'm not going to be picking anything up off the floor as an authentic memento. Removing anything is forbidden, although clearly it happens. Looting has been a problem, even in the immediate aftermath of the disaster. Elena Filatova reported that the motorcycle dealership in Pripyat was cleared out at the first opportunity, and radioactive television sets soon began to appear in the shops in Kiev. In the early 1990s it wasn't unusual for Ukrainians to check the radiation levels of goods they brought at market, to help determine their provenance. A quarter of a century after the disaster, Sergey Chernenky, a Liquidator responsible for catching looters, gave testimony concerning two individuals who stole a car, but died during their getaway. The vehicle they chose was 'hot' and had a reading of 6,000 roentgens.

We tour the town, exploring the police station and dark cells, the scrapyard of vehicles, the swimming pool, kindergarten, and amusement park, with its desolate bumper cars and iconic Ferris wheel. Due to open on May Day 1986, it never turned. In the middle school we skirt the floor of strewn gas masks, tipped from their boxes, noting children's dolls with their dirty faces

Tour group view a wrecked piano.

Part of a fireman's uniform, Pripyat hospital.

strategically positioned by other tourists to photograph. The town feels very much like it has been picked over. All the radiators have been stripped for scrap, leaving just their carbon shadows on the walls.

In the foyer of the hospital Igor gathers us around an innocuous looking piece of cloth. He tells us one of the "idiot" 'S.T.A.L.K.E.R.' fans entered the basement, where the firemen's radiated equipment was kept, and brought it upstairs. This strip of material comes from one of their uniforms. Igor doesn't say what happened to the rest of the uniform, or the idiot who retrieved it, but instead waves his Geiger counter towards the fabric, which screams in protest. We take a collective step back from the cloth as if confronted by a spitting cobra. Igor continues to conduct the banshee wail, moving his counter to and fro, and we cautiously edge forward to see the reading. It's not 0.15, or 2.8. From the relative safety of over someone else's shoulder I can see it's registering 1666 point something, and it will remain like that for centuries to come. I wait until the counter is a couple of feet away from the cloth to take a photo of the comparatively safe reading of 140.1.

If it wasn't clear before, it is now. An experienced guide with an instrument to monitor radiation is essential here. Igor is able to show us the best bits, whilst protecting us from our own curiosity. Pripyat may well be the ultimate Urbex[1] destination, but it contains hazards like no other. Well, none other than Fukushima to be fair. As a dark tourist visiting Chernobyl you are being exposed to the same level of radiation the locals live with on a daily basis, but at the end, you get to go home, to somewhere less radioactive.

We enter a sixteen-storey apartment block, heading for the roof and the view over the town it affords. Naturally there's no working lift, so it's up thirty-two flights of stone stairs, with the occasional pause to photograph the partially destroyed piano, or to poke round an abandoned apartment. Invariably they're empty, just a solitary armchair with peeling wallpaper for company.

The last flight to the roof is a suspicious iron ladder, but the panorama is worth it, because it's like nothing else on earth. Building blocks hemmed in by trees, some now higher than the roofs, the forest stretching away into the distance, its distinctive red scar glowing in the afternoon sunlight. On the horizon the mysterious giant cat's cradle of Duga-3, the so-called 'Russian Woodpecker' radar system, also known as 'Chernobyl 2'. Phil Donahue, the first western journalist to visit Chernobyl after the disaster, asked what the structure was, and the story goes that after a long pause his guide told him it was a "hotel".

The advantage of taking a weekender to Chernobyl is the additional time, which affords us the opportunity to explore the vast Duga-3 complex tomorrow, a luxury denied to the day-trippers. Crossing the roof, pretending not to notice the saggy feel underfoot, the reactor imperceptibly ticks away in the distance, the huge silver arch shield to contain the ailing sarcophagus still under construction alongside. We gather for a group photo, whilst Igor clambers precariously onto a broken sofa to get the desired elevation to show the reactor and containment in the background.

From this rooftop you can see that Pripyat is truly lost. It just took time. It's had thirty years; what will it look like after thirty more, or a century from now? This is way beyond Biblical and our likely recorded future. As we continue our tour back at ground level we see saplings puncturing through benches, weeds and bushes piercing the pavement, and without Igor's local knowledge, pointing out the floodlights, I'd be oblivious to the fact that the fledgling wood we pass through was once the town's football pitch.

We stop on the road to the reactor to view and photograph from a distance, before Igor utters the immortal line:

"Let us go closer to the nuclear reactor..."

Five minutes later we assemble under the watchful eye of camouflaged personnel to pose before another memorial in the shadow of Block 4. Standing at a tangent with a reading of 3.48 we are allocated just eight minutes to snap away, although this might be because of the sentries on duty, rather than the exposure to this particular level of radiation.

---

1) Urbex: Urban exploration. This is the exploration of man-made sites that have been abandoned and fallen into ruin. Photographic documentation is fundamental to the pursuit. Popular sites include factories, schools, asylums, and amusement parks. In Japan it is referred to as 'Haikyo'. Urbex is associated with abandonment, rather than death, which is associated with dark tourism.

Construction of the enormous arch shield takes place behind a protective wall, which enables workers to carry out shifts of five hours per day for a month, before taking fifteen days off. When completed in 2017 (it was originally envisaged to be in place by 2005) the 'New Safe Confinement', the largest movable structure ever created, will be piston driven on rails over the original sarcophagus, the ends will be sealed and internal robotic arms will then begin to dismantle the original structure. They've got a century to do this, which is the projected life span of the new shield. It's like something out of *Thunderbirds*.

As we disembark from the minibus back at the hotel, a woman at the door points to the sleeves of my jacket. They're chalked from where I've leant against the walls inside the buildings to photograph scrolls of peeling paint. Feeling foolish I retreat to a suitable naughty step in the corner of the car park to brush the dust off, grateful that at least I remembered to bring latex gloves to avoid handling anything that might be contaminated, such as my own jacket.

After another excellent dinner Igor leaves us to our own amusement. We've all loaded up with Ukrainian *hryvnia* in Kiev, and given that no one seems enamoured by the souvenirs on offer, we're all desperate to buy each other

drinks, but although the vodka is world class, and would put a sloppy smile on any face, it is ridiculously cheap. Worse still, we're informed the bar will shut at a miserably early 10 p.m., and they're true to their word. Our enforced curfew extends to being locked inside the hotel. We are having an early night.

SUNDAY MORNING AND IGOR IS UP EARLY, WASHING THE BUS down with a broom and soapy water. While it's common practice for tour drivers to ensure their clients have clean windows through which to view the scenery, I can't help but wonder if, in this particular destination, it's being done to remove contamination. We head off to tour the cooling tower, viewing the vast structure from the inside, and drive through forest roads to an even larger one, the gargantuan Duga-3 radar installation. Igor leads us through the seemingly endless underground complex before we emerge back into daylight on the sandy soil to see the giant mesh up close. Some of our party decide to climb the vertical caged ladders onto the higher stages to look back over the trees towards the reactor, reversing the view from the roof of the apartment block from yesterday. Blow that for a game of soldiers, I'm on holiday, and anyway I need a bush.

Whilst both structures present unique sightseeing opportunities, I have a

Panorama over Pripyat.

sense that this morning feels more akin to 'Urbex' than to 'dark tourism'.

Lunch is taken in the Chernobyl workers canteen, accessed through radioactive scanning turnstiles, strange contraptions that would not look out of place in a 1930s science fiction B-movie. Everyone passes through, fortunately undetected. Before Igor drives us back to Kiev we have time to take the bread provided by the dinner ladies to feed the huge catfish that wait expectantly under the bridge.

A trip to Chernobyl is the opportunity to experience time travel. From 26th April 1986, the clocks ran down until they stopped. The zone has not been 'frozen in time', because nature has been busy during the intervening years. Now it represents both a portal to the past, and into our collective future, to a time when humanity is no longer here, just the crumbling remnants of our once great civilisation, which will go the same way as those we have discovered under the sands, waves and jungle. How we will reach our collective end is uncertain. But there was a time, not so very long ago, when I genuinely believed I'd get the chance to find out, and as ridiculous as that comment may seem with hindsight, I assure you, I wasn't alone.

So my next stop is a visit to the 'The Dark Site at the End of The World', to speak with a man who promotes the reality of an English Country Armageddon to tourists.

THERE IS SOMETHING QUINTESSENTIALLY BRITISH ABOUT THE brown signs dotted around the UK, directing the tourist to places of historical, cultural, or geographical interest, and none more so than the one I'm approaching, which informs me that the 'Secret Nuclear Bunker' is 150 yards away. I know the road only too well and start indicating early, dabbing the brakes before the rollercoaster road dips, then blind bends left over the rise, hoping the 4x4 looming large in the mirror is paying attention. I take the hairpin turn off, leaving the 4x4 and the A128 to meander their own way to Chipping Ongar.

The sealed lane skirts the field. When I first visited, years ago, it was just a lurching, bone-jarring, slightly nervous route created by tractor. The landscape expands as I dribble towards the hollow, then brake, as a herd of deer with fawns roam leisurely across my path. You wouldn't describe Essex as the most beautiful county the British Isles has to offer. It's not the Cotswolds, or Cumbria, but it does have its moments, although few and far between, which is why I just stare in wonder as if witnessing the migrating wildebeest of the Serengeti.

In fairness to the much-maligned county, Essex is not the end of the world, nor is the village of Kelvedon Hatch, population 2,541 according to the 2011 census. It boasts a picturesque church, and the land here has been farmed long before the Domesday Book was written. Which segues nicely into what it has to offer today's dark tourist. Deep under the hill topped by the radio mast before me, lies the bunker from where the last great battle between the forces of supposedly good and evil was to be conducted, with no winner guaranteed.

The footpath winds into the trees and the signpost switchbacks me down an incline towards an incongruous chalet bungalow at the foot, more suited to a genteel estate on the outskirts of new town Basildon than a copse in Kelvedon Hatch. It was supposed to look like a typical farm cottage, and is nothing like one. Although I know this is merely an illusion, it's still difficult to comprehend what lies inside, up the steps and beyond the porch. Walking through the doors is like stepping through the looking glass into another time, one of fear and paranoia, leading inexorably towards a dystopian future.

The claustrophobic lobby plays host to a small telly screen, broadcasting a looped introduction from the face of the bunker's owner, Mike Parrish, which is a brilliant Orwellian touch, and I do hope that was the intention. Mike, in his role of benign Big Brother, instructs the visitor in the use of the 'wand', a hand-held playback device with keypad, stacked in racks, that allows you to self guide at your own pace, in conjunction with visual colour-coded arrows throughout the underground installation. There are separate wands available for children who will be following a tailor-made presentation. The tour was originally self-guided with a Walkman and headphones, but this upgrade is very 1984.

Mike provides succinct commentary, advising when to turn off the wand between points of interest. His narrative is informative, and adroitly droll when discussing the chances of surviving nuclear war.

It all started back in 1952, when the Air Ministry paid Mike's grandfather a visit. They offered to pay £25 per acre for the land in the middle of his farm. Mike tells me:

"My grandfather had fought in two World Wars. He didn't want to fight in a third. Kids today don't understand there was this chilly relationship between Russia and the West, and yet they didn't have a war. But when Churchill came back (as Prime Minister) in 1951, one of the first things he did was build this, because he knew Stalin couldn't be trusted."

So the Ministry took up residence on the farmland in October 1952, pouring concrete twenty-four hours a day, completing the enormous bunker by May the following year, and encouraged Mike's grandfather to farm over the top to project an aura of normality, with 'nothing to see here' despite the large radio mast giveaway. The bunker was initially commissioned as an early warning air defence station, before it became a Regional Seat of Government for London in the event of nuclear attack in the late 1960s. It was a live station with posted guards, ready to accommodate up to 600 personnel, until finally decommissioned in 1992, after the Cold War thawed, when the Parrish family purchased the bunker back, opening it up to the public in 1994.

The reception room leads down into a tunnel, 120 yards long, with an offset bend at the end before the main blast doors, to deflect and reduce any shock

'Fake house' entrance to the Kelvedon Hatch Secret Nuclear Bunker, Essex.

wave. This kink simultaneously functions as ideal cover for the bunker's armed guards to pick off would-be marauders. Intruders would most likely be the local population who knew there was a secret underground bunker on their doorstep, and who were seeking shelter in the run up to, or aftermath of, any nuclear exchange. Whilst the pragmatic view amongst the general public during the simmering Cold War may have been that there would be no survivors, some estimates projected that there might be as many as three–four million of us left after the UK's 200 presumed targets had been obliterated.

Whilst the security at the bunker was concerned with keeping people out, it also had to keep people in. Those on duty would likely have family and loved ones outside, and the pressure to be with them at the end would have been considerable.

The bunker is huge. There are three floors, with reinforced walls, ten feet thick. It lies 100 feet under the hill, embedded in gravel to absorb any shock, and is surrounded by a Faraday cage to counter the electro-magnetic pulse associated with a nuclear explosion. The installation is completely self-contained: generators, diesel to run them, water, air conditioning providing a controlled environment, several thousand phone lines with which to communicate with the rest of the world, or the outposts still responding, and a BBC studio to broadcast from. Even after a nuclear attack on the UK, there would be a politician to tell you what to do. You'd just need to remember to turn your tranny off before the 'Big Bang' (and retract the aerial), otherwise you might not be able to hear what the politician was telling you.

Moving up the staircase your tour takes in the giant plotting room, with several exhibits from the civil defence era, protective clothing, and a mock up DIY fallout shelter, an example of what the general public were expected to construct within their homes. There's also an area provided for dressing up in period fallout costume, where you can have your Nuclear Bunker souvenir photograph taken for a suggested 'honesty' donation. I gaze wistfully at the wardrobe and accessories provided; I really want this. It's a legitimate opportunity/any excuse to get into heavy rubber and use a respirator, but I'm alone, and there's no one to operate the Polaroid camera contraption in the improvised studio. I could wave to the CCTV for assistance, but then notice the temporary 'Out of Order' note tacked to the camera. I'm crestfallen.

Dotted throughout the bunker are several films relating to the impending nuclear holocaust. Seating is provided, and some of the transmissions are nearly an hour long. Yet they are well worth watching, not only because they are historical documents, simultaneously chilling and hilarious, but because of the setting in which you are viewing them. It adds a certain resonance, which will likely wipe any patronising smile off your face.

If you didn't live through those times then I appreciate that they're difficult to comprehend. Now, with the benefit of hindsight, the only meaningful conclusion to be drawn is that we were all completely insane. Mutually Assured Destruction. Never has an acronym been so apt. Unfortunately this period of genuine tension, ramped up with rhetoric and propaganda by both sides, coincided with my own teenage angst. But back then it was all so different, and a time of 'what if?' rather than today's dismissive 'so what?'

DURING THE EARLY YEARS OF THE 1980S, THE FEAR OF ARMAGEDDON was pervasive. Former Catholic priest-cum-activist, Bruce Kent, was marching under homemade bed sheet banners with the Campaign for Nuclear Disarmament (CND), who rallied across our television screens on a regular basis, in time and tune with the pop culture of the day. New Wave synthsters Orchestral Manoeuvres in the Dark (OMD) released a single in September 1980 entitled Enola Gay, after the B-29 Superfortress that dropped the bomb on Hiroshima. The single reached number eight in the UK pop chart, and number two in Switzerland. The respective chart positions aren't particularly relevant, but it is worth noting that the Swiss record buying public had access to public fallout shelters, whilst we in the UK did not. I imagine if you were Swiss at that time, you were entitled to feel ever so slightly smug. It would at least provide some consolation for the fact that you had to import decent music for your kids.

Frankie Goes to Hollywood released Two Tribes in 1984, with an accompanying video of Ronald Reagan and Konstantin Chernenko lookalikes wrestling to the death in a bear pit, while the rest of the world egged them on. The single went straight to number one in the UK and stayed there for nine weeks. It is worth noting that the single had a savvy running time of three minutes and fifty-seven seconds, meaning there would just be time for a final play, come the dreaded four minute warning.

Ultravox produced Hiroshima Mon Amour as early as 1977, then Dancing With Tears In My Eyes in 1984, a case of 'New Clairvoyance', rather than new wave, given Chernobyl duly fulfilled their prophetic lament in 1986. Heaven 17 cut Let's All Make A Bomb, and Bowie's 1983 comeback number one Let's Dance featured an erupting mushroom cloud in the video. Even Sting wrote a song; what more evidence do you need? Popular music was agog at the prospect of Armageddon.

While pop going to the well of nuclear holocaust for inspiration might be dismissed as frivolity, the BBC's flagship documentary, *Panorama*, and its reporter, a certain fresh-faced Jeremy Paxman, could not. Originally broadcast in March 1980, *If The Bomb Drops* can be seen in perfect context on the Kelvedon Hatch bunker tour, which itself features in the film as "an innocuous bungalow, a building so secret we cannot show it to you."

The documentary is incontrovertible proof that I am not making this stuff up. It focuses on the UK's lack of preparation for nuclear attack, in stark contrast to that of Switzerland, and demonstrates that our reluctance to contemplate any chance of survival appears in step with the government's reluctance to spend any money on providing us with any opportunity. The undoubted gallows humour highlight is the vox pop where Paxman, strangely neutered in this early incarnation of 'Grand Inquisitor', asks a Cockney old boy under a flat cap if he would know what to do in the advent of a nuclear attack?

"Waste of time, innit? Goin' anywhere... You've 'ad it, aint'cha... 'ad it, aint'cha — "

"Would you take any preparations at all?"

"Well what preparations you got?... You've 'ad it, aint'cha... You've 'ad it, aint'cha... No messin' about, is it... You've 'ad it, aint'cha... No use crying over spilt milk, is it..."

If The Bomb Drops was commissioned at a time when the symbolic 'Doomsday Clock' was set at seven minutes to midnight, the highest state of alert since the Cuban missile crisis in 1962. Whilst the majority of the British public were either resigned to their fate, or in denial about the possibility of a nuclear strike, the government clearly did not share this view, otherwise there would be no regional command centres playing war games with nuclear attack scenarios, and no command bunker in the first place. The one at Kelvedon Hatch cost £1.5m to build, in 1952. Had it not been decommissioned it would have required a further £10m to modernise in the 1990s, when it was already costing £3m a year to keep on standby.

If government planning failed, and regional centres collapsed, then there would likely be total anarchy. However the BBC documentary showed former Paratrooper Major Tony Hibbert organising volunteers Dick, George, Amanda, and Margret, all dressed in 'hazmat' suits, in a drill which involved them driving a Landrover through a Devonshire village, shouting warnings of impending fallout through a loudhailer.

As Paxman observes during the clip, accompanied by the theme to *The Great Escape*:

"If this looks funny now, remember, after an attack it may be all we have."

What wasn't funny in the slightest was the BBC *Q.E.D.* documentary, *A Guide to Armageddon*. Broadcast at peak-time in July 1982, it detailed the effects of a single megaton nuclear device detonating above St. Paul's Cathedral. Based on scientific assessments, it brought terrifying footage into the nation's living rooms. Effects from the blast, radiating out miles from the epicentre, were illustrated by an exploding pane of glass lacerating a pumpkin, intercut with the kindly faces of elderly ladies in headscarves. This hazard would ripple out as far as Hornchurch, so I still had a few miles grace, provided it was only a one megaton bomb, and it was bang on target. If it exploded off centre, for example over Tower Bridge, there'd be no point drawing the curtains, or sticking tape over the window.

Several years later, having leapfrogged Hornchurch to take up residence in a Romford bedsit, I reasoned that if the bomb dropped I wouldn't be shredded by flying glass, but would be slapped in the face by flying, charred cardboard. On the downside I was now much closer to St. Paul's and the predicted 'Ground Zero'. The bomb would be far greater than a single megaton, there would be multiple warheads, so the house, street, and Romford, would simply explode under the pressure. I'd be conveniently evaporated along with my neighbours and millions of bricks, decorated by Victorian chimney pots, reduced to hundreds and thousands.

Watching the *Q.E.D.* documentary again, thirty years on, there was clearly no escape, unless you contracted one of thirty UK companies at the time, and paid them £10,000–£20,000 to install a fallout shelter in your back garden, providing you had both the money and the garden. Then hopefully, when the sirens wailed, you'd be close enough to access it and possess both a suitable weapon and the requisite moral fibre to repel your neighbours.

Once again, any such contingency was only postponing the inevitable. Food and water will run out, further proof that the sensible would not wish to survive. The Kelvedon Hatch bunker contains a strong room, which held not only state secret documents to be kept from the eyes of those who carried out the orders issued by the bunker commissioner, but also a supply of cyanide capsules. These were presumably to be used once 'retaliation' had been concluded, and all the food eaten, at which point both the bunker and its personnel were redundant, and would be left to their own devices.

Ascending the bunker, the tour takes in the separate accommodation for the top brass: the commissioner, who would be a cabinet minister, an assistant, who would be another cabinet minister, and the Prime Minister. From the roped doorway to his room you can see 'John Major' lying in bed. Everyone else had to use a 'hot bed' system, across the three eight-hour shifts. The washrooms contain 'ER' soap and 'Government Property' toilet paper, and there was even a field medical centre equipped for operations, and a supply of body bags and collapsible cardboard coffins so bodies could be neatly stacked, out of the way.

Retrospectively the public consciousness of the early 1980s can only be seen as embarrassing, and I include myself in this, because I was part of it, fretting with all the other headless chickens. Although I couldn't write a thought-provoking song, which was best left to Sting, I slavishly read about Hiroshima and what would happen in the event of a nuclear attack, and at no point during this time did I ever stop to question what was fuelling my obsession, or how I'd been caught up in the mass angst. Why worry when the truth was, "You've 'ad it, aint'cha..."

FASCINATION WITH A NUCLEAR STRIKE AGAINST THE UK APPEARS TO stem from the Home Office pamphlet *Protect and Survive*, originally published in 1976, then reprinted in May 1980, and made available to purchase in response to a series of articles in the *Times* newspaper from January of that year, and I know what you're thinking, but Rupert Murdoch didn't buy the paper until 1981. It advises the householder how to make both their home and family "as safe as possible under nuclear attack".

The pamphlet is now an historical document. All the characters are Caucasian, and torches and tin openers have changed radically in design. In essence *Protect and Survive* was an exercise in keeping the 'Gen Pop' occupied with tasks such as whitewashing windows, building a fallout shelter under the stairs, and cutting a trench to lie down in, which now looks exactly like what it was: a convenient DIY grave and burial service in one.

The government wanted people to stay at home, not block the roads heading for caves and caverns. The booklet was very short change for the population, to the point that inducing fear appears the primary objective. I still have my copy, and although too old to be concerned by the sabre-rattling of nations, it serves to remind me how the government values those they represent.

The newspaper articles, the prime time documentaries, the award-winning TV drama *Threads*, Raymond Briggs' graphic novel *When the Wind Blows* (turned into a feature length animation), a plethora of pop songs with emotive videos, CND marches, and the Greenham Common Women's Peace Camp, opposing cruise missiles on UK soil, all contributed to or fed the tension. There was even a parody poster of *Gone With The Wind*, featuring Margaret Thatcher as Scarlett, in the arms of Ronald Reagan as Rhett, the mushroom cloud rising behind them, with the tagline, 'She promised to follow him to the end of the earth, He promised to organise it!'

As a result I don't stress about climate change, because back in the day we only had four minutes. You wouldn't even get that nowadays. They've removed all the sirens after disbanding the Royal Observer Corps in September 1991 at the end of the Cold War, saving £6m annually. The government once spent less than 50p per head on civil defence. Now it's all down to your local authority. Given the challenges faced by Kensington council in the aftermath of the Grenfell Tower fire, no one can be confident if any council were faced with a major incident of a CBR (chemical, biological, radioactive) nature.

My own council, in reply to a Freedom of Information request regarding their ability to alert residents of a localised emergency, informed me that the primary means of communication to residents is through "social media and our website". Perish the thought anyone might be asleep at the time, as was the case with Grenfell Tower. Fallout might not come from a nuclear strike, but an accident, like Chernobyl. Or Fukushima, in case you thought something like Chernobyl could never happen again. It's all down to which way the wind blows.

The money is still found for the weapons and the submarine delivery systems to deploy them, and there are four bunkers on standby for those who are going to implement retaliation in our name, or most likely in our memory.

W E'RE SITTING IN WHAT MIKE CALLS 'THE NAFFERY' AT THE top of the bunker, a combination of self-service cafeteria and gift shop. His Labrador plods over for some fuss as Mike explains his bunker mentality.

"The ethos is that they were here yesterday (bunker staff) and they've just all walked out. I've tried not to make it like a museum with cases and cases of gas masks. I wanted to create that atmosphere for people to think what it would be like to live down here for three months, with their families left outside. Very austere, all green and magnolia."

He's certainly succeeded in creating the *Mary Celeste* effect. Visit during wintery midweek, and you may well have the bunker all to yourself, which is simultaneously eerie and exciting. It's a far cry from when they had to repel protesters at the door:

"CND used to march here regularly. We used to have mounted police charging all over the place!"

He smiles nostalgically.

"It was quite good. CND would march here, they would get their pliers out and cut the barbed wire, and a policeman would clap them on the shoulder and arrest them for damaging government property. The press were all there taking photographs and honour was served. Everyone went away for a couple of years and then the same thing happened again. They never actually got into the bunker, and it was all done for publicity."

Sometimes it wouldn't be a 'demo', but a lone intruder.

"When the bunker was still active, we used to have a lot of poachers here, and one Sunday morning I saw a guy, very odd, very suspicious, so I accosted him and called the police, and Special Branch came down. He was a reporter, I think for the *Morning Star*, all very exciting for me as a young lad, being interviewed by Special Branch. And because of that they made it public, and then Paxman turned up."

Although the farm had purchased the land over the bunker back from the government, the bunker itself was a different prospect. When it was decommissioned, the sale was conducted by sealed bids. There were two open days for prospective buyers, and over 400 people attended. There was no indication as to who was just having a look out of curiosity, and who was genuinely interested in submitting a bid. It was also difficult to calculate what a winning bid might be, given the nature of the installation. However as the farm owned the land on either side of the access road, they erected tight fences, to make it appear as 'user unfriendly' as possible.

Fortunately Mike's bid won, which is why we now have a dark tourist site, rather than an electronic testing facility, or a firing range.

"When we bought it, it was in all the newspapers, and so many people wanted to come and see it, so we opened it for a weekend, and it was total mayhem and chaos!"

Mike indicates over his shoulder towards the rear lobby outside 'The Naffery', and explains the vexing problems facing those who open dark tourist sites. The bunker was designed to withstand Armageddon, not accommodate the general public.

"We had to make this tunnel[1] for 'Health and Safety'. That took a lot of discussion, because of course there was no criteria for a bunker, so they based it on a theatre. We had no idea how many people we would have down here at any one time, and we needed a fire alarm system. We had visit after visit from the fire brigade, and gradually the rank got higher and higher, until we eventually got to the white collar level, and that was much more sensible, because he devised a route, which was much better than putting a door in here and here — you end up with people going round in circles. Once that was sorted it was a piece of cake, but it took about three to four months to make it safe for the public, which of course it now is."

"How did you go about promoting the bunker?"

---

1) There is a tunnel in the rear lobby, just through the doors of 'The Naffery', that provides a rear exit from the bunker. It leads to an outdoor area with a few benches, and an example of a typical Anderson shelter from WWII. They were commonplace in the back gardens of my youth.

The Anderson shelter was made of galvanised corrugated steel panels with an arched roof and could accommodate six. It was partially buried four-foot deep in the soil, which was then piled over the top. People decorated the banks with flowers. Neighbourhoods held competitions for the 'best dressed'. In the winter the Andersons were very cold and wet. They were situated away from the house, in case the property took a direct hit, and debris blocked the single door, which was set at the base of steps cut into the ground. Postwar they were returned for scrap, or bought back by the householder, to serve as sheds.

Diorama of a family DIY fall out shelter, Kelvedon Hatch Secret Nuclear Bunker.

"We didn't have to! It was in all the national newspapers. The reason we actually opened it as soon as we got it was because we were inundated with people wanting to visit — we couldn't use our telephones — there were that many people who wanted to come! So it built its own momentum. We had the people who had served down here, so we held an open day, for them, and we got all their histories and stories — my sister is an amateur historian — and it just blossomed. What set us back was when we applied for planning permission. The council only gave it to us for three months — which means you can't afford to spend the £100,000 they wanted to build this exit here — (waves to the tunnel over his shoulder) — because you might be closed in three months. They then extended it to six months and we thought, 'Well we're going to have to do this', so we spent the money, but it was always with this uncertainty, and it took about seven years to get full planning permission."

"How do you get the brown road signs?"

"You apply for them and they charge you a fortune. When we first started we had a chalkboard at the side of the road. But we couldn't apply for the brown signs before we got planning permission. When we've done surveys, and asked people how they found out about us, the greatest is 'word of mouth'. The second is, 'we saw your brown sign'. Certainly our brown signs have gone round the world on the web several times."

The Kelvedon Hatch Secret Nuclear Bunker is a prime example of a dark site that responded to public demand. I'm interested in how they managed to equip the bunker so realistically, with period artefacts?

"We were very lucky. They (Government) spent two years throwing everything out, despite us saying we wanted it, so we went to other bunkers they were closing and rescued stuff from those. We employed one of the former guards who worked here — he was very tight on the secrecy — 'Surely you can tell us if there were tables in here?' — it seemed a bit daft. But we got some stuff from him. There was a bunker in Scotland, much smaller than this, that I did go and visit, but we were one of the first."

Originally Mike and his father led the tours, but self-touring became a more practical idea, which is when the portable cassette players and headphones were introduced. However they "went through thousands of batteries", so the wands were appropriated. They are ex-Millennium Dome, and can be recharged.

"So what's involved in the day to day running of a nuclear bunker attraction?"

"Drinking coffee — lots of it! We have lots of filming down here — we've had a feature film, *Let's Be Evil*, which has been released as we speak, and there was a red carpet thing, which unfortunately I couldn't attend."

Mike indicates the film poster. *Let's Be Evil* is a British sci-fi horror film (2016), directed by Martin Owen, staring Isabelle Allen.

The adjoining land caters for 'Nuclear Races', an endurance and obstacle course for those hardy souls who like racing each other through the cloying Essex mud. The bunker is also a setting for futuristic, post apocalyptic LARP, live action role-play. Mike describes something that sounds like the *Stargate* movie.

"They go off and jump through, do a mission and come back".

The bunker also provides a suitable backdrop for interviewing a military talking head if there is a media story regarding Russia. The hundreds of brightly coloured neckerchiefs hanging from the ceiling indicate the number of Scout troops that have visited. They also have 'All Nighters' for the 'Paranormals', or ghost hunters, following on from the television programme, *Most Haunted*, who also came to the bunker.

"But nobody actually died here, did they?"

"Well they poured concrete back in the fifties, and one morning they found the foreman's hat where they'd been pouring, and he was never seen again. So is he in the walls, or did he do a 'Lord Lucan' and do a runner?"

While 'The Naffery' is essentially a self-service canteen with a coffee and tea machine, soft drinks cabinet and a selection of cake and snacks, two sides are racked with baskets of souvenirs. How does Mike select what to sell?

"We have very limited room here in the bunker, even for a big bunker."

"And you need to exit through the gift shop?"

"Well that's why we have it here. We could put some in there [room off to the side] but then we'd be taking away our conference and green room facilities. And mostly we have families with children, so I wanted things the children could spend their pocket money on, so nothing too expensive. They might buy granny a tea towel —"

"You have a tea towel? I am *so* buying one of those!"

"Funnily enough there aren't that many things around. There are twelve million types of pen, but at the end of the day they're a biro, and I don't see the point in having more than one type of biro."

"What does sell really well?"

"Bullets. We have bullet key rings — the kids love those. Bullet necklaces..."

Souvenirs also include Russian hats, which also do good business, and there are fridge magnets, thimbles, mugs, and other novelty knick-knacks, copies of *Protect and Survive*, and assorted postcards, eight for £1. There is even a Russian translation of the bunker guide available for visitors from the former USSR. The whole operation is covered by an "honesty box system", so when you return your wand at the end of the tour you can buy a drink, snack, and souvenir whilst paying your entrance fee. There's a basket of change available. And it works. Mike says that although they have CCTV throughout the bunker, "99.9% of people are honest." He estimates they get around 60,000 visitors a year, and they aren't all captive audience school kids.

"It's now in the National Curriculum, stages 2, 3 and 4[2] —the Cold War — so we find we are getting more schoolchildren here.

"You probably know they produced another *Protect and Survive* about ten years ago? Everyone got one through the post, but nobody kept it. They reinvented the wheel, but if you speak to anyone they say, 'I don't even remember!'"

"I don't even remember!"

---

2) This covers the development of the Cold war, the Cuban missile crisis, and the collapse of Communism.

"Every household got one, but they didn't call it *Protect and Survive*, they called it something else..."[3]

"I've still got the original. I keep it in my desk."

Mike laughs.

"Just in case! Very prudent, quite right, Sir!"

---

3) The thought of there being an updated version of *Protect and Survive*, especially one that I would have received, that I couldn't remember, troubled me. When I returned home from Kelvedon Hatch I rifled through my desk, and found it, still in the original envelope. Now I remembered it, because it was rubbish. No illustrations, nothing about tagging any bodies.

Circulated in 2004, and entitled *Preparing for Emergencies: What You Need To Know*, it was the same size as Protect and Survive, but in a landscape format, with a white cover bearing six circular icons. It is based on common sense, so there's no instruction for building DIY shelters, and you can leave your internal doors on their hinges. The theme is 'GO IN, STAY IN. TUNE IN'. The orange icon on the cover isn't 'Pac-man', it's actually the dial of a radio, depicting 'TUNE IN'. There's a section on fire, explosives, then — A-ha! — CBR — that's chemical, biological or radiological incident.

The provisions on this page aren't going to help against any mega-tonnage warhead. Apparently Fire and Rescue can, "decontaminate large numbers of people quickly. This involves showering with soap and water and then dressing in temporary clothing that would be provided."

This sounds like the scene in *Dr. No* (1962), where James Bond and Honey Ryder are successfully decontaminated with soapy brooms and showers on a moving conveyor belt.

"It is important that this takes place where the incident happened so that other areas, including homes, are not contaminated."

There is now increased baggage and passenger screening at UK airports, which was obviously in response to 9/11, and according to the booklet over the last three years (2001–2004) "security around vital national resources, such as water, energy and transport systems has been improved".

In July 2005, the terrorist bombings on the London transport network claimed fifty-two lives. There is, after all, only so much any democratically elected government can do.

The booklet is predominantly concerned with terrorism. There is absolutely no mention of nuclear attack, or a Chernobyl-esque fallout scenario, and keeping a radio and spare batteries to hand appears to be the only thing that has survived from the original orange 'Doomsday Booklet'.

It is available in Braille, Bengali, French, Chinese, Urdu, Arabic, Welsh, Somali, Geordie, Punjabi, Gujarati, Arabic, Greek, Kurdish, Farsi, Turkish, Vietnamese and Hindi. The UK demographic has demonstrably moved a long way from the days of *Protect And Survive*, and if you are keen to collect the whole set, or get one just in case, you can contact: 'Planning For Emergencies', Freepost CN2223, Croydon, CR9 4WZ, or phone 0800 88 7777 — or in 2004 'newspeak', textphone 08000 859 859.

Incidentally, the online version, where you can download a copy < www.preparingforemergencies. gov.uk > now lists audio tape and large print versions.

Have you got yours? Otherwise, well, "you've 'ad it, aint'cha?"

THE UNDERWATER CORTÈGE

"The sea is the largest cemetery, and its slumbers sleep without a monument. All other graveyards show symbols of distinction between great and small, rich and poor: but in the ocean cemetery, the king, the clown, the prince and the peasant are alike, indistinguishable."

George Bruce, 1884, St Andrews

I T'S A BEAUTIFUL MORNING. OUR BOAT SITS BLINDING WHITE AGAINST cobalt blue, as the sun scatters a million diamonds on the glass-like surface of the Egyptian Red Sea. Conditions could not be better for the final dive of the week, yet some of our party are sitting this one out, because just over the rail, lying on the seabed below, at a depth of thirty metres, is the wreck of the *Salem Express*.

On the night of 16th December 1991, the roll-on roll-off ferry was heading for Safaga, Egypt, from Jeddah, Saudi Arabia, overloaded with pilgrims returning from Mecca. Captain Moro was experienced, and knew the route well, to the extent that he'd even pioneered his own course between the mainland and the Hyndman Reefs to shorten the voyage.

So in the face of the deteriorating weather conditions that night, he naturally took his regular shortcut to protect his deck passengers from the elements, although in the aftermath of the ensuing tragedy there was the suggestion that the shortcut was taken so the ship could berth earlier, which would afford the crew more time for sleep. Slightly off course, possibly driven by the gale, the ferry rammed the reef, punching a hole in the starboard side, forcing the visor bow doors open. The sea rushed in and swamped the car deck.

The ferry sank so quickly there was no time to launch the lifeboats. Those in the water only had their life jackets to save them. Those below decks had very little chance of escape. The power failed, it would have been pitch black, the corridors rammed with panicking passengers, tripping over each other and their luggage. Despite the extensive recovery programme, which lasted for three days, it was likely there were still undiscovered bodies within the bowels of the ship when the Egyptian Navy decided the operation was too dangerous to continue. The wreck of the *Salem Express* was effectively abandoned as a tomb, with the official death toll from the tragedy set at 470. The actual total may have been nearly double that. When the official 470 dead is added to the 180 who survived, it totals 650, the *Salem's* recommended capacity. It was reported that there may have been as many as 1,000 aboard when she went down.

It would be easy to describe the mood on our wreck 'safari' as sombre, that we hardly spoke as we assembled our kit, each lost in our own private thoughts, that the sun shrank behind a threatening storm cloud, or that the crew, fearful of a curse, started to pray. It would be evocative, melodramatic, and the sort of thing Clive Cussler might conjure for one of his 'Dirk Pitt' novels. But it would be disingenuous.

It is quiet this morning, but that's because there are fewer of us going in. The couples have packed their equipment away and headed for the sun loungers, and although some of us have been lobbying to dive the *Salem* for the past week, the decision to go rested with our Egyptian skipper, and he only confirmed over breakfast. All those going down to the wreck are single men. The only sounds emanating from the dive deck are clanking tanks, snapping neoprene wetsuits, and the purging of air as we run through our pre-dive checks.

Of course this is a sensitive wreck, and therefore we won't be undertaking any penetration to venture inside the shell. Nonetheless, I really want to dive the *Salem*. I'd already made the decision to go before we embarked, if the opportunity arose, and had been at my persuasive best in order to engineer it. Having made the choice to dive this particular wreck I've already squared away the morality and ethics of what I'm doing. This dive might be considered as ghoulish by some of our party, who don't fancy it, and no doubt the crew would secretly prefer it if we gave the *Salem* a miss. However first and foremost this is a wreck, so it draws me like a magnet. I'd be up for diving her if she'd been sunk intentionally, as an artificial reef, having plied her trade for decades without encountering so much as a squall, or been responsible for even a single case of *mal de mer*.

We congregate on the dive deck, cumbersome with our tanks, a collective sense of anticipation, keen to escape the sun and return to our underwater environment and become weightless once again. There's the initial shock upon hitting the water, which is always colder than it looks. I dump the residual air from my dive jacket and sink into the blue. A glance at the computer to ensure it's registering the descent, then adjust my trim and head down after the others with a flick of the fins. With excellent underwater visibility of at least twenty metres, the wreck dominates the view, stretching away into the distance as I approach the stern and sedentary twin propellers.

There's the rush of adrenaline as the spectacle unfolds, and the sheer size of the *Salem* becomes apparent, we divers little more than wasps pestering the carcass of a metal giant. Ever since my first proper wreck dive on the WWII Japanese freighter, *Italy Maru*, when the superstructure emerged from the gloom, like a twisted wrinkled face, craning its neck enquiringly towards me, I've been addicted, bitten by the rust.

It would be foolish however, not to address the moral aspect while adding the *Salem* to my logbook, bearing in mind it's a tomb, and a relatively

Wreck of the *Salem Express*, Safaga, Egyptian Red Sea. Photo: Rick Ayrton

recent one at that, and because I'm already finning over the once personal possessions that now litter the seabed in the shadow of the behemoth, resting on its starboard side.

There's an encrusted ghetto blaster, the obligatory and evocative solitary shoe, then a suitcase, it's rotten lid gaping wide, rictus-like, trapped in time, journey and purpose unfulfilled. Passing over the debris field littered with dysfunctional lifeboats toppled from their derricks is sobering, and even respecting those topside on the sun loungers, and the crew, no doubt extra-busying themselves, none of us currently fanning out below the upturned deck are going to be punching the air with elation when we return to the surface. Bragging rights will be discreetly supressed, confined to knowing looks between those of us who went. I won't have any regrets about diving the *Salem*. There again, there won't be any triumphal exclamation marks in my logbook either. Indeed, digging it out from the short stack at the back of the cupboard nearly a decade later, the entry recording dive No. 127 remains resolutely blank.

Yet the *Salem Express* isn't the first wreck I've explored where lives were lost. It's not even the first this week. Thirty-one went down with the *SS Carnatic* in September 1869, when she ran aground and broke her back; nine were killed when the *Thistlegorm* was attacked by German bombers; two more died when her sister ship, *Rosalie Moller*, suffered the same fate, just days later, in October 1941. Our party all dived those wrecks, with no moral

Luggage in the wreck of the *Salem Express*. Photo: Christian Llewellyn

objections against exploring any of them. So clearly there is a timeline, drawn by individual divers, as to when they are prepared to entertain a wreck where there has been loss of life.[1]

With the passing of time, the distinction between tomb and legitimate tourist wreck has already become blurred. Increasing numbers of divers are now venturing inside the *Salem*, their adventures reported in the *Daily Mail*, without condemnation, rather supplemented with lavish photography. The Egyptian dive boat crews would prefer the *Salem* to be left alone, but the Red Sea dive industry is highly competitive, and in the face of fluctuating tourist numbers due to sporadic upheavals in the region, those that come to dive get to call the sites.

Personally I don't have an objection to diving a wreck whether lives were lost in 1941 or 1991, whether there are remains inside, be they military personnel, or, as with the *Salem Express*, pilgrims, although I don't envy those divers who carry out the recovery of victims in the immediate aftermath of a sinking. I've spoken to one, and the memory of his encounter with dead

---

1) To put this moral timeline into context, consider that on land, in the aftermath of a disaster, sites are cordoned off, investigated, and subsequently sanitised for reuse. Examples would include the terraces at Hillsborough, where 96 Liverpool football fans were unlawfully killed as a result of police mismanagement, and in the aftermath of a terrorist attack, such as those carried out on the London transport system in July 2005. Memorials to the victims are put in place, anniversaries are observed, and life goes on. It is simply not feasible to take such sites out of service permanently.

Propeller, USS New York, Subic Bay, Philippines.

children, locked together in fatal embrace, has not faded with time in the way that it might for recreational divers encountering disjointed skull and bone.

I've dived wrecks where there were no fatalities, although the loss of a ship itself is still a catastrophe, given the hopes, dreams, liberty and livelihoods invested in them, and the shipwreck graveyards littered across the world's ocean bear testimony to our dependency on seafaring trade and passage through the ages. Masts, funnels and bridges rise like headstones, hulls, decks, and railings, all as intricately decorated as any of our 'top side' cemetery tombs. It can be no coincidence that when diving a shipwreck, being able to see the actual name of the vessel is so highly prized. They are effectively underwater markers and mausoleums.

And it is primarily the grave I dive for, where the ship itself has fallen, although the thrill is tempered according to the circumstances surrounding the loss. So diving the wreck of the SS *New York* in Subic Bay, the Philippines, a WWI battleship scuttled by the Americans, fearful of it falling into the hands of the advancing Japanese during WWII, was a fabulous experience. I didn't know who to thank when I surfaced: the Japanese for advancing, the Americans for scuttling their ship, or the current US Navy for being at sea when I arrived, thereby permitting me to dive the wreck. My eyes were like dinner plates when I surfaced, delirious with childish excitement:

"The size of those GUNS! That propeller — Mickey Mouse ears! The Art Deco crow's nest! Beautiful... And that prow! Like something out of *Jason and the Argonauts* — steampunked! THAT is the best wreck in the Philippines, by an absolute MILE! I'm diving that again this afternoon."[2]

It wasn't like that for anyone after we exited the water from the *Salem Express*, which is at the black end of the dark spectrum of wreck dives, and I'd always respect those who say, "No thanks." Most who choose to visit the *Salem* will dive it once, and that will be enough.

The majority of wrecks I've dived have been losses inflicted during WWII, in the Pacific theatre, and it didn't take long before being compelled to confront the realities of what it must have been like for the protagonists, as their island burned, listed, and sunk beneath them, sucking them down into the depths. From the testimony of survivors, and the newsreels of the time, you could only try to imagine the horror, the drone and whine of the bombers, angry flecks in the sky, homing in on the kill. Then the blast, lifting men off their feet, the fires, the heat, choking, acrid smoke, the confusion, the panic, and the stench of burning, followed by the groans of the ship in her death throes, the hiss as the wreckage slipped below the surface, men trapped below decks, the waters rushing in to close like a curtain, leaving just a trail of flotsam in its wake.

Then, some sixty years later, I descend, the latest in a long line of divers to seek out the wreck, now a dinosaur, fossilising in the silt, silent and at peace, yet in the inexorable process of metamorphosis, the metal now encrusted with coral, feathering and softening the outline. There is a parallel with the body, the soul departed from our world into the next, leaving just the husk, now in a state of corrosion and transformation, providing both sanctuary and nursery for marine life. The wreck also provides an underwater dark tourism attraction, albeit somewhat elitist, from which revenue is derived.

Even surfacing from dives in the more obscure corners of the Pacific, there will be a local who will take you to see their dark tourism baggage, inherited from a war they neither cared for nor asked for, yet which was thrust upon them. A one room museum of recovered artefacts in the local social club, Japanese tunnel systems, gun emplacements, even the skeletal remains of scavenged aircraft, buried in the undergrowth, some with metal skins so paper-thin they've been white washed for protection, literally held together by the paint, so they can be proudly presented by a posse of local kids in return for a few bucks.

It should be noted that not all scuba divers entertain wrecks. Many admittedly find them creepy, and avoid them altogether, or focus their attention with a magnifying glass on the Petri dish marine life that dwells upon them, rather than explore the 10,000 tonnes of rusty habitat. Perhaps

---

2) I need to be honest. There was a life lost on the *SS New York*. There's a memorial plate fixed to the wreck by an open hatch that leads to the interior and the engine room. It commemorates Glen Acker, a highly experienced diver of the wreck, who lost his life there.

this reticence is in part due to visiting sites where people were trapped and drowned, and for the diver, aware of the personal risks whilst underwater, that is simply too close to home.

I've dived a worryingly large number of shipwrecks where divers have lost their lives, although admittedly I don't mourn their passing in the way I'd reflect on a passenger, or a member of the ship's crew. A memorial to a lost diver fixed to a wreck actually has the beneficial effect of heightening the awareness of safety, because, inexplicably, many of those divers lost on wrecks are highly certified and vastly experienced. The reality is we're thrill-seeking tourists who can afford our adventurous recreation at a glamorous destination, and, despite our addiction, we still have a choice whether or not to enter a wreck. As the sign sometimes placed at the point of penetration notes, "There is nothing to see in here worth dying for."

Underwater wrecks are mysterious by nature. They present the opportunity to see something recognisable since childhood, be it a boat, or a plane that now inhabits a landscape it was never intended for. They are surreal, hypnotic, and it's a privilege to see things once lost that by rights we weren't meant to see again. This gives wreck diving a certain frisson. You get to see a sunken *Mary Celeste* every time. The experience is voyeuristic in the extreme.

THE DISASTER OF THE *SALEM* WILL FADE AWAY WITH THE PASSING years, as it has with its more established Red Sea neighbours, such as the *Thistlegorm*. Survivors of the trauma will pass away, and the wreck and its debris field will deteriorate and diminish. Inevitably it will be souvenired. Sometimes the t-shirt, photos, video, and stamp in the logbook are not enough.

The idea of divers taking keepsakes from a wreck site, like modern day tomb raiders, seems repugnant, but that fate has already befallen the *Thistlegorm*, an underwater time capsule from WWII, which is slowly being looted. The Bedford trucks in the hold have long since been relieved of their highly prized steering wheels. The wreck is such a draw for dive tourism that there can be as many as twenty boat loads of divers over it at a time, and many vessels moor up by tying directly to the structure, which, given the strong currents, is detrimental to *Thistlegorm's* integrity.

The *Salem Express* will go the same way. Items have been moved on the wreck, positioned intentionally to present a better photo opportunity, in order to tell or sell the story, so it's just a matter of time until the moral parameters surrounding the wreck are sufficiently eroded, then waiting for that moment, when everyone's looking the other way. The signal flags from the bridge that dive guides retrieve to show their clients underwater, before returning them to their cubbyholes, will vanish, if they have not done so already. That piece of crockery, temporarily recovered to show those aboard the dive boat before being released to sink back to the bottom, will one day adorn a diver's trophy cabinet, or suburban shed instead.

I've dived a Japanese merchant vessel sunk in WWII, where on the sunset boat ride home, one of the Brit 'wreckies' presented a sake bottle he'd found, now destined for his mantelpiece. As he stepped from the boat to the dock in the half-light, he dropped his prize, which smashed to pieces. It had lain in the wreck for sixty years undisturbed, and now no one had the opportunity to see it. What legislation against souveniring is going to stand up in the back of beyond, and realistically, who is going to know? The guide cannot be expected to police experienced clients, spread out along a wreck 100 metres long, 40 metres down, and besides, he's counting on his clients for tips. It would be foolish to make a scene; there are six of them, and I'm Billy No-Mates.

Within the wreck diving fraternity there's a collective moral outrage when illegal trophy-taking is exposed, certainly in the case of war wrecks, most definitely if they're one of 'ours', and especially when the blame can collectively be laid on Russian divers. Conversely it seems acceptable when trophies are lifted from wrecks where no lives have been lost, and where commercial salvage has already taken place, and we positively sanction the recovery of artefacts retrieved under archaeological supervision for subsequent public display.

Even after the artefacts have been pilfered, and the wreck has been pillaged, divers have a rare opportunity to see sites of tragedy that have not been sanitised, and can therefore experience the unique perspective a shipwreck affords them, as amateur accident investigators. The metal remembers and shows us, so we can see the evidence of how catastrophe unfolded with our own eyes. When we dive the *Thistlegorm*, we see the deck peeled back like a sardine can, caused by the explosion when a bomb hit the ship's magazine, and the locomotive engine, once aboard, now spun to rest on the seabed.

Divers will continue to visit watery memorials as long as there's something to see, bragging rights to be had, or booty to grab. Yet truthfully most of the names of those who went down with their ship we'll never know, and frankly won't care, whether they're our brave lads or not. Divers do lay commemorative wreaths on wrecks. This is invariably recorded and published, to ensure the diving community knows it has been done, and who to thank.

Some wrecks are protected from divers by law, as they fall under Ministry of Defence protection, and are known as controlled wrecks. They are effectively war graves, or are being monitored due to their extremely hazardous cargo, as in the case of the SS *Richard Montgomery*, sunk in shallow water in the Thames Estuary off Sheerness, a wreck laden with hundreds of tonnes of explosives. Notably in Hawaii, the USS *Arizona*, one of the first casualties of the Japanese attack on Pearl Harbor, is a memorial and mass grave, where tourists are ferried from the shore to the floating pontoon, so they can look down upon the shallow wreck to pay their respects. Absolutely no diving is permitted, unless carried out by US Navy personnel. Those members of the ship's company that survived the attack are afforded the opportunity to have their remains interred within the wreck, to be reunited with their comrades, when their time comes.

U NLIKE THE MAJORITY OF TERRA FIRMA DARK TOURISM SITES, sanitised specifically to accommodate the public safely, with directional signage, cafeterias, and conveniences, there are inherent risks incurred in the pursuit of dark tourism diving, which can lead to experiencing one's own tragedy.

Most landlubbers are familiar with the condition known as the bends, which divers refer to as DCS, decompression sickness. The risk of DCS (micro bubbles in the blood) is increased by diving at depth or for extended periods, and ascending too quickly without the requisite decompression 'stops'. These stops allow the diver to reduce the gas they've absorbed under pressure at depth, simply by continual breathing.

But once divers penetrate wrecks, risks increase exponentially. When entering what is known as an overhead environment, there is no longer a direct route to the surface. Inside it's easy to get disorientated, especially on larger wrecks, such as the *Zenobia*, a Swedish roll-on roll-off ferry, which sunk on its maiden voyage in 1980, and lies less than a mile from the harbour at Larnaca, Cyprus. Justly rated as one of the top ten wreck dives in the world, this huge vessel has three enclosed decks — a passenger deck, upper and lower car decks — filled with articulated trucks, which are also scattered over the seabed, as if toys abandoned by a child. Inconsiderately shipwrecks don't always come to rest at a convenient depth of twenty metres, neither do they always settle 'right' way up. 'The *Zen*' lies on her port side, so the carpet, which once dressed the floor, now adorns the 'wall' like a tapestry, and doorways have become human sized letterboxes for posting yourself through. If you're thinking of taking the stairs, remember they'll be sideways. No lives were lost when the *Zenobia* sank, and the only bones visible are those on a truck that was carrying a cargo of frozen butchery. Yet divers have periodically perished exploring the confines of her decks and engine room.

It is recommended when entering wrecks to lay a line to follow. Think Theseus in Daedalus' Labyrinth. During the wreck course, required to certify a diver for interior access, there is an exercise to lay a line within an enclosed area, during which the instructor deliberately silts the compartment, creating a blizzard of muck. Visibility vanishes instantly. Even with a torch you can only see an inch of your laid lifeline. That beautifully lit blue doorway has disappeared. How long will the sediment take to settle for it to reappear, and do you have sufficient air left in your tank to wait. The object of the exercise is to remain calm when you suddenly can't see your hand in front of your face, and return along the line to exit.

There are multiple hazards within wrecks. Cables hang and snare and abandoned cargo can shift and become unstable after storms. There are sharp

Trucks on the wreck of the Zenobia.

edges. The only diver lost during the salvage of the *Costa Concordia* died as a result of a cut to his leg. Exhalations can disturb rust on ceilings, which falls like rain, reducing visibility. Interiors can be dark, corridors and shafts confined, where the diver in front can unintentionally kick you in the face, dislodging your mask. Areas such as the bridge, with open doorways, can be prone to surge, which can suck and throw a diver into the walls, akin to being inside a washing machine. War wrecks contain unexploded munitions, which become unstable over time and leak picric acid, or drums of aviation fuel, which seep into the surrounding water, so even if you don't touch anything, you're exposed to potential chemical reactions.

When a wreck lies at a depth of thirty metres or more, divers encounter a condition called nitrogen narcosis, also known as 'the rapture of the deep'. This is an alteration in the state of consciousness as a result of breathing air with a higher concentration of nitrogen, because the air in your tank is compressed. In practical terms narcosis can impair judgement. Threading a line through a loop the size of your fist at depth becomes surprisingly taxing, as does solving a numerical sequence an eleven-year-old would find a doddle. Narcosis has a debilitating effect, and although symptoms disappear on ascent they will be present when inside any wreck below thirty metres, where being 'narced' and making poor decisions could cost your life.

If these potential risks weren't enough, you have to keep a watchful eye on your air consumption. Wreck divers mentally divide their full tank into thirds. The first third accounts for the maximum extent of the dive internally into the wreck, allowing two thirds to retrace the route and ascend. Spare tanks are ideally left outside the entrance to the wreck, or are slung from the line that leads back to the surface.

Land-based dark tourism feels easier and safer, where the inherent risks are likely abuse from neighbours of a 'House of Horrors', or having your coins and cigarettes cadged by a cemetery rent boy.

I F THE INVENTION OF THE AQUALUNG AND THE POPULARITY OF scuba diving have allowed us to dip our toes into the underwater world, then the development of deep sea exploration technology has allowed mankind unfettered access to the seabed.

The wreck of the *Titanic* lies two and a half miles down, 370 miles southeast off the coast of Newfoundland, after she hit an iceberg on the night of 14th April 1912, during her maiden voyage, and sank with the loss of over 1,500 lives. *Titanic* attained legendary status, not only because she carried the 'Upstairs Downstairs' set on a state of the art liner saddled with the unfortunate tag of 'unsinkable', but because, as Lennon and Foley noted in their book, *Dark Tourism*, *Titanic* was the first truly global disaster of the fledgling media age.

The public certainly bought into the disaster, snapping up the memorabilia produced in the wake of the sinking, including six postcards issued as a collectible set, ubiquitous commemorative plates and mourning teddy bears. Crowds flocked to the cinema to see the newsreels. The liner would have been forgotten over time, but her story and subsequent public fascination was rekindled with the 1958 movie spin off, *A Night to Remember*, following the publication of the book of the same name by Walter Lord.

However the jaw-dropper came in September 1985, when it was announced to the world that the wreck had been located and positively identified. The footage of the ghostly bow rail, rusting away on the ocean floor in the darkness was pure televisual glue. As if that wasn't enough, recovery of the debris field between the two halves of the wreck commenced, and in October 1987 Telly Savalas, TV's *Kojak*, presented a television special, *Return to the Titanic*, live from Paris, window dressed with armed guards and periodic dry ice, where the artefacts were presented to the world. The show culminated with the opening of the Assistant Purser's safe, which transpired to be somewhat anticlimactic, as Savalas ran out of scripted pathos, and ad-limped towards the tele-prompter for the summing up and closing credits.

While the idea of recreational divers removing artefacts from wrecks where lives have been lost may be considered as grave robbing, the *Titanic* trove attracted less condemnation. There were objections, most notably from Eva Hart, a survivor of the sinking, who was opposed to any salvage from the grave. However an American judge had sanctioned the salvage rights in international waters, and the talk was of 'saving' the finds, and preserving them, so they could be 'shared' with the wider paying public. There was a sense that no matter how heartfelt the objection, these treasures were going to be raised regardless. Eva Hart passed away on Valentine's Day, 1996.

There are no discernable human remains to be seen on the wreck, according to James Cameron, director of the Oscar-winning motion picture, *Titanic*, who has visited the site over thirty times. However to coincide with the centenary of the sinking, photos were released to the media showing pairs of boots and clothing, laid out in such a fashion as to be worn by a ghost, indicating that they were transported to the sea floor by a person who went down with the liner, and whose remains are now embedded in the silt.

For the most part the wreck now appears to be a battleground for conflicting interests, which will continue until *Titanic* rusts away into a heap. Dr Robert Ballard, credited with the discovery, is in favour of using technology to light and film the scene for online tourism, perhaps similar to the way we can view Dealey Plaza in real time. However there's now less to see at the site. Since RMS Titanic Inc. obtained the salvage rights they've removed in excess of 5,500 items from the site, which are displayed in various exhibitions.

For recreational wreck divers *Titanic* is the elephant in the room. It is unquestionably the most famous shipwreck of all time, but the vast majority of us will never 'dive' it, given the cost, and the increasingly rare excursions to the site. A couple of divers from New York were married in a submersible on the wreck in 2001, after the groom won a *Titanic* 'free dive' competition. Ballard described the wedding as "over the top". Objections to the ceremony being conducted on the submerged mass grave were countered by comparisons with people marrying in churches, where they would also be in close proximity to graveyards. Spin, like water, tends to find the path of least resistance.

With the wreck effectively out of their reach, and to compensate for any envy, wreck divers have a tendency to dismiss *Titanic*; "It's only famous because it sunk." There is some truth in this, because few would recall the names of her sister ships, the liners *Olympic* and *Britannic*, the former providing nearly a quarter-century of service before being scrapped, and the latter striking a mine in the Mediterranean in November 1916 and sinking, claiming thirty lives.

Titanic's legacy is big business. Even if the $60,000 to access the wreck is out of reach to most, there are a plethora of exhibitions offering 'an experience'. RMS Titanic Inc, who salvaged the wreck, are a subsidiary of Premier Exhibitions. They have travelling *Titanic* shows in addition to their permanent exhibition, at the Luxor Hotel and Casino in Las Vegas, Nevada, which includes a section of the hull, luggage, a bottle of unopened champagne, a replica of the Grand Staircase, and outer promenade deck, which comes complete with freezing temperature to match that of the fateful night.

Naturally there's a range of merchandise, including apparel, three different shot glasses, a Captain Smith teddy bear, and jewellery, such as a pair of exquisite '*RMS Titanic* Goldtone Earrings w/Genuine coal', your price $25. RMS Titanic Inc. recovered coal from the debris field and incorporated it within the souvenir range, thereby offering more people the chance to afford their own actual bit of *Titanic* history. If earrings don't suit you, then there is the four-inch *Titanic* Hourglass, which includes a quarter inch piece of coal, along with a certificate of authentication.

Titanic: The Artefact Exhibition has received over twenty-five million people worldwide, and it is not the only *Titanic* venture. There are dedicated *Titanic* museum exhibitions in Tennesse, Massachussetts, and Missouri in the United States. The Maritime Museum of the Atlantic, in Halifax, Nova Scotia has a permanent exhibition. So too does the Merseyside Maritime Museum in Liverpool, and the SeaCity Museum in Southampton, UK, which also provides a '*Titanic* Trail' walking tour, which sensibly incorporates a public house that members of the crew frequented.

The liner's legacy continues, and thrives. *Titanic* Belfast museum opened in 2012, in time for the centenary of the sinking. It includes a walking tour of the Harland & Wolff drawing offices and the shipyard where *Titanic* was constructed. The museum, a stunning piece of architecture in its own right, and built at a cost of £77m, does not include any artefacts lifted from the wreck site on 'ethical' grounds. Over 800,000 people visited in its first year, nearly double the number initially expected. It should be noted that, after correspondence with its press office, *Titanic* Belfast acknowledges itself as 'a dark tourist attraction'. *Titanic* was a disaster, so there's no ambiguity. All these exhibitions are drawing from the dark tourism pool.

It is remarkable to think that this one ship is responsible for an industry, a century after it failed to complete its maiden voyage, yet although it's financial legacy is considerable, so is the investment required to maintain it. Hiring a submersible to work two and a half miles down is not cheap, whether it recovers a section of hull or a basket of bric-a-brac, nor is keeping a support vessel on the surface of an inhospitable North Atlantic, or the continued conservation of recovered artefacts from the salvage expeditions. Indeed Premier Exhibitions diversified in 2004, with Bodies, touring 'plasticised' cadavers from China to rival Gunther von Hagens' Body Worlds.

In 2009, the company reported that Bodies was the more profitable venture, and in 2012 they put their entire collection of *Titanic* artefacts up for auction. The collection had to be sold as a job lot, with the proviso that the new owners would present the cache for periodic public display.

At the time of writing, the Premier Exhibitions *Titanic* collection remains unsold. It was reported on 14th June 2016 that the company filed for bankruptcy protection, and was now seeking judgement to split its collection, so it could sell selected artefacts to assist with its financial predicament. After eighteen years, Premier Exhibitions is facing financial difficulties, saddled with artefacts, controversially recovered, that it cannot sell. It seems unlikely, given the attendance figures garnered by the *Titanic* Belfast museum, that the public have become jaded with the story, more likely just in the way that it is told.

From the moment the wreck and mass grave was discovered, it was never going to remain undisturbed. Unfortunately discovery has had a price.

A S LEW GRADE, AND ANYONE WHO SAT THROUGH THE TOE curling film-of-the-book, *Raise the Titanic*, will appreciate, bringing a wreck to the surface is a very tricky business indeed. But it has been achieved, most notably in 1982 with the recovery of the *Mary Rose*, the pride of Henry VIII's navy. The ship sank into the ooze of the Solent in 1545, with massive loss of life, and spent 473 years on the bottom before being raised live on television in a £4m salvage operation, unintentionally dramatic, when a pin on the specially designed lifting cradle supporting the timbers sheared, threatening to send the wreck back to the depths. After extensive restoration the ship has finally been preserved and is on display in a purpose built museum in Portsmouth.

A section of the VOC[3] ship *Batavia*, lost in 1629, was also recovered in the 1970s, along with human remains, and is now impressively exhibited in the Western Australian Maritime Museum at Fremantle.

As recently as December 2007 the Chinese raised the *Nanhai One*, a merchant ship that sank in the mouth of the Pearl River approximately 800 years ago. The wreck is in excellent condition and there are reportedly over 60,000 items on board. The ship resides in an aquarium on Hailing Island, lying in sampled water that had preserved it prior to discovery. Visitors can watch the continuing archaeological work through the glass sides of the holding tank.

The reclamation of these sunken time capsules after centuries underwater have attracted wonderment and fascination worldwide, rather than the

---

3) Vereenigde Oost-Indische Compagnie (Dutch East India Company).

controversy that you might expect from disturbing a final resting place, reinforcing the fact that the passage of time determines our response. Bringing these vessels to the surface allows a far greater number of tourists to see them, rather than just those who dive.

So what about a fatal wreck raised in living memory?

Like most English schoolboys of the sixties, I'd grown up with *Bluebird*. Her pilot, Donald Campbell CBE, was the stuff of *Boy's Own* legends and cigarette cards. He'd broken world speed records in both the 1950s and 1960's, then went on to set both land and water speed records in 1964. He is to this day the only individual to set both records during the same year. In 1967 he took his jet-propelled hydroplane, *Bluebird K7* onto Coniston Water in an attempt to smash his own water speed record, but on the second run, disaster struck. Travelling in excess of 300 mph, the nose lifted, the boat somersaulted, hung for an instant at the apex of the arc, then disintegrated on impact with the water. The nation saw the black and white footage and heard his last words.

The wreck lay undisturbed until 'Bluebird Project', a team of divers led by Bill Smith, discovered and raised the wreckage and Campbell's body from the lake between October 2000 and May 2001. What was of particular interest was that the craft had been raised initially against the wishes of some of Campbell's surviving family. I duly contacted Bill Smith to ask him how he had managed to resolve the moral issues inevitably attached to the project. His reply:

"If I had a pound for every time an attempt has been made to drag me into this argument..."

He would not be drawn further, suffice to say, "It can be done."

His comments reinforce just how many people find the issue of recovery controversial, whether they might be directly connected to the deceased, or as provocateurs with the intent to muddy murky waters further still. However as diving has increased in popularity, becoming both more affordable and accessible, so too has underwater exploration and detection equipment, therefore allowing more recreational divers to hunt with a greater chance of success for relics, treasure, or, as in this case, for legends. One Coniston local commented on the sheer number of divers in the lake, searching: "It has become like looking for the Holy Grail, trying to find Donald Campbell's boat."

The stark truth is that if it had not been Bill Smith and his team that discovered and recovered *Bluebird* and her pilot, it would have been someone else. There's only a finite amount of bottom, so it would have been found eventually. In a worse case scenario, the wreck could have been discovered and raised without the commitment, care and sensitivity exercised by the 'Bluebird Project'. It is easy to imagine the find being picked to pieces, ending up in a shed, along with the odd porthole, only of importance to those who recovered them.

So the wreck of *Bluebird* could never be left in situ, given what has happened to *Thistlegorm* and other wrecks around the world. The very existence of the souvenir hunters provides the perfect justification for bringing the wreck to the surface for its own protection, thereby eroding any moral objection in the process. It is very much a choice between having the wreck recovered with care, or letting it be stripped to the bone and scattered to the winds.

The Campbell Family Heritage Trust donated *Bluebird K7* to the Ruskin Museum in Coniston. Bill Smith and the '*Bluebird* Project' team continue their work to restore *K7* to running order, and permission has been granted for a proving run on Coniston Water when completed. The boat will then be housed in a purpose built wing of the museum, which already contains a display of memorabilia, including Campbell's helmet recovered from the crash site. Donald Campbell was laid to rest in Coniston cemetery on 12th September 2001. The motif of a blue bird adorns the headstone.

I T IS ESTIMATED THAT THERE ARE APPROXIMATELY SIX MILLION DIVERS worldwide. In America, DEMA, the Diving Equipment and Marketing Association, calculates that in 2014 diving contributed $11 billion to the USA gross domestic product. The state of California alone accounted for some 1.35 million dives that year, with a projected income of $161–$323m.

Scuba diving in Florida contributes some $900m to the annual local economy, much of it due to the lure of their 'artificial reef', the largest in the world, the decommissioned aircraft carrier, USS *Oriskany*, known as 'The Mighty O'. Intentionally sunk in May 2006, twenty-four miles south of Pensacola, the wreck, which took several years to prepare at a cost of $20m, now rests in seventy metres of water, with the island tower at a depth of thirty metres, within the range of recreational limits. The hope is that over time the wreck will be colonised by organisms, and provide a habitat for marine life. Although divers from all over the world are drawn to 'The Great Carrier Reef', the revenue generated by local divers from Escambia and Baldwin Florida counties alone is estimated to be worth $2.2m annually.

While 'The Mighty O' does not have a dark history as such, it illustrates the popularity of wreck diving, and the tourist income it generates. The US programme of sinking decommissioned ships for the diving industry continues, with demand for 'new' wrecks far outstripping supply.

In 2014 it was estimated that dive-related spending in Australia was worth $2.2 billion Australian dollars. It's also estimated that Australia's domestic diving tourists spend three times more than their non-diving counterparts, and, better still, international dive tourists stay a third longer than their non-diving counterparts, and consequently spend 80% more.

The majority of diving tourists head for Queensland, for the Great Barrier Reef, and I was no exception, for although I didn't care for the reef itself, there was a world class wreck there, one recognised by UNESCO, visited by about 10,000 divers annually, that had a dark history, and one which had recently become darker still.

I DON'T BELIEVE IN GHOSTS, BUT IF I DID, THEN THEY'D BE HERE. YOU can still see their faces, sepia tinged, large as life, stuck to a wall in memoriam. They're the officers of the SS *Yongala*, posed for the photographer, captured for posterity, now benignly watching over the glass-cased model of their beautiful Edwardian ship.

The small gallery in the Maritime Museum of Townsville creaks underfoot. It's like a ship inside and out, so no great surprise to discover this was once the office of the Pier Master in a former life, before they moved the building to its present location on Palmer Street, overlooking Ross Creek. Admission is $6 for adults, $3 for children aged three to fourteen. I have the place to myself and the staff very kindly set up a chair so I can watch a video of the wreck filmed by underwater explorers Ron and Valerie Taylor from the early 1980s.

The artefacts the Taylors recovered are housed here, lovingly curated: deformed skylights and portholes, stained glassware and porcelain, the ship's bell, a photograph of the racehorse Moonshine, *Yongala's* most celebrated victim, and an artist's impression of the ship on the brink of oblivion, swamped by the sea. I can barely bring myself to look at the photograph of Captain Bill Knight, head cocked with a trace of a smile. He looks too kind for this end. Tomorrow I'm going to dive the ship that became his grave, and that of his crew and passengers, and I feel guilty, because the truth is I can hardly wait.

The Greyhound bus takes me south along the Bruce Highway towards the small town of Ayr, just over an hour away. I journey in the company of Max Gleeson's detailed account of the SS *Yongala*, *Townsville's Titanic*, purchased at the Maritime Museum gift shop. She was commissioned, along with a sister ship, *Grantala*, by the Adelaide Steamship Company to meet the demand of the Gold Rush coastal routes in the late 1890s.

Built in Newcastle-on-Tyne, launched in 1903, she was a beautiful 363 foot long vessel, state-of-the-art for her day, fitted out in walnut and oak with the capacity to carry 110 first class and 130 second class passengers, plus cargo. She boasted state rooms, smoking room, music room, saloon, and a magnificent staircase in the dining room, all whisked along in fine style at an impressive sixteen knots. Her name came from the Aboriginal word meaning "broad watering place", in line with the company's policy to christen their ships in the indigenous language.

As the Gold Rush panned out in Western Australia, the company switched to ply the northern coast, and *Yongala* commenced the Melbourne to Cairns run in 1907, with Captain Knight in command. Experienced and respected, his portrait was centre stage amongst his contemporaries in the line's promotional literature.

The bus pulls into the crossroads at Ayr, and within a minute I'm left standing alone in balmy single storey rural Australia. A radio plays to itself through an open window. I call *Yongala* Dive. They'll send someone to pick me up when their dive boat returns, in an hour, maybe two. No dramas then. Sat

Model of the SS *Yongala*, Townsville Maritime Museum.

on my bench at the bus stop I turn the page to *Yongala's* final voyage.

She departed Melbourne for Cairns on 14th March 1911, making her usual scheduled stops, and at Brisbane received a racehorse trainer with his new acquisition, Moonshine. Livestock as freight was not unusual, and the horse joined the Lincoln Red bull already aboard. *Yongala* departed Flat-top Island for the 200 mile leg north to Townsville, early afternoon on 23rd March, and was sighted five hours later by a lighthouse keeper in deteriorating weather. The vessel and the 121 on board were never seen again.

Other shipping sought shelter having received storm warnings, but the *Yongala*, without radio, sailed straight into a cyclone. Overdue at Townsville, the assumption was that Knight had taken refuge, but when other ships arrived and there was still no word, an extensive land and sea search began. The lighthouse keeper at Bowling Cape Green found a bag of chaff on the beach, and a steamer arrived in Townsville having recovered detritus, including an inscribed door from *Yongala's* promenade deck to the music room. Then the badly decomposed remains of a horse, presumably Moonshine, were discovered, washed ashore.

With the ship now lost beyond doubt, the tragedy was observed in churches and village halls, and a disaster fund was launched. Yet again, with the passing of time, and with no sign of the wreck, *Yongala* slipped into maritime mythology. There was the odd ghost story featuring a rusty doppelgänger, but it wasn't until 1947, when the Navy took a closer look at an obstruction discovered by minesweepers during the war, that they realised they'd found a wreck, and one with dimensions that matched those of the lost *Yongala*.

It was the Queensland Underwater Research Group, with their new scuba diving equipment, who finally established the wreck's identity. In 1958 they recovered a safe, and although the contents had been reduced to sludge, the serial number was sent to the manufacturer in England, who duly confirmed that it did indeed come from *Yongala*. With the mystery finally solved, the scuba club dumped the recovered artefact into the river.

Yongala Dive picks me up for the fifteen minutes scenic drive to Alva Beach. There's not even a crossroads here, just a small residential community bolstered by the transient tourists of the local trailer park. I've arrived in the Twilight Zone on the fringe of a beautiful white beach. The *Yongala* Divers Lodge accommodates a dozen guests in neat dorms, or a double room, with a lounge, kitchen, and a picture postcard sunset thrown in for good measure. The dive shop is downstairs, so you can roll out of bed, grab some 'brekkie', and you're good to go.

Having sorted the kit, a dive briefing[4] takes place under the shade in the garden, where the forthcoming highlights are detailed on the whiteboard, including the hole into the wreck through which various assembled bones can be seen with the aid of a torch. Due to the fragility of the structure, no penetration of the wreck itself is permitted.

Then it's into the 4x4 to off-road along the beach to the waiting *Yongala Express*, a 10m rigid inflatable. We're tractored into the surf, where our skipper navigates the shifting sand bars, before opening up the throttle for the exhilarating half hour dash to the wreck. This is where diving from the remote outpost of Alva Beach to access the wreck comes into its own, as boats from Townsville only run when full, and with their crossing to the site taking three hours over notoriously choppy waters, when they do eventually arrive, the majority of their clients are seasick.

As our diving party is comprised of gap year tourists, I have the honour of rolling in first with Jamie, a dive instructor from Sydney. He's coming off the back of a week diving the *SS President Coolidge*, the US luxury liner converted into a WWII troop carrier, sunk off the beach of Espiritu Santo, Vanuatu, after it was holed by sea mines. I've had three weeks diving the wrecks of Papua New Guinea, including '*Blackjack*', the intact B-17 bomber at Tufi, indisputably the world's greatest plane dive. So we're quits in terms of bragging rights, both 'salty', and won't need a guide.

There's little discernable current as we descend the line towards the bow at a depth of fourteen metres, which is clearly visible from the surface. I'd

---

4) Dive briefings include a potted history of how the ship went down, especially if the evidence of how it was lost can be seen. The guide will highlight interesting features on the wreck, likely marine life, potential hazards, and the 'profile', or route, of our dive tour. Briefings tend to be no more than ten-fifteen minutes for most wrecks within thirty metres.

viewed plenty of underwater footage of the wreck, and over the years had enviously sat through first hand accounts of others who had dived *Yongala*, so I knew this was going to be an aquarium dive. In truth, neither footage nor word of mouth could adequately convey the sheer quantity and quality of life present. Dive operators who sink ships to make artificial reefs can only dream of this. The wreck is an oasis in an underwater desert, and every living creature from miles around is drawn to it, with every available inch colonised by a greater variety of coral than can be found on most reefs. It is as if the *Yongala* has a living exoskeleton.

We descend over the bow, across the deck, the carcass upright, although listing heavily towards starboard, and past the forward cargo hold, where the femur bones can be seen. Continuing our tour requires concentration to avoid ploughing into the prolific black coral trees that have supplanted the lifeboat davits. *Yongala* moves. Everywhere. It heaves with life. Shoals bomb back and forth. A hawksbill turtle grazes on the wreck, seemingly obliviously to our close quarters attention, ignoring us in favour of food.

We drop down onto the flat white sandy bottom, between masts that lie like fallen maypoles. I follow Jamie along the starboard side, where he's shadowed by an olive sea snake that bounds through the water after him like an enthusiastic puppy. We round the stern, hanging back to take in the view of the majestic curve, somewhat blurred by the frenetic fish traffic hugging the wreck. Sinking down into the shadow of the stern, a ceiling now rising above my head, bedecked with jewel-like growth, where a curtain of trevally screen a huge sedentary flowery cod. This is the maximum depth of our dive, and with my hand on the sand the computer registers 28.3 metres.

As we ascend to cover the port side it's possible to peer into the bowels of the wreck to spy the cast iron bath and toilets, and the obligatory decorative anemone fish, before traversing the companionways to the coral grotto structure that was once the first class dining room. *Yongala* is a grave, and also a fitting memorial to those who were lost, although there is no commemorative plaque to mark it as such, and coral would quickly smother it if there were. It is a beautiful final resting place, thanks to nature, and it comes as no surprise that Australian diving legend Valerie Taylor said that if she had just one more dive to make in her life, she would chose *Yongala*. Tragically Christina Mae Watson didn't get a choice.

S HE'D ONLY TAKEN UP SCUBA DIVING TO PLEASE HER FIANCÉ. AFTER their fairy tale wedding in Alabama in 2003, she and husband David 'Gabe' Watson travelled to Australia for their honeymoon, including a Queensland liveaboard and a dive on *Yongala*. Watson, a qualified rescue diver, claimed 'Tina' quickly got into trouble, knocked his mask askew, and in the time it took him to recover she had sunk to the bottom. Unable to save her, he ascended to the dive boat for help. Recovered by a guide, attempts to resuscitate Tina failed.

It might have been a tragic accident. Or it might not. There appeared inconsistencies in Watson's statement to the Townsville police. In a further macabre twist that brought the story to international prominence, a photograph taken by another diver on the wreck emerged, with Tina's body, prone on the seabed, unintentionally captured in the background. She had been married to Gabe Watson for just eleven days.

In 2007 the Queensland government launched an inquest, and the following June the Townsville coroner returned a verdict. The court charged Watson with Tina's murder, and a warrant was issued for his arrest. It was alleged that he had restrained his wife underwater, turned off her air until she lost consciousness, then turned the air back on, before letting her fall to the bottom and making a controlled ascent to the surface to raise the alarm. Tina's family suggested the motive behind her death was a life insurance policy, which Watson is alleged to have asked his wife to increase in the weeks prior to their wedding.

Back in Alabama, out of reach of the Queensland authorities, Watson remarried a Tina lookalike and periodically visited his first wife's grave to remove the flowers left by her family. He was finally caught on a police surveillance camera using bolt cutters to cut away plastic floral tributes that had been secured with wire to prevent vandalism.

Following the case gave diving *Yongala* a contemporary resonance. Around the time I was completing my fourth and final dive on the wreck, Watson was turning himself in to the police in Brisbane, having voluntarily returned to Australia to clear his name.

Tina's family flew to Australia for the trial in June 2009, hoping for answers. However the prosecution accepted a deal for Watson to plead guilty to the lesser charge of manslaughter. There was no trial and he served eighteen months of a four and a half year prison term. On his return to the US he was arrested and charged with murder.

The trial was set for February 2012. The judge soon acquitted him for lack of evidence. Watson's full dive history revealed he was not sufficiently experienced to hold a rescue certification, and had not been diving for a year prior to the *Yongala*. The diving expert for the case stated: "He had no hope of being competent, he could barely save himself, let alone his wife", and suggested Watson was likely a coward, not a murderer. Tina had a heart condition, which she failed to disclose, and no open water experience. The liveaboard company pleaded guilty to contravening safety standards by not providing the couple with a qualified divemaster, and was fined.

I pitched an article on the *Yongala* to dive magazines in both Australia and the UK. The centenary of the sinking was approaching, which made the wreck topical, and I was an established contributor. Both markets ran the article. All mention of what happened to Tina Watson, included to give the article contemporary resonance, was edited out. It was as if her contentious death, which had been widely reported in the mainstream media, both here and in Australia, had never happened, and both editors were less than forthcoming about why they'd excluded this intriguing case from the history of the wreck, much to my chagrin. It appeared *Yongala's* 121 victims in 1911 were the only ones worthy of note, and Moonshine the racehorse predictably got top billing.

Diving magazines are effectively promotional tools for tourism, filled with trip reports and advertising for exotic locations and the operators that supply them. No one is going to rock the boat by highlighting a tragedy that portrays diving in an unfavourable light.

Although wrecks may be considered dark tourism sites, (if not then what are they?), the diving industry does not promote them as such, preferring to focus on the exploration, adventure, and seemingly selected history. If some wreck divers are surreptitiously, or subconsciously, seeking out shipwrecks where fatalities have occurred, no one is volunteering to discuss it.

I wouldn't want to leave the subject of watery graves on such a cynical note, that all those who follow the underwater cortège are self-centred glory hunters, diving wrecks for that souvenir WWII Coke bottle, trophy photograph, commemorative t-shirt, hard-core penetration bragging rights, or to be in proximity to drowned souls.

So the final reflection comes from Rod Pearce, who's been searching for, and discovering, war wrecks in the waters of Papua New Guinea for the past forty years.

"The hardest part is the letters. I still get letters from people looking for their relatives, missing in action. They want to know if I've found their father... their grandfather."

It's a reminder that there are people seeking out wrecks for very different reasons, and that for some, the passing of time changes nothing.

THE PROMISE

UNSPOKEN ETIQUETTE DICTATES WE COME TO A COLLECTIVE HALT in the gravel, before the gate, below the sign. Our guide addresses us, but in truth not all are paying attention. Some drift to take photographs, and like a drone, I follow suit... I have no idea why I took that... or that, for that matter. Do I really need photos in portrait *and* landscape format, and why am I taking pictures anyway? To prove I was here? Who cares? Perhaps I'm just snapping away as a means to decompress before walking inside. No idea.

The sign, the iconic wave, hangs above our collective conscience like a guillotine as the guide brings her narrative to a close, and the only thing I've learned standing here is that I will never see a silver birch tree in quite the same way again. It towers above the sign. Venerable, beautiful, it reminds me of someone I used to know, and the reason why I'm here.

One last habitual look behind, in part to disguise the smile at the memory, and to make sure I remember our coach livery amongst the many. Then we funnel forward, crunching underfoot with a slow, slightly uncertain gait, perhaps trying to reconcile ourselves with what we've chosen to do today. No one wishes to appear over eager to satisfy their curiosity, but there again no one wants to be left behind, in case they miss out. Miss out on what, exactly? The highlights? As we approach the blocks I can't resist a snatched look back at the sign, black against the cascading branches and a flat, seal-white winter sky. From here it has lost its resonance, meaning, symbolism, power, and the hypnotic aura that compelled us to capture it in the first place. Now it can be seen for what it really is.

ARBEIT MACHT FREI

It's just an illegible metal scroll.

Before us lie, as in the words of the song, 'Avenues all lined with trees', fringed with neat two storey buildings under pantile roofs. It looks administrative, orderly, European, nothing untoward, other than the ancient electrified fences. Phalanxes of concrete posts, cast like dinosaur necks, strung together with rotting barbed wire, and Cyclopean lights on distended stalks, the squat watchtower in the distance, skulking under a witching hat.

We arrive at the first block and politely file through the door to the museum, tramping the granite steps, ridiculously bowed under the footfall of the millions who've come before, furtively searching for clues in the faces of those on their way out. The strip lit corridors upstairs are lined with stark black and white photographic portraits of the inmates, mug shots really, hanging three deep, taken when their captors had time for such formalities, before all the silver in the world threatened to run out, because there were simply too many faces to record. So they dispensed with the formality of portraiture, and reduced everyone to numbers instead. All had their own unique combination, locked in with ink and a needle.

Huge glass display tanks stretch along the walls in the upstairs rooms. They hold cutaway chalk grey models of the crematoria and gas chambers, a collapsed mountain of old suitcases, identified with hopeless, hand painted optimism, a sea of shoes, bric-a-brac prosthetics, and a morass of wire spectacles, as if an angry child had gone berserk with a black crayon. And the empty canisters, branded with the faded *totenkopf*, that once held the pellets of pesticide, now displayed for our collective consideration. There's even a solitary tin in a separate case, so we can see the pellets, poured, to show Zyklon B in its solid form, before it was tipped into the chamber.

There is so much of everything, yet it is but a tiny fraction of what was wrought here. There's a disturbing thought; these displays, the remains and artefacts of mass murder, might not even account for a day's worth.

A USCHWITZ-BIRKENAU[1] BECAME THE WORLD'S MOST NOTORIOUS killing factory in part due to the railway network, established in the nineteenth century, which served the small, innocuous town, long before the rise of the Nazis and their 'Final Solution'. A camp for migrant workers was constructed in 1916 on the site, with the intention of using the railway to transport labourers to distant estates to work the land. When Poland regained independence in 1919, the town was christened Oświęcim, and the army was billeted in the camp. Germany invaded Poland in September 1939. The railway network was still in place. Now the hub intended to disperse people throughout Europe in search of a living would become a terminus, and the proverbial end of the line.

The former barracks at Oświęcim were used to detain Polish political prisoners, the first of whom arrived in May 1940, swelled by other undesirables, such as homosexuals and Jehovah's Witnesses.

Rudolf Höss was appointed commandant of what would now be known as Auschwitz I (not to be confused with Rudolf Hess, the Deputy Führer and long-

---

1) The main camps were Auschwitz, Birkenau, and Monowitz. In addition there were over forty subcamps. The United Nations officially changed the complex to the collective name of 'Auschwitz-Birkenau, German Nazi Concentration and Extermination Camp (1940–1945)' in 2007, in order to clarify that Poland had nothing to do with the camps, or the running of them.

Auschwitz I. Photo: Larah Vidotti

term inmate of Spandau prison). Höss was experienced with concentration camps, having served at both Dachau and Sachsenhausen. He moved his wife and children into a villa on the site, and set about expanding the camp's potential, evicting any remaining locals from the vicinity, refurbishing and extending the existing structures, with many buildings given a second floor. As the year drew to a close, the site encompassed some forty square kilometres, fortified with barbed wire and watchtowers.

By March 1941 the inmate population had grown to 10,000, predominantly Poles. The camp needed to expand. I.G. Farben, a petro-chemical company, planned to build a factory in the area. The environs provided water, lime, and coal seams needed for the production of synthetic rubber and fuel, and with the railway infrastructure and a huge pool of renewable labour already in place, Auschwitz was the perfect location. Reichsführer Heinrich Himmler wanted I.G. Farben's business, and ordered the camp to expect 30,000 detainees.

To build the factory, workers were initially marched several kilometres from Auschwitz I to the construction site, but were later transported by train to save time. A labour camp was eventually established next to the factory, saving the daily commute, and would become known as Auschwitz III, or Monowitz.

The expansion of Auschwitz was also necessary in the wake of the German invasion of the Soviet Union in the spring of 1941, and construction of what became known as Birkenau began in October, to absorb the influx of Soviet prisoners of war. Thousands were put to work building the camp extension. Few saw the following spring.

Auschwitz II-Birkenau was built on exposed, boggy ground, and the accommodation for the inmates consisted of wooden huts with no sanitation or insulation. Each hut had capacity for some 500 prisoners, but hundreds more were crammed inside. Many perished due to the conditions, especially during the harsh winter months, through brutality, starvation, and rampant disease, such as typhus. Then Birkenau morphed, from a camp where prisoners died to a factory facility where they were systematically killed.

This change was implemented after the Wannsee conference of January 1942, convened to ensure cooperation across all departments of the Third Reich with the 'Final Solution to the Jewish question', essentially that all Jews under Nazi control would be killed. Bullets were expensive and impractical for the scale envisaged, and the Nazis recognised that they needed to protect their own by providing more than an arm's length from mass murder.

In occupied Russia, the Nazis conducted experiments using carbon monoxide, fed from the exhaust pipes of motor vehicles into a sealed room. At Auschwitz they turned to a pesticide already employed at the camp for the decontamination of clothing, a prussic acid called Zyklon B, a pellet that dissolved in contact with the air.

Initial gassings were carried out in the mortuary, adapted for the purpose, but the facility was too small, and too central. In the BBC documentary series *Auschwitz: The Nazis and The Final Solution*, an eyewitness reported that motorcycles were revved in a futile attempt to drown out the screams from within. The gas took approximately twenty minutes to take effect, then the bodies were taken to the on-site crematorium for disposal.

While four large purpose built gas chambers and crematoria were under construction at Birkenau, two secluded farmhouses, The Little Red House and The Little White House, were adapted for the purpose. According to Höss, these farmhouses could take 800 and 1,200 prisoners respectively.

The first gassing of Jews in The Little Red House began on 20th March 1942. This was the day after Alzbeta 'Sissy' Meisl, a Slovakian seamstress, married Pavel Wienwurm, who worked in textiles. There would be no honeymoon for Mr. and Mrs. Wienwurm. A deal had been struck between Slovakia and the Nazis. The paperwork was in place, the freight cars coupled. Deportations of the Slovakian Jews would begin on 25th March.

Initially it was able-bodied men and single women, but on 11th April the Ministry of Transport began shipping out whole families, including Sissy's, under the cover of night. For most it was a one way, 150 mile trip north from the Slovakian capital, Bratislava, to the *Judenrampe* at Auschwitz-Birkenau, and then to the gas.

According to a census of December 1940, there were approximately 88,000 Jews in Slovakia. It is estimated that only 17% survived the Holocaust. Sissy was one of those who made it, and nearly seventy years later, she would send me through the gates of Auschwitz-Birkenau, as a tourist, to keep a promise.

I WAS INTRODUCED TO SISSY, AND HER SECOND HUSBAND MARTZI, AT a friend's family party in Berkshire in the mid 1980s. Born less than twenty years after the end of the war, I'd been raised on Airfix Spitfires and Messerschmitts and gran's tales of 'The Blitz'.

But when Sissy pushed back the sleeve of her party frock to show the number officiously tattooed on the inside of her arm, it was a first. This was the Home Counties on a beautiful afternoon, forty years after the events, and the serial number was in context, on a living arm. It was both jolting and surreal. Against her ageing skin, the blue pigment had an ugly purplish tinge, with a hint of turquoise. In truth it was a colour I'd never seen, or even imagined. I'd assumed it would be black. The font looked official, almost Gothic. I had to resist the temptation to take her wrist, wet my thumb and try to rub it out.

When Martzi passed away, Sissy moved into an apartment in Brentwood, Essex, only a few miles away. We would visit her in the evenings, where she would stuff us with steaming goulash and sauerkraut, picking our brains on current affairs, or something she'd heard on LBC Talk radio.

"Children... we should abolish all religions. Let us discuss this."

Thanks, LBC.

Sissy never spoke about her experiences during the war, or the camps, and we were far too deferential to ask. She never defined herself by those times, to the point that we forgot. One evening we chided her for saving a piece of cling film, then realised we had no comprehension of what it was truly like to be without. Sissy waved our apologies away, saying this way she could give more pocket money to her grandchildren.

It was the evening I visited alone that she showed me the black and white photograph of her family in Slovakia, in a garden setting before the war. Even allowing for my memory playing tricks over time, there must have been over thirty people, spanning the generations, formally posed for the camera.

There was only one question to ask.

"How many of the others survived?"

She raised one finger.

I had no connection with Judaism, the victims of any persecuted group, or even the perpetrators. I could not be any further divorced from the reality. After regaining my composure, Sissy suggested I visit Auschwitz.

"You should go, Aitch. Go for me."

And so, there and then, I promised. I'd made promises in the past, and broken a few, unintentionally or otherwise, when common sense prevailed. But when Sissy asked me to go to Auschwitz on her behalf and I said I would, it was one promise I couldn't break.

AUSCHWITZ II–BIRKENAU IS SITUATED A COUPLE OF KILOMETRES from the original camp of Auschwitz I, and there's a free shuttle bus if you are pressed for time or don't fancy the nondescript walk. Between November and March there is one bus every half hour, otherwise it's every ten minutes. However on a day trip package from Krakow you can re-board your coach for the short hop between the two.

The arch of the notorious gatehouse, through which the condemned from every corner of mainland Europe passed, has been described as 'The Hole in the World'. We're swallowed into the symmetrical gatehouse one by one, climbing the metal spiral staircase, echoing the footsteps of those who planned and oversaw the nightmare scenario. At the top we disperse into the windowed gallery. What today's tourist sees, or is shown, is not entirely original. Buildings have been constructed, postwar, on land that was originally part of the camp, and some features within are reproductions. It is important that these distinctions are made and noted. However my first thought when I saw the panorama from the watchtower was:

"Oh! — For! — Fucks! — Sake! Look at the fucking SIZE of it!"

Through the glass on three sides, the sheer scale of the institution dwarfs preconceptions. The photographs, maps and models I'd seen beforehand couldn't adequately convey the scale of the Birkenau facility. Row upon row of barracks, many in a state of decay, regimented demented chicken coops as far as the eye can see. The expanse is such that it's easier to focus on the railway tracks, plumb centre, running three quarters of a kilometre to a vanishing point amidst a comb of spindly trees. Concentrating on the rails wards off a sense of moral vertigo the panorama induces. I'd read that it's Birkenau, rather than the camp of Auschwitz I, that has the greater impact on visitors. Although Auschwitz I has the gallows, standing cells, the 'Wall of Death' for those facing the firing squad, and Block 10 for medical experimentation, a place so repellent that it's off limits for tourists, Auschwitz II–Birkenau is something else.

Standing in this dystopian god spot, where the architects surveyed their panacea, hammers home what we, humanity, are truly capable of when we put our minds to it. It is frightening because it wasn't some anarchic creation, born from insanity or evil, but constructed on the basis of trial and error, until it worked.

As a result the world has a full-scale museum model of how to factory farm, kill, and cremate people. With deference to those who highlight the disparities between the original functioning complex and today's tourist site, does anyone descend from the gatehouse disappointed, expecting it would be bigger?

The camp is too large for tourists to see everything anyway. The tour is tailored to present Auschwitz-Birkenau within a realistic time frame of a day trip from Krakow, showing the key elements and exhibits within the complex. Tourists don't have the inclination or budget to spend multiple days there, not

Gate sign, Auschwitz I.

when there's the salt mines at Wieliczka to see. Incidentally, there is a 'Super Saver' tour, readily available, where you can do both Auschwitz-Birkenau *and* the Wieliczka salt mines in a day, so although Auschwitz-Birkenau may not wish to be considered a tourist attraction, this double-header tour suggests that is how it is perceived and marketed by the supporting tourist industry.

Auschwitz-Birkenau faces similar issues to the National September 11 Museum and Memorial in New York; both are graves, memorials, and although neither institution would care for the association, both are major tourist attractions.

Naturally to accommodate tourism the camp has had to undergo some changes, in terms of adding a cafeteria, a bookshop, and a place to screen film. Having initially been set up to accommodate some 500,000 visitors annually, it received over two million in 2016, so further expansion to facilitate actual tourists will be necessary. The existing buildings have already been mapped, allowing computer-based tourists a virtual representation.

Some parts of the camp, including gas chamber and crematoria, were reconstructed by the Soviet Union postwar, after the retreating Nazis tried to destroy evidence of their crimes. This reconstruction seems pragmatic, and not unreasonable, in order to convey the nature of what took place, and to counter the attempts of the guilty to eradicate the physical evidence of their crimes. The act of reproduction and reconstruction suggests this has been done for the benefit of tourists, and tourism, rather than for historians and history.

The iconic Arbeit Macht Frei sign, set above the gate at Auschwitz I, was stolen in December 2009. Although the perpetrators were caught, convicted, jailed, and the sign recovered, it had been cut into three pieces. What visitors at the gate see now is a reproduction, as is the corresponding sign at Dachau concentration camp, which was also stolen, then subsequently recovered in Norway, with no suspects or arrests.

The Arbeit Macht Frei replicas are necessary. It is a known highlight. Visitors come expecting to see the iconic sign, and the authorities obviously want them to see it. Everyone with a camera in my tour group photographed that sign, as did I. Portrait format, landscape format, one with the raised barrier, wide angle of the tour group to give scale, one from behind with everyone walking underneath to provide narrative, before playing catch up for the next photo opportunity. You can scroll through the multiple images later and delete as required. It matters not a jot to the tourists that the sign is a replica. Thankfully the fact that it is doesn't change what happened here either.

The 'Work Sets You Free' banner headline over Auschwitz is iconic, but also ironic. The only way work set the inmates free was when they died as a result, and many did. This then is surely an example of gallows humour at a site of mass murder. There was international outrage after the sign was stolen, the theft seen as a desecration. Yet the museum authorities have permitted it to be filmed and photographed until it has attained its desired status, presumably to illustrate the mind-set of those implementing mass extermination.

Tourism, the media, and the museum itself, have all contributed to give the sign resonance. Its theft, instigated by a neo-Nazi, demonstrates its power, symbolism, and spell, under which most would not wish to fall. So why have we? Perhaps when the last survivor has passed, our generation's legacy could be to invert the sign, and record that it was done in order to ridicule those who established it, to deny it and them any continued influence. This would show that we learned from history, and took responsibility to implement change as a result. The perpetrators failed, after all, didn't they?

DURING 1942 THE NAZIS COMBED EUROPE FOR JEWS TO CONTRIBUTE towards the Final Solution. By the end of the year, approximately two million had been isolated into ghettos, with some 200,000 interned in various camps, where 70% went straight to the gas, including children.

At Auschwitz-Birkenau, disposal of the corpses was problematic. The dead had been buried in a giant pit, but the decomposition in the summer heat was such that the corpses were subsequently exhumed and burnt on pyres. It is important to note that Auschwitz-Birkenau was not solely a killing factory, like Treblinka, where it's estimated that 99% of inmates were killed within two hours of arrival. At Auschwitz -Birkenau the fit and strong were put to work, although they would likely die through natural wastage from the extreme conditions they were subjected to. Those designated for work were registered with a tattoo, and some were dispatched to work at camps elsewhere. Children were killed, or sent before Dr Josef Mengele, the 'Angel of Death' who carried out medical experiments, with a predilection for twins.

Rudolf Höss, who had been removed as Auschwitz commandant in November 1943 for a supervising desk job, returned to his infamous post in May 1944, to oversee the execution of the Hungarian Jews. He added a spur to the railway line, so the tracks ran through the gatehouse, directly down to the crematoria.

An estimated 438,000 Hungarian Jews were killed between May and July, before the Hungarian authorities sensed the winds of change and halted the transports. The course of the war had turned decisively. Intelligence provided by the Polish resistance had alerted the Allies to the existence of the camp in the summer of 1942, and although representations from Jewish organisations to bomb the railways leading to Auschwitz-Birkenau were made, these were rejected,[2] in favour of bombing the I.G. Farben factory, which was carried out in August 1944.

By November 1944, with the Red Army now in Poland, gassing ceased, and three of the four crematoria were dismantled, the last converted into an air raid shelter. On 17th January, approximately 58,000 prisoners were sent on a 'death march' to Loslau, fifty kilometres away, through snow in freezing temperatures. A survivor of the march described the roadside as littered with bodies of those who died of exhaustion, or were shot for not keeping up. When the Red Army liberated Auschwitz on 27th January 1945, they found thousands of survivors who'd been left to die, including children, and hundreds of corpses.

The site was designated a museum in 1947, and former commandant Rudolf Höss, who'd been captured in hiding after his wife gave him up, was

---

2) It should be noted that the decision not to bomb the railway tracks remains a contentious issue to this day. However there are salient points that deserve consideration.

British and American aircraft were not within bombing range of the camp until December 1943, after the Allies captured the military airfield at Foggia.

The first planned bombing raid on the I.G. plant took place on 20th August 1944, during which seventy-five prisoners were killed with a further 150 injured. One prisoner managed to escape. This illustrates that aerial bombing was far more likely to kill prisoners than to free them. In addition, Auschwitz-Birkenau was a railway hub, meaning numerous tracks would have to be destroyed, which could have been replaced easily due to the massive pool of slave labour available.

A railway line is less than 2m in diameter. The US air force considered a bomb had landed 'on target' if it fell within a 300 metres radius of a designated target. That's an on target diameter of 600 metres. Only 20% of US bombs actually fell within the designated target radius anyway. Sabotage by the local resistance was more effective. In April 1943, the Belgian resistance stopped a train containing Jewish and Romani prisoners, bound for Auschwitz, some of whom were able to escape.

Thus bombing was high risk, with a low probability of success, that gave no return for the war effort, and any damage would be quickly repaired. Even after the atomic bomb was dropped on Hiroshima, parts of the city's tram network were operational within three days.

End of the railway tracks, Auschwitz II-Birkenau.

tried, convicted, and executed on the gallows at Auschwitz I, on 16th April of that year. Of the 7,000 members of the SS who survived the war, some 90% evaded prosecution. It has been accepted that some 1.1 million people, predominantly Jews, died at Auschwitz-Birkenau. The date of liberation, 27th January, is now marked as Holocaust Memorial Day.

THE TOUR GROUPS PICK THEIR WAY OVER THE RAILS AND SLEEPERS, past wooden guard towers and endless barrack huts, one of which is presented as a tourist display, so we can step inside to view the conditions. It is rammed with bleak bunks, nothing more than wooden planking, shared by multiple prisoners at a time.

At the end of the train tracks lies the International Monument to the Victims of Fascism, flanked by the remnants of two of the gas chambers and crematoria. Set on cobblestones, a line of plaques carry a set statement in every major European language, and Yiddish.

FOR EVER LET THIS PLACE BE A CRY OF DESPAIR AND A WARNING TO HUMANITY, WHERE THE NAZIS MURDERED ABOUT ONE AND A HALF MILLION MEN, WOMEN AND CHILDREN MAINLY JEWS FROM VARIOUS COUNTRIES OF EUROPE. AUSCHWITZ-BIRKENAU 1940–1945

A shallow flight of steps, ideally suited for group photo opportunities, leads to a nondescript monolithic memorial, with a jumble of black hewn stone blocks. Several hundred artists entered an international competition to design the memorial.[3]

This winning design is woeful. It's been here since 1967, and already looks terribly dated, uninspiring, and poorly sited, totally anonymous against the backdrop of trees. While it does not glorify death, it provokes apathy, and a feeling of 'Is this the best we can do, here, of all places?'

It was so disappointing that I did some research, in the hope that there might be an explanation as to why the International Monument was so abject. It transpires the memorial was a mishmash compromise of several shortlisted designs, which might explain its lack of vision, resonance, and impact, and why it reflects a nod to the work of the memorial jury chairman, British sculptor Henry Moore. This compromise was necessary because the competition was restricted by the law of July 1947, which stated that any memorial could not physically alter the camp.

The visionary submissions flouted this, so were rejected. What intrigued me, as a scuba diver, was the suggestion to flood the entire camp under a lake,

---

3) Comedian Dom Joly didn't visit the Nazi concentration camps in his travelogue *The Dark Tourist*, but I don't need him to tell me that the International Monument to the Victims of Fascism is... *shit*.

and to provide bridges and pedestrian walkways above. However there was one particular rejected design that stood out, which Henry Moore described as 'exceptionally brilliant'.

The proposal came from Polish architect Oskar Hansen and his team. It was for an environment, an anti-monument, both visionary and genius in its simplicity. Called 'The Road', the concept was to construct a black paved walkway, seventy metres wide, a kilometre long, running diagonally through Auschwitz II-Birkenau, where everything that fell on the road was preserved, and everything off the road would be allowed to fall into disrepair, in the manner of a 'biological clock'. The plans alone look stunning, and by comparison make the current compromised memorial look pitiful.

The simple stacked pyre of railway tracks and sleepers that provides the memorial at the Belzec concentration camp has far more impact than the memorial at Auschwitz II-Birkenau, because it shows and conveys clarity of thought, consideration of its physical placement, symbolism, empathy, and understanding.

"Now that... is brilliant."

The Auschwitz-Birkenau camp is disintegrating. The original huts were built to fulfil a short-term goal due to Nazi efficiency. There was no need to provide durable accommodation for prisoners worked to death, claimed by disease and starvation, or summarily executed *en masse* on arrival. Now those inadequate huts are leaking, the wire is rotting, the human hair in the display tanks is losing its colour, and even the granite steps are being worn away under our combined footfall, so preservation is being carried out for the benefit of tomorrow's tourists.

Implementation of 'The Road' would have solved the majority of these problems, by limiting the amount that needed to be preserved, as well as providing a truly timeless memorial. It still could, but won't. The dedicated Facebook page for the Auschwitz Memorial has announced major conservation work, using a fund of €120m from the Auschwitz foundation, to preserve what is there as is.

However as Lennon and Foley noted in *Dark Tourism*, tourists flocked to see Steven Spielberg's temporary set for *Schindler's List* over the two years it remained in situ after the film was shot, which suggests that the majority of tourists are unconcerned by a Holocaust site's provenance or authenticity, never mind its permanence.

THE HOLOCAUST HAS BEEN EXPORTED FAR AND WIDE, BEYOND THE European borders where the event actually occurred, commemorated on continents where no killing or deportations took place.

There are Holocaust centres in Montreal, Canada, founded in 1979; Melbourne, Australia, founded in 1984; Buenos Aires, Argentina, founded in 1993; Cape Town, South Africa, founded in 1999; and London, at the Imperial War Museum, founded in 2000. There is also a Holocaust

Spectacle artefacts, Auschwitz I.

Education Centre in Fukuyama, Japan, although there are fewer than 1,000 Jews in Japan. However local Japanese pastor, Makoto Otsuka, met with Otto Frank, father of diarist Ann, in 1971, and consequently opened the centre in 1995. It exhibits the obligatory suitcases, a striped prisoner's uniform, and the shoe of an unknown child from the gas chambers.

There are in excess of fifty Holocaust memorials and museums in the USA alone, fronted by the United States Holocaust Memorial and Museum, located in Washington, D.C. Entry is free, and it is in part federally funded. The reported budget for 2016 was $57m. The museum has a replica of the Arbeit Macht Frei sign, as seen at Auschwitz I, and a Facebook page. Since opening in April 1993 it has received forty million visitors, while its "traveling exhibitions have appeared in 195 US cities and 49 US states and in Canada, Croatia, Germany, Hungary, Israel and Serbia."

While the United States Holocaust Memorial and Museum receives a third of its annual footfall from schoolchildren, in Laxton, Nottingham, the National Holocaust Centre and Museum, opened in 1995, currently receives 80% of their annual 25,000 visitors through education. Of this 25% come from primary schools, and 55% from secondary schools and universities, illustrating the symbiotic relationship between dark tourism, in this instance, the Nazi Holocaust, and education. Nottingham also has a collection of suitcases, and soil from each of the six 'death camps' lies underneath an inscribed black and gold pillar, which includes the name of Auschwitz-Birkenau, although I understand Auschwitz-Birkenau as a concentration and extermination camp, rather than a 'death camp', hence the process of selection in the first place.

It is unclear what revenue is accrued from the Holocaust globally, or indeed how much Holocaust tourism costs to run. The accounts for Auschwitz-Birkenau in 2017 detailed that the museum generated €9.8m, which accounted for 57.6% of its total €17.1m budget, the shortfall covered by various grants and funding from the EU, the Auschwitz-Birkenau Foundation, and others.

Academic and political scientist Norman G. Finkelstein has coined the term 'Holocaust Industry' to describe what he details as the expansion and exploitation of the event.[4]

Shoes and suitcases have been packaged and presented in countries not only disconnected from the actual events, but, as with 'Museo Del Holocausto Buenos Aires', Argentina, as an attempt to change perceptions about the country itself. For surely Argentina is most commonly associated with senior Nazis, such as Eichmann, Roschmann, and Mengele, escaping justice along so-called 'Ratlines', rather than a popular destination for Jews emigrating after WWII.

Clearly Krakow and its tourist infrastructure has capitalised on its dark heritage, although not solely from the world famous concentration camp on its doorstep. It should be stressed that although there is a charge levied at Auschwitz-Birkenau, this is for a guided tour. It is possible to enter the grounds for free, without a guide, although the facility does levy a charge of 1.5 zloty to use the bathroom.

There are other museums and memorials related to the Holocaust within the city, including the Krakow Ghetto and Deportation Memorial, brilliantly simple with empty chairs arranged in an open square, and the converted Oskar Schindler factory, which contains a mind-numbingly extensive exhibition on Krakow under Nazi occupation.[5] Never mind a couple of hours, you could spend days in there.

While Krakow has not forgotten its Jewish history, or how to market it, anti-Semitic graffiti still scars its suburbs. It's shocking, having toured the

---

4) According to an article by Seth Freedman in the *Guardian*, December 2007, Finkelstein suggests American Jewish groups are manipulating collective guilt regarding the Holocaust for political and financial advantage. Finkelstein is a controversial figure, although both his parents survived the camps, and his claims haven't been refuted, only abused.

5) Playing devil's advocate, what are places such as Krakow and Dachau to do with their dark heritage? Destroy historical sites and pretend nothing happened? As extensively reported by the BBC online, the Austrian authorities have a quandary with the house in the town of Braunau am Inn where Hitler was born.

There is no tourist infrastructure, dark or otherwise, for this particular building yet tourists visit regardless. Even if the authorities reduce Hitler's birthplace to rubble, those wishing to pay homage will move onto other sites, or, as illustrated with previous demolitions of 'Houses of Horror' in the UK, the committed will still travel to the site, regardless of whether there is something to see or not.

Holocaust memorials and museums, to then see anti-Semitism blatantly expressed. This illustrates that despite the lucrative tourist industry, the educative legacy of the Holocaust appears to have had no discernable success in some quarters, including the tourist hub for its cornerstone museum.

If Norman Finkelstein's exposure of a 'Holocaust Industry' is challenging, or uncomfortable, the proliferation of Holocaust museums may reflect the need to record survivors' testimonies and curate their artefacts before they pass away. Clearly there was a surge in dedicated museums in cities totally unrelated to the atrocities, between Montreal in 1979, and the permanent exhibition at the Imperial War Museum, London, in 2000, although this period also coincided with the fiftieth anniversary of the Holocaust, which in turn gave the media an opportunity to revisit the events and reawaken public interest.

That this expansion of Holocaust education coincided with the recognition of the dark tourism phenomena, with the publication of Lennon and Foley's paper in 1996, may be purely coincidental, as may be their use of the railway track and Birkenau gatehouse on the front cover of *Dark Tourism*. Alternatively the foundation of multiple museums and permanent Holocaust exhibitions in cities unrelated to the events during this relatively condensed time frame may have drawn academic attention, and thus been a contributing factor in the acknowledgement, prevalence, and prominence of dark tourism in our contemporary society.

Coincidentally, the Cambodian genocide from 1975–1979 may have also focused attention on the need to resurrect, remind, and promote the Nazi Holocaust, to ensure it would not be relegated in the public consciousness by the unfolding atrocity in Southeast Asia.

What is beyond doubt is that the Nazi Holocaust is the single largest provider of dark tourism.

It is open to the public on six out of seven continents. In the US there are over fifty representations. The state of Texas alone has five, the state of Florida four, California and New York, seven each. There are museums in Canada, Argentina, Europe, South Africa, Japan, and Australia, in addition to the concentration camps themselves. The Jewish Virtual Library lists nine camps in Germany, nine in Poland, two in Austria, one in France, three in The Netherlands, and Terezín, or Theresienstadt, in the Czech Republic.

On the pavements of many German cities are the *Stolpersteine*, cobblestone brass plaque memorials, commemorating victims of the Holocaust including gypsies, homosexuals, and political dissenters. The project, created by German artist Gunter Demnig, accounts for over 48,000 cobblestone memorials, which are also found in Austria, The Netherlands, Hungary, Belgium, Czech Republic, Norway, Switzerland, Slovakia, and Luxemburg.

In July 2017, the *New York Times* reported that Auschwitz artefacts would now go on tour for the first time, with fourteen dates in cities across Europe and North America, over a period of seven years. Piotr Cywinski, director of Auschwitz-Birkenau said that it was no longer enough to "sit inside four walls, stare at the door and wait for visitors to come in."[6]

Holocaust sites, be they original camps, themed museums, or memorials, face a dichotomy in relation to dark tourism. Although Auschwitz-Birkenau is arguably the cornerstone for this particular demographic, the committed dark tourist visits regardless of the narrative the site presents. Whilst the administrative gatekeepers are naturally cautious that some of their visitors may have an anti-Semitic bent, or are there to indulge in Holocaust denial fantasy,[7] hard-core dark tourists are likely present in an entirely different capacity, one which may be equally unwelcome to many of the sites they visit, not just those related to the Nazi Holocaust.

They are there because such sites are associated with death, and in this case, death on a massive scale. There would be considerably less draw for the dark tourist visiting Auschwitz-Birkenau if no one had died there, and I would suggest that it makes no difference whatsoever to these particular tourists that the majority of those killed were Jews. They would still visit the camp if the majority of those killed had been Russian prisoners of war.

I would also suggest it is fundamentally the manner, the numbers, the notoriety of the site, and *the nature of the killers* that draws visitors, rather than one specific demographic within the victims.

That might be a thorny issue for sites investing and projecting a specific educative message. It's not that committed dark tourists aren't listening, but they're not there specifically to receive it. They will tour the sites associated with 9/11 with the same degree of interest, and potentially the same motivation, that would take them to the concentration camps and memorial centres of the Nazi Holocaust, or through the gates of any cemetery in the world.

There appears no discernable discrimination between the particular sex, age, race, or status of the victims, or the numbers of the dead, as far as the ardent dark tourist is concerned. The likelihood is that they're there in order to tick another site off their list, as well as fulfilling their own personal motivations for visiting in the first place.

---

6) Presumably this was said without irony, having stared at the very door through which 2,053,000 visitors had entered during 2016: a record attendance in the seventy years since the memorial's creation.

7) During my tour in 2011, the official guide mentioned that samples had been illegally taken from the remains of the gas chambers at Auschwitz in order to debunk the gassings conducted as part of the Holocaust. Researching this, I discovered that one analysis was carried out by an American execution technician, Fred A. Leuchter, who was working to provide 'expert' testimony to defend Ernst Zündel, a German publisher in Canada who'd gone on trial for producing a pamphlet espousing Holocaust denial, written by Richard Verrall. Leuchter's credentials as an expert witness were quashed. Subsequent authorized Polish forensic examinations established that cyanide had indeed been used in the chambers.

The 'Holocaust Industry' is well aware of these issues. Glasgow University hosted a conference (28th June–1st July 2017), 'Dark Tourism Sites related to the Holocaust, the Nazi Past and World War II: Visitation and Practice.' The event was partnered with the United States Holocaust Memorial Museum.

Eye-catching topics under discussion included:

'Understanding visitation: Audience perceptions of "dark tourism" sites'

'Places with "big economic potential" — the rediscovery of Nazi crime sites in Czech Republic'

'Selfies at Sites of Violent Death'

'Sites of Holocaust memory and the question of dark tourist *transformation*' [my italics]

The 'Holocaust Industry' knows dark tourists are coming, and the baggage we bring with us. There is intent to change us into something more acceptable. One wonders why they are so keen to invite us along in the first place.

I T TOOK TIME FOR ME TO MAKE GOOD ON MY PROMISE, OVER A DECADE after Sissy passed away in hospital, following a stroke, her hair still a magnificent silver mane against the pillow. She'd not stirred when I visited the night before she slipped away. I sat alone to her right. Her number was on the left. She never allowed it, or the experience surrounding it, to define her. There wasn't much to say, other than I would never forget her, and that it had been my privilege to know her. I kissed her forehead and left her to rest.

Sissy's testimony was part of the 'Survivors of the Shoah' Visual History Foundation, founded by film director Steven Spielberg. It had been recorded in May 1998, a year before she passed away, whilst Sissy was on a trip to Teplice, in the Czech Republic, and was conducted in Slovakian. There were no subtitles. So my friend and I paid to have it translated into English, to finally discover what we'd been too deferential to ask.

Sissy was born in 1922, in Malacky, thirty kilometres north of Bratislava. Her mother, Paula, was a single parent; Sissy's father, Arpad Grossman, remained frozen in time in a wedding photograph from 1920, dressed in his military uniform. With an elder brother Janko, and younger sister Gertruda, the family lived with their grandparents, who owned a print and bookbinding business. Sissy described an idyllic childhood, swimming, playing tennis, mushroom picking, and skiing in the winter.

After leaving school she became an apprentice seamstress, but in 1938 division began, when her brother's former schoolfriends, Sissy's potential suitors, appeared in the uniform of the Hlinka Guard, the new militia attached to the Slovak People's Party led by Jozef Tiso, a Roman Catholic priest who declared Slovakia independent, whilst under German protection. Once Slovakia's independence was established, Germany invaded the remaining Czech lands the following day.

Tiso and the pro-Nazi government immediately introduced the Jewish Code, laws designed to isolate the Jewish community from the rest of society, enforced by the Hlinka Guard. Jews were excluded from holding public sector employment, could not participate in cultural or sporting events, were barred from state education, and were no longer allowed to have property on a main street. Telephones and radios were also prohibited, and a curfew introduced. After the outbreak of war in September 1939, the confiscator, or arizator, came calling.

"You must bring all jewellery, furs, skates and skis to the Slovak Sports Centre."

Under the Code, Jews in Slovakia could not own luxury goods. Sissy recalled hauling the family's possessions on a sledge.

In August of the following year, Adolf Eichmann, then working in the Office for Jewish Emigration, sent a deputy to Slovakia, and the following month the government established a *Judenrat*, or Jewish Centre, in Bratislava, the only official institution allowed to represent Jews, effectively a conduit to transmit official edicts to the Jewish population, and to ensure compliance.

By September 1941, the Slovakian Jews were defined in law as an undesirable race. Sissy remembered it as, "The time when we had to wear the stars."

Everyone was scared. She recalled a friendly German soldier, Wiesner, who spoke of his own fear and helplessness in the face of the tide sweeping in from Austria and Germany. Young and old were taken away, with no idea of what became of them. Jewish men were forced to sweep the streets amidst mounting abuse from passers by.

Then the transports began. The Hlinka Guard beat the hands of the deportees, so they dropped their luggage, or cut the straps holding packs to backs. They were allowed to take one suitcase and food for a couple of days, but on arrival at their destination they were subsequently stripped of everything of value, including matches. Anyone trying to pass food or a keepsake onto a friend or relative aboard a departing train was likely to be beaten, or immediately added to the manifest. Although bribery could, in theory, secure exemption from deportation, in practice the transaction would likely culminate with those individuals being relieved of their payment and sent on the next train out.

So effective were the deportations that the Reich sent a letter of recognition to the Slovakian Ministry of Transport and Public Works. Little wonder, because Slovakia was willing to pay 500 Reichmarks 'resettlement cost' for each deportee. They paid to have their Jewish population removed, hanging out white flags when communities were 'Jew-free', and recouped the money paid for the deportations from the vacant property and goods they'd seized. So Sissy found herself with her family, packed on a train.

What is so infuriating about Sissy's testimony is that there is no mention of Auschwitz-Birkenau, other than a solitary reference.

"Then we learned that they started to burn people. In 1943 we learned this. People said, 'In Oświęcim they burn people.' We could not believe it."

Now I was cursing myself for being deferential. The interviewer wasn't asking the salient questions, or didn't have the required background knowledge in order to ask them.

Because Sissy must have been to Auschwitz-Birkenau, at least for 'Anmeldung' (registration) because, according to Auschwitz-Birkenau, only prisoners selected for work from that particular camp were tattooed, and the tattooing of female prisoners only commenced in March 1942 when over 7,000 Jewish girls arrived from Slovakia, including Sissy. Around 200,000 were sent to other camps, after being registered, which again must have included Sissy, because she, her husband, and brother were all returned to Slovakia and interned in a forced labour camp at Nováky under the Hlinka Guard.

The Slovak Jewish Centre had convinced the Ministry of the Interior that labour camps were a worthwhile solution to containing a population the state didn't want, whilst simultaneously saving at least some of their people. Nováky was the largest and most profitable of the three forced labour camps in Slovakia, thanks to its skilled workforce. They enjoyed exceptional privileges, including a swimming pool, and a drunk for a camp commandant who Jewish leaders were able to manipulate, although they were still vulnerable. Friday's weekly 'appel' still saw interns join transports dispatched back to Poland.

"At that time we had the feeling that we were lucky, because we were working very hard. People that were able to work stayed. We had to stand there, and they said, 'This one, that one and that one, are going.' And that was that."

Sissy's husband had some immunity from the cull. He had contacts with textile factories and some freedom of movement to purchase material. The camp produced uniforms, which is where Sissy's skill saved her from being returned to Auschwitz-Birkenau. The transports from Slovakia ran until October 1942, when the Vatican informed President Jozef Tiso of their true nature. Two more trains still went after Tiso ordered them 'stopped'. In Nováky the Hlinka Guard continued with their brutality.

"One night it was pouring with rain and I wanted to use the toilet. And I was running, but I didn't acknowledge the guard, 'Na stráz!' as I was supposed to. So he took me and beat me. Even today I still have terrible pain in my pelvis where I was kicked."

The guard forced Sissy to run round the building a dozen times as further punishment. Relief of sorts came in August 1944, when the camp was liberated during the Slovak National Uprising by the Communist and Zionist resistance. When the gates were thrown open Sissy remembered chaos:

"What now to do with that freedom? People were running and running, and they did not know where they were running to. Where to go? What to do?"

Slovakia was still under Tiso's rule. He was a committed Nazi collaborator who'd ostracized and persecuted the Jews under his control. Hitler would come to his aid, and there'd be reprisals. Outside the camp, life would be even more uncertain. With her husband's cousin Ervin, Sissy took four elderly interns, those left behind who could not run, in a hay cart to the nearby village of Kos and paid the villagers to look after them.

Ervin joined the partisans. Around 200 prisoners from Nováky joined the rebels to fight the Germans who, wary of Soviet forces encroaching the border, suppressed the insurgency and took control of the country. Some 19,000 rebels were taken prisoner, including an estimated 5,000 Jews, although small pockets of resistance survived. In October 1944 a second wave of deportations began. By the end of the war in May 1945, a further 13,500 Slovakian Jews had been sent to Auschwitz.

Sissy dyed her hair and travelled to Bratislava on false papers under the name 'Alzbeta Vesela'. Now hiding in plain sight using money she'd sewn into her coat lining, she found a place to rent.

"I had to be very careful. They were doing house searches and catching people."

She met a former inmate, now part of the resistance, who asked for help. Sissy purchased food and clothing, recalling her fear at the rendezvous.

"He told me where we would meet, and we did, and I delivered everything to him, but we said good-bye very quickly, because everyone was so scared. I do not remember his name."

Equipping the resistance effectively burnt Sissy's bridges in Bratislava. A single woman in rented accommodation, buying provisions, with the occupying force conducting house-to-house searches, made hiding in plain sight untenable. Under cover of night she returned to Malacky to seek refuge with Pavel and Anna Novota, who'd been hiding Sissy's mother-in-law and sister-in-law in their cellar, along with other Jews, since the round up for transportation began in March 1942.

"I was shaking with fear. I was sure I'd be caught, but I got there. I really got there."

Her husband, who'd been away sourcing fabric when Nováky was liberated, also made his way to Malacky, and the Novata's cellar. They were reunited in hiding, but sanctuary was shortlived. Rumours began to circulate that the Novotas were hiding Jews. Fearing blackmail, betrayal, and knowing the risk to their hosts should their presence be detected, they slipped away to Gajary, a one church village twelve kilometres to the west, to shelter with their former housekeeper from before the war.

February froze over in 1945. There they stayed hidden underground in what Sissy described as "a well" for three months. To pass the time they learned the Lord's Prayer in Hebrew. In May, the housekeeper came to tell them the war was over. Sissy and her husband returned to Malacky, along with other refugees, many of whom were liberated from the concentration camps, some little more than skin and bone. Sissy took in two women; Magda Simkova and Gertruda Bednarova. The doctor had given up on both. "It's hopeless," he told her.

Undeterred, Sissy took a baby bottle and filled it with a solution of water and saccharin, and after several days added a little milk. When Sissy gave her testimony to the Shoah Foundation on 25th May 1998, over fifty years later, both Magda and Gertruda were alive. The only member of Sissy's family to survive the war was her mother. Taken from Nováky to Terezín (also known as Theresienstadt), a concentration camp to the north west of Prague principally reserved for musicians, writers and artists, she developed typhus but recovered. Sissy's brother Janko joined the partisans after the liberation of Nováky, and was killed fighting in Kremnicka. Her sister, Gertruda, went on the transports, to Bergen-Belsen, and was never heard from again.

D ARK TOURISTS VISIT DARK SIGHTS FOR A VARIETY OF REASONS. One individual may visit a number of sites, and do so with totally different motivations for each one. Although I'd been visiting dark sites for years, I'd never been asked to visit on someone else's behalf. On reflection I wondered why Sissy asked me. I wasn't family. The black and white photo taken before the war was to hand, not tucked away in a drawer, so she'd already decided on our topic of conversation in advance. It wasn't like she was asking me to take her shopping at Sainsbury's. There's a big difference between going to Auschwitz-Birkenau for someone, and taking them to Sainsbury's, yet the reality was I did both, simply because Sissy asked. At the supermarket I could push the trolley and reach items from the high shelves, so she could study the contents with the magnifying glass she carried as her eyesight deteriorated.

Auschwitz-Birkenau is truly a dark site in every sense. I didn't need a specific reason to go there, although it transpired I had the best one imaginable. So when I walked through the camp it wasn't under an oppressive pall of gloom and doom, self-induced or inherent to the location. On the contrary, I found the experience uplifting. If that seems egotistical in a place of so much death and suffering, it's because in part I had kept my word, and because I was honoured to have been asked to go by Sissy on her behalf, not because she was a survivor, but because of the lady she was.

I wasn't sure what Sissy wanted me to do when I was there, she never said, so I left a white paper crane at the Wall of Death, for all of those that didn't make it out alive. I don't do candles. That's the Pope's job.

Sissy was a reminder that people, seemingly chosen at random, had not only survived, (and in Sissy's case, thrived), but over time, despite the physical and mental scars, had been able to send designated representatives back. That my friend never allowed the Holocaust to define her life means that I don't wish for it to define her memory. Sissy was so much more than her story within the Holocaust, which I only learned after she'd passed away. There's another tale to tell, one that always makes me smile.

After her testimony Steven Spielberg sent a letter of thanks, standard practice for all of those who contributed to his Shoah Visual History Foundation. Nonetheless we were impressed that one of the world's foremost film directors had sent an acknowledgement, although Sissy appeared indifferent. I tilted the letter in the light, examining the signature:

"This isn't printed... He's actually signed this..."

She remained unimpressed.

"Sissy, this is the man who directed *Duel*, one of the greatest films ever made!"

She gave that Slavic shrug that appears theatrical, but isn't. A few weeks later, and it was a completely different story.

"Children! Children! Come in! Come in! I must tell you! The most AMAZING thing has happened!"

She'd been shopping at the local branch of Marks & Spencer.

"I was going down the stairs, and I dropped my walking stick. This young man immediately came over and picked it up for me. I looked up, and — OH! — MY — GOTT! I could NOT BELIEVE IT! ... STEVE!... DAVIS!"

When Sissy moved to England she fell in love with snooker. Even when her eyesight deteriorated she would sit closer to the television, totally enthralled. Steve Davis OBE, had won six world titles during the 1980s, three Masters titles, six UK Championship titles, and had brought the sport to the attention of the masses. He also happened to be a Brentwood resident.

"He took my arm and walked me down the stairs and through the store! Everyone was looking — *everyone!*"

As Steve Davis escorted Sissy into a taxi as if she were the Queen, she told him:

"Mr Davis, I would like to thank you for helping me. You have been a perfect gentleman, and I think you are a wonderful player — but to be honest, I prefer Jimmy White."

I still smile, trying to imagine the look on Steve Davis's face as Sissy laid a perfect snooker before her taxi pulled away.

I HAD INTENDED TO RETURN TO AUSCHWITZ-BIRKENAU, SPECIFICALLY for this book, rather than fulfilling a promise. It would be wonderful to see the camp under snow. Holocaust Memorial Day, now branded as 'HMD' by the Holocaust Memorial Day Trust, fell on 27th January, and although I'd have to cross my fingers for snow it seemed an appropriate time to visit. I'd changed money into Polish zloty in preparation. However there were reservations, and they were growing.

Auschwitz-Birkenau, specifically their media team, were resolutely ignoring my emails regarding dark tourism. I wanted to know how the museum viewed people actively coming to the site because people had died there, regardless of any particular demographic or narrative. Clearly they didn't wish to engage, but Auschwitz-Birkenau is undoubtedly a dark tourist destination. Arguably, until 11th September 2001, it was *the* dark tourist destination, and for old school dark tourists it probably still is and always will be.

Naturally the media department weren't obligated to cooperate. It should be noted that their colleagues dealing with the research of former inmates had been incredibly helpful, back in 2011, when I had been filling in the Auschwitz-Birkenau blanks in Sissy's testimony.

Having now read Finkelstein's book, *The Holocaust Industry*, the machinations he exposed were totally at odds with the inspirational lady I'd known. My visit to Auschwitz-Birkenau had been a positive, life-affirming experience. Now there was a risk that might be soured. The presentation of the Nazi Holocaust, strung across the world with a proliferation of sanitised sites and learning centres, complete with replica signs, shoes and suitcases, had the feel of an identikit global 'franchise'.

Pawel Sawicki, Press and PR officer at the Auschwitz-Birkenau State Museum wrote a piece for Forward.com in January 2017, 'How Auschwitz Can Be Both a Memorial and a Center for Education', in which he opined:

"We are aware that tourists visit the Memorial, but from our perspective the Auschwitz Memorial is not a tourist attraction."

This is perhaps why Pawel ignored my emails relating to dark tourism. He concluded:

"But we also truly believe that many people who begin their visit as tourists later become messengers of remembrance, and that this happens thanks to experiencing the authenticity of the site as guided by educators. Visiting the former camp itself is a valuable personal experience which can teach and change people. The fact that visitors might initially attend the site as tourists does not change that."

The museum was intentionally distancing itself from dark tourists, portraying them as malleable, to be transformed into "messengers of remembrance", thereby instantly justifying and sanitising their own presence.

This metamorphosis of the tourists' perceived role could possibly be a counter-punch to Sergei Loznistsa's 2016 documentary *Austerlitz*, where tourists had been filmed wandering round both Dachau and Sachsenhausen concentration camps. Filmed in black and white from fixed camera positions, the tourists appear "unnervingly indifferent", according to one review in the *New York Times*. There is a sequence in the film where tourists take selfie after selfie by the Arbeit Macht Frei sign on the front gate.

Sergei Loznista had an answer to what this behaviour illustrated: "It means that Goebbels won."

I've now had the benefit of watching *Austerlitz* several times. Ninety minutes of tourists wandering round concentration camps sounds boring, but presented in this goldfish bowl format, the tourists themselves take on a macabre fascination. One wears a 'Fucking Fuck Happens' t-shirt, another 'F**kin' 99 Problems'. A dog is wheeled in a child's stroller, and one girl tries to balance a bottle of water on her head. Others stand by shooting posts, having their pictures taken in silhouette, arms above their heads.

The documentary offers no clues as to why these people visited the camps in the first place. The tourists themselves seemingly have no idea either, because they appear resolutely disengaged, although they presumably chose to go. So it can only be to say that they had been. It's a tick. Perhaps when they relate their experience they will tailor it to fit a pre-existing perception of the camps. I don't think this is evidence of tourists becoming 'messengers of remembrance'. That is wishful thinking.

I do think the 'messengers of remembrance' tag is an attempt to 'transform' tourists, because we aren't fulfilling the wishes of the 'Holocaust Industry', at least not in our current state.

Despite being the largest provider of dark tourism, with a corresponding footfall to match, the 'Holocaust Industry' is still unhappy.

Further evidence of this emerged in the 2015 University College London report, entitled, 'What do students know and understand about the Holocaust? Evidence from English secondary schools'.

I was interested in how education was being used by various dark sites to justify tourism, and if there was any benefit to those receiving it. As the Holocaust had been part of the National Curriculum for twenty-five years in the UK, the report would gauge how effective education was, not from a guide on-site, but in the more receptive classroom environment. Furthermore the UCL report was the most extensive study ever carried out into young people's understanding of the subject, with contributions from over 8,000 eleven-eighteen year olds. Many of the findings were 'surprising', and 'some deeply troubling'.

The report was at pains not to apportion blame to students or teachers, whilst bemoaning the lack of time given to Holocaust education within schools, although it overlaps into Religious Studies and English in some instances. Concern was expressed at the increasing number of secondary schools becoming 'academies', thereby allowing them to 'opt out' of having to teach the subject. There was no mention of what had been dropped from the curriculum to accommodate the Holocaust in the first place. There were reservations about myths infused from popular culture, with John Boyne's 2006 bestselling novel, *The Boy in the Striped Pyjamas*,[8] subsequently filmed in 2008, frequently cited.

The good news was that 83% of schoolchildren believed the Holocaust was an important subject, and more than 70% who'd studied it wanted to learn more. Looking for pluses, the report also singled out a specific group:

"Also contrary to popular belief, Muslim students appear just as positive about studying the Holocaust as other students across the country."

---

8) It's a novel. As was *Fragments*, by Binjamin Wilkomirski, initially published as an acclaimed, award winning Holocaust memoir in 1996, before it was exposed as a fabrication. So too was Misha Defonseca's bestselling memoir. She claimed she set off alone aged six, across Belgium, Germany and Poland, to find her parents who'd been taken by the Nazis, before being adopted by a pack of wolves.

Now, the bad news.

"Even after studying the Holocaust in school, only 37% of young people surveyed knew what the term 'antisemitism' means."

It was also noted that students hadn't perceived the culpability of the average German in the *Straße*, or the inaction of the British:

"Only 6.7% of students appreciated that — while the British government did have knowledge of the killings — its response was limited to a declaration to bring the perpetrators to justice when the war was over."

The use of the words 'only' and 'limited' appeared to imply disappointment, a desire for more of today's students to apportion blame towards the UK wartime government, after they became aware of the extent of the Holocaust in the summer of 1942.[9]

The report essentially complains that the Holocaust is not being studied enough, nor in sufficient detail, and that there are no examinations at the end. While it is unclear from the report how many of these 8,000-plus children had visited a Holocaust dark site, exhibition, or educational facility, which may have enhanced their studies, they still received far more education in the classroom than the tourist does at a site, and the Nazi Holocaust is the longest standing dark subject taught within UK schools, despite the fact that genocide has continued into contemporary times.

However the real revelation came on page 218.

"Despite the repeated inclusion of the Holocaust in the history curriculum in England, at no point in the last twenty-five years has a formal rationale been provided for why the Holocaust should be taught (Russell 2006; Pearce 2014)."

That this salient point has been highlighted, both in 2006 and again in 2014, and has yet to be addressed, is incomprehensible. The report states most teachers were confused about what the principal aims of Holocaust education were, and this had been known since the work of Pettigrew *et al.* in 2009.

So according to the UCL report, UK schools have been teaching the Holocaust, albeit ineffectively, for a quarter of a century, with no idea why they are teaching it in the first place, and this has been recognised for over a decade, during which time no one has provided an answer. If you don't know why you are teaching the subject in the first place, why hold up Holocaust centres, museums, and the dark sites of the camps themselves as 'educational', and take school parties there in the first place?

The report had, in the words of Sir Peter Bazalgette, Chairman of the UK Holocaust Memorial Foundation[10], "played a critical role in informing the recommendations of the Prime Minister's Holocaust Commission", who

---

9) There was presumably no education relating to the military considerations, previously highlighted within this chapter, as to why this was impossible until December 1943, and even then impractical.
10) Sir Peter quietly resigned without explanation in April 2018. The role is now co-chaired by Sir Eric Pickles and Ed Balls.

also said that meeting the challenges it highlighted would be central to the work the Foundation was currently undertaking: to build "a proper National Memorial to the Holocaust together with a world class Learning Centre."[11]

Which begs the question: If Holocaust education has been ineffective over time, and no one knows why it is even being taught in the first place (as the report clearly states), then why dig a big hole to construct a new learning centre when the one in situ across the river at the Imperial War Museum has failed in terms of the educational impact desired? I emailed the UK Holocaust Memorial Foundation to ask them. They did not reply. No education forthcoming there.

So there will be yet another Holocaust memorial and "world-class Learning Centre", in which the UK government is reportedly investing £50m of taxpayer's money. Given the failings highlighted in the report, that is a risible use of public money by any government.

Holocaust fatigue had set in. What was I going to learn by returning to Auschwitz-Birkenau, when my fingers were primarily crossed for snow: watch other tourists in the hope of catching them misbehaving? I'd previously seen a couple of girls photographing each other, gurning through the wire.[12]

Door-stepping the media department with an inventory of ignored emails wouldn't lead to my questions being answered. Besides, in light of the UCL report I now had some new ones:

What, exactly, did the Holocaust Industry want?

Did they even know what they wanted?

Hadn't they already got it?

I'd lost heart. Resigned, I swapped the zloty for dollars, picked a suitably sober Hawaiian shirt, and booked a flight to Phnom Penh to visit the Cambodian sites of genocide instead.

Realistically the only certainty about returning to Auschwitz-Birkenau would be that I'd end up taking yet more photographs of that bloody sign.

---

11) The site is proposed for Victoria Tower Gardens on the Embankment. Memorial topside and learning centre underground, following the National September 11 Memorial and Museum iceberg configuration.

12) Bizarrely when writing this, an online site entitled 'Yolocaust' (a cut-and-shut of Yolo, 'You only live once', and 'Holocaust') published a series of action 'selfies' taken at the Berlin Holocaust Memorial. Yolocaust doctored these selfies, so the performers were superimposed on a background wallpaper of emaciated people and corpses from the camps.

It was an exercise in so-called public shaming, encouraging the selfie 'victim' to establish contact to 'undouche' themselves and have their face pixelated. A number of media outlets carried the story. The memorial's architect, Peter Eisenman, pointed out that the memorial was not a grave, nor sacred ground, and he personally had no problem with the memorial being used by the living in their various pursuits.

All the selfies featured contacted the site in contrition, and were subsequently 'undouched'.

You can still search for 'Yolocaust' and find some of the original un-pixelated photos in the results.

9/11 souvenir shot glass set.

Hello Kitty Hiroshima souvenir pin.

Ferris Wheel, Pripyat, Chernobyl.

Salem Express: Original artwork by Ric Oldfield (Rico) prepared for Ned Middleton's book, 'Shipwrecks from the Egyptian Red Sea' and reproduced by kind permission of the author.

Scene of a suicide, inside the 'Sea of Trees', Aokigahara. Photo: Adam Tuck

Video introduction by Mike Parish, Kelvedon Hatch Secret Nuclear Bunker.

Marc Bolan's shrine on the 40th anniversary of his death, Queens Ride, Barnes, London.

Killing Caves, Phnom Sampeau, Battambang.

The cut through once occupied by 25 Cromwell Street, home of Fred & Rosemary West. Nine murdered women were buried in this space.

Personal items belonging to Fred & Rosemary West, exhibited in the Crime Through Time Collection, Littledean Jail, Gloucester.

Peace Memorial Hall, Hiroshima Peace Park.

Killing Tree and mass grave, Choeung Ek.

Foundation Hall, National September 11 Museum.

Portrait lined corridor, Auschwitz I.

YEAR ZERO

I T WAS A FRONT PAGE LIKE NO OTHER, COVERED WITH SKULLS. JOHN Pilger broke 'Year Zero', the story of the Cambodian genocide, on September 12th 1979 in the *Daily Mirror*. The edition sold out. Not only had Pilger's exclusive made the front page, it monopolised the inside, and ran over into the following day's edition. Once the other news carried by the *Mail*, the *Express*, and the *Telegraph* had been delivered through the letterboxes of small town suburbia, there was just a copy of the *Mirror* left for No.19. Tucked into a doorway in the still slumbering high street, I read every word.

When Pilger flew into Phnom Penh over the deserted paddies, he found the once beautiful French colonial capital devoid of life. The populace had abandoned their city years ago, evicted at gunpoint, leaving behind a rusting ziggurat to consumerism: cars, televisions and white goods, piled sky high in a temple of scrap. All trappings of modernity became worthless once the Khmer Rouge entered Phnom Penh on 17th April 1975, reset the clock, and renamed Cambodia 'Democratic Kampuchea'. It has been estimated that some 2–2.2 million people died under their revolutionary rule, approximately one fifth of the population.

Pilger, photographer Eric Piper, and film director David Munro picked their way through a surreal cityscape. The Roman Catholic cathedral, built in the 1860s, had disappeared, leaving behind a vacant lot. As a symbol of capitalism, religion and colonialism, it had three strikes against it, and was removed, physically dismantled, stone by stone, the first of over seventy Catholic churches razed to the ground throughout the country. The National Library was trashed onto the street, its books burnt, and countless worthless banknotes ran in the gutters when it rained.

When the Vietnamese army liberated Phnom Penh on 7th January 1979, the Khmer Rouge fled to their jungle refuge, leaving the capital to rot. There was no running water, limited electricity, and the only residents were nomadic scavenging children. Following in the liberator's footsteps, the journalist found the Chao Ponhea Yat High School, which had been converted into what became known as the Tuol Sleng Security Prison (S-21).

Between 1975–1979, approximately 17,000–20,000 people were imprisoned here, behind electrified wire, photographed, tortured and killed, including former members of the Khmer Rouge themselves who were 'suspected' of being spies for the 'CIA', or the 'North Vietnamese'. In reality they were just victims of a leadership ruled by paranoia, feasting on its young.

T HERE'S LITTLE POINT GOING TO BED. IT'S BARELY LUNCHTIME. The map suggests a twenty-minute walk for a tired man spat from Heathrow in the early hours of yesterday morning. The tuk-tuk drivers lounge in their chariots under the shade of the tree-lined boulevard, offering a languid wave to welcome business, and although there's a pang of guilt for not contributing to Pasteur Street's pavement economy, the desire to walk off the confines of the plane seat is greater. The shower and change of clothes has helped, although my shirt is already limp in the oppressive heat.

The streets are bustling hives. It's hard to imagine this was once a ghost town as traffic swarms around me as I cross the roads, counting down the blocks. Southeast Asia assaults the olfactory senses on the bridge over a perfumed 'river', then it's hang right into the peaceful sanctuary of Street 113, leaving the capital to wrestle with its perpetual pneumatic drill headache. The tuk-tuk taxi rank stationed outside the Tuol Sleng Genocide Museum takes an interest, gathering round, pitching the Killing Fields of Choeung Ek for tomorrow, at $12 return. Although I'm at Tuol Sleng now, technically ahead of schedule, I explain to the touts that I intend to return tomorrow, to spend the day inside.

"Yes. Two hours here, then you go to Choeung Ek in the afternoon."

They give me their number to call, written on a scrap of paper.

"Tomorrow afternoon, yes?"

I can't be bothered to explain about my research, or that I don't have a phone. I might as well tell them I have no intention of visiting Angkor Wat.

The blocks of Tuol Sleng are visible over the barbed wire that decorates the perimeter wall. The entrance is sited at the corner, with a ticket office set back inside, under a fabric sunscreen to keep the queue in the shade, although currently there isn't one. I pay $6, which includes $3 for the audio tour, and take the paperwork round the corner to pick up the headphone set.

Both the entrance ticket and the audio guide leaflet bear a striking design, reflecting the site, using the gold chequered floor tiles, overlaid with a simple motif of barbed wire and frangipani flowers, whose pearl petals lie scattered in the courtyard oasis. Serenaded by bird chirp, Phnom Penh already feels very distant, rather than lying 500 yards away beyond the prison walls at the intersection.

There is an immediate encounter with a small neat cemetery of fourteen anonymous whitewashed graves, which the audio guide reveals are those bodies discovered in the prison after its liberation. One of the survivors of Tuol Sleng was told that those final victims had had their throats cut by the guards before the prison was abandoned.

The self-guided tour proceeds on a clockwise route through blocks A, B, C and D, each with ground, first, and second floors, although some of the upper floors are not accessible to tourists. Building A includes a room containing three metal bed frames, and a large black and white photo on the wall showing how the room was originally discovered, with one of the beds bearing a tortured

Audio signpost, S21 Tuol Sleng, Phnom Penh.

corpse. On the corner of Block B stands an ominous tall timber frame, cup hooks screwed into the underside of the crossbeam. Initially a school climbing frame, it was subsequently used to hang prisoners by their ankles. When they passed out, the guards systematically lowered and dunked them into large ceramic pots, filled with effluent, to revive them, so they could be hoisted up for the process to begin again. A mannequin of a prisoner, arms secured, head wrenched back, sits below the 'gallows'.

Building B continues the story with photographs of the leaders of Angkar, 'The Organization', the S-21 staff and prisoners, including those overseas nationals caught up in the revolution, and rows of ugly shackle racks used to hold the interns in place.

Building C has been preserved in situ, swathed in barbed wire to prevent prisoners jumping to their deaths from the upper gallery, after one succeeded in doing so. The interior is divided into single cells, those on the ground floor brick built, those on the first floor constructed from hardwood. The partition walls that once denoted classrooms have been crudely knocked through, in order to give the prison guards an unrestricted view of the landing. It was in these cells that two of Tuol Sleng's survivors, Chum Mey and Bou Meng, were held.

On the second floor of building D is the White Lotus Room reserved for peaceful meditation and chanting, although when I try the handle it is locked. A sign says that although there are mats and cushions within, this is not a room intended for sleeping in. The ground floor contains endless photographs of the victims mounted on boards, and the implements and apparatus of torture, which included waterboarding. The specialist chair acquired from the French police, with a protruding rod to be guided into the nape of the neck in order to fix the position of the inmate for their identikit mug shot is, seen in this context, a torture implement in its own right. At the end of D block, panoramic photographs of the excavations at Choeung Ek, the Killing Fields beyond Phnom Penh, a display of skulls in glass cases showing evidence of impactions, and a small shrine with a notice asking for incense to be burnt outdoors in the receptacle provided.

Throughout the blocks run the chequered floor tiles of Old Gold and oyster white. The large classrooms, fronted by a veranda, have bars across the windows, curtained by Louvre shutters in duck egg blue, and the impression is of a hangover from French colonial rule. The discoloured plaster walls are ochre. You wonder how many times the surfaces have been washed and scrubbed. There was dried blood on the floor when Pilger entered in 1979. Stains are still visible, and imagination does the rest. Conditions inside the prison were barbaric: speaking between inmates was forbidden, and the latrines were simply empty ammo boxes. There's a rotten one on display. Reportedly any excrement or urine

spilled had to be licked off the floor.

The stairwells of S-21 are iconic. Art deco cast concrete, the rear walls vented by a geometric letterbox grid. The rooms on the upper floors of Building C are empty. It was here prisoners were shackled to the floor, packed like sardines, depicted in a painting by survivor Vann Nath, a powerful image amongst many he created, displayed both here at Tuol Sleng and at Choeung Ek. These rooms and landing were also the stage for a re-enactment so bizarre as to be beyond comprehension.

Before coming to Cambodia I'd watched the 2003 documentary *S-21 The Khmer Rouge Killing Machine*, by Rithy Panh, himself a survivor of the genocide. The film reunites Vann Nath with fellow Tuol Sleng survivor, Chum Mey, bringing them together in the prison with their former captors, those who were just teenage guards at the time, and the men who carried out the interrogation and torture.

Under questioning from Vann Nath, the perpetrators see themselves primarily as victims, those they killed as secondary victims, and seemingly cannot relate to or take ultimate responsibility for their actions, to Vann Nath's understandable frustration. They had been indoctrinated to a level of blind obedience, detaching

Stairs and landing, Tuol Sleng S21 prison, Phnom Penh.

Cells, Tuol Sleng

themselves from the physical brutality they inflicted on a daily basis. A former guard reprises his nightly routine for the camera. It is a chilling re-enactment, as a 'prisoner' is handed over to him, post-interrogation, at which point it is as if a switch is thrown and he becomes an automaton, providing a running commentary detailing the minutiae of his detail, jabbing his finger through the bars, shouting threats at the ghosts of prisoners he can still visualise within the communal cell.

"If you spill it, I'll get the club!"

He's berating an empty room and an imaginary prisoner who needs to relieve himself. The gaoler, transported back in time physically, mentally, and emotionally, is himself a trauma victim, seemingly beyond help and redemption, imprisoned in Tuol Sleng along with the other survivors. From the evidence of Rithy Panh's documentary it appears unlikely that any of them will ever leave.

In the courtyard garden stands a *stupa* (a domed memorial shrine) to the victims of Democratic Kampuchea, and a secluded souvenir stall set in the far corner, where books and DVDs relating to the reign of the Khmer Rouge are prominently displayed. The rest of the store is devoted to traditional Southeast Asian paraphernalia, including old wristwatches, ubiquitous Zippo lighters and fridge magnets.

The tree-lined path towards the exit is interspersed with benches, and there's a display board detailing the trials of the leadership who lived long enough to eventually be brought to account.

In 2009 Kaing Guek Eav, known as 'Comrade Duch', the director of S-21 and a former school teacher, became the first Khmer Rouge leader to face a UN-backed tribunal charged with war crimes and crimes against humanity, "personally overseeing the systematic torture of more than 15,000 prisoners". He is sentenced to thirty-five years in jail, having already served over a decade in detention. The tariff is later extended to life imprisonment, with no possibility of appeal. At the time of writing he is seventy-four-years-old.

In 2014 two other Khmer Rouge leaders, Nuon Chea, aged eighty-eight, and Kheiu Samphan, eighty-five, are also sentenced to life imprisonment for crimes against humanity. Nuon Chea was known as 'Brother Number Two', second in command to the Khmer Rouge leader Pol Pot. Kheiu Samphan served as president under the regime. Two other defendants were reprieved: Ieng Sary died awaiting justice, whilst his wife, Ieng Thirith, was declared unfit to stand trial.

The leader of the Khmer Rouge and 'Brother Number One' Saloth Sar, known to the world as Pol Pot, was facing an international tribunal after suffering a stroke in 1995. Unsurprisingly he absolved himself from any guilt for what happened under his rule, claiming the mass deaths were down to those he appointed. They were the real traitors. His only admitted responsibility was for taking things too far to the political Left. Pol Pot died under house arrest on 15th April 1998, aged seventy-two, and was cremated without an autopsy, fuelling speculation that he took an overdose of prescribed medication to avoid the show trial.

Thus justice dictates just three elderly men live out their remaining days in custody to pay for the repression, torture and mass murder inflicted on Cambodia under the Khmer Rouge.

ASMALL SHADED STAND SELLS SOFT DRINKS, PRE-PACKAGED snacks, and water, which I'm grateful for, still trying to acclimatise to the heat. Opposite there's a single storey administration block, the porch area given over to a lady at a table selling t-shirts, baseball caps, and tote bags. The tees are black with a white frangipani motif and the words 'We remember' on the reverse, and 'Tuol Sleng Genocide Museum' over the breast, with Khmer script in red below, and they even have my size. The souvenirs are sold under a handwritten sign: 'Your contribution will be reserved for research and training activities,' although this has no bearing on my decision to purchase one. I like the design, which cleverly incorporates the museum into the umbrella theme of genocide, and there's the added benefit that it will postpone doing any laundry.

I know of the gentleman who sits in a chair beside a stack of books. His kindly worn face looks out through the prison bars on the covers. It is Bou Meng, an artist, one of a handful of recognised survivors from S-21, who'd initially supported the insurgency and produced early propaganda posters on their behalf.

When 'Comrade Duch' discovered that one of his tortured prisoners, and supposed 'CIA sympathizer', was an artist, he set him to work to reproduce a photograph of Pol Pot as a portrait, under threat of death if it wasn't lifelike. Suitably motivated, Bou Meng took his time to create the likeness: three months. Other 'commissions' followed. Bou Meng's artistic talent undoubtedly saved his life. He was finally marched out of the prison on 7th January 1979 along with several other inmates, until their guards abandoned them in the face of the advancing Vietnamese. Bou Meng eventually returned to work in the Tuol Sleng Genocide Museum in an administrative capacity in 1981, examining the comprehensive documentation his captors had left behind. He's now retired, but returns to the site of his former incarceration on a daily basis, to sell his book.

A young girl sits next to him to keep him company, sort which language version is required, and convey his thanks in English. His book costs $10, and is worth it purely to see his delight when it is purchased, as if it were the first one he's ever sold. Bou Meng signs and dates my copy, then performs a *sampeah*, the Cambodian greeting, hands together in prayer and a bow of the head. His 'Girl Friday' asks if I would like to have my photograph taken with Bou Meng, but instead I ask if it would be possible to take one of him with his book. I haven't got the heart to ask him to return to pose in the cell he once occupied for a portrait, which he's done on numerous occasions for the media. He's in his seventies, and it's likely been a very long day for both of us.

Diagonally across the path sits fellow survivor and bookseller, Chum Mey, a man who survived because he could repair the typewriters required to smash out the copious 'confessions', and the routine is the same: the beaming smile, the *Sampeah*, the signature and date. Mr Mey's assistant, a smartly dressed young man, supervises the transaction. After I've photographed Chum Mey with his book I ask him how he feels about tourists now visiting a place where so many atrocities were perpetrated. His assistant says he is glad, because he wants people to know what happened here. Chum Mey can follow English well enough to nod his consent.

While superficially this appears a stock answer for those who survived, eyewitness testimony is often the only way the rest of the world will ever know what happened. Who would want to have endured torture, have found the courage to speak out, only to subsequently be ignored, the cruellest form of torture we've ever devised.

While I'm interested in the layers beneath superficial dark tourism, and the exploitation of tragedy by the living, both commercial and political, I feel neutered in the presence of survivors at dark sites, as if they only survived in order to benefit tourism and to cater for my curiosity. At least here in Tuol Sleng there is a symbiotic financial relationship between the survivors, the museum, and the tourist. Messieurs Meng and Mey each have my $10 (how can you buy testimony from one, and not the other?) and the museum has the cache of genuine survivors on-site daily.

I SIT WITH A DOZEN TOURISTS ON PLASTIC PATIO CHAIRS IN A SIDE room, cooled by a whirring fan. Norng Chan Phal tells his story standing up, hands clasped nervously in front. A Cambodian lady stands to the side, ready to translate into English. His father was a member of the Communist Party of Kampuchea, working in a timber yard, until he was sent to Phnom Penh in 1978. Norng Chan Phal, who was eight-years-old at the time, his younger brother, aged four, and their mother, were taken to the capital on the pretence of joining him. Instead they found themselves in S-21.

Norng Chan Phal witnessed his mother being beaten and kicked. Blood came from her nose. She was told that she'd have to clean it up before she was photographed. The two brothers were separated from their mother and placed with three other children, one around three years old, one younger, and a baby who was still being breast-fed, minded by an elderly woman in the workshops occupied by the artist and carpenters. The baby soon died of malnutrition. Norng Chan Phal once saw his mother at a window, her hands gripping the bars, but that was the last time he ever saw her.

When the Vietnamese advanced on S-21, the guards evacuated the inmates, but the children hid under a pile of clothes until everyone left. Norng Chan Phal wandered the deserted prison looking for his mother, but instead found a fly-swarmed corpse chained to a bed. The sight was so disturbing he ran back to hide with the others until they were discovered by the Vietnamese soldiers. The youngest child had died from suffocation while in hiding. The three surviving children were placed in the care of an orphanage. Later Norng Chan Phal would revisit S-21, now the Tuol Sleng Genocide Museum, because he missed his mother. Only a case file on his father was recovered from the prison archive.

He returned to the museum permanently after an accident at work, realising that as a survivor his future lay there, despite it being the source of his childhood trauma. He's been employed at the museum since 2014, and says talking about his experiences has become easier after two years. At the end of his testimony, we are asked if there are any questions for Norng Chan Phal. There are none. We nod in acknowledgement and mutely file out.

Later, when reading a report of his testimony delivered at the tribunal of Comrade Duch, it is noted that Norng Chan Phal rarely responded to a question about his mother without breaking down.

I wander towards the exit to return my headset, reflecting on the fact that whilst these men endured so much, they've still chosen to return daily to be within the walls that took so much from them. It is difficult to subscribe this to a form of institutionalism, because they earn an income from being there. Yet Tuol Sleng provides the survivors with a sense of purpose that transcends its confines, and reminds those of us fortunate enough to come that despite these very real Room 101s, truths and dignities worth saving have survived.

They've shut the main gate, so I take the wicket route, and walk the back blind

Tuol Sleng prison, Phnom Penh

side of the block before merging in with the traffic on the main thoroughfare, thus negating the tuk-tuk rank, although I suspect they've already moved on or forgotten me, just another anonymous tourist. Twenty minutes later I arrive back at the crossroads on Pasteur Street. Western fast food outlets occupy every corner plot, surely the nadir for the Khmer Rouge in the city that once capitulated to their warped ideology. It is an unusual justification for ordering a 'combo meal', yet simultaneously entirely appropriate.

I PRESENT MYSELF AT THE TUOL SLENG INFORMATION OFFICE THE following morning, having already sent an email through the official website media contact tab, and received no reply. So now I'm door-stepping, wondering if there is anyone available to take my questions. I'm directed to take a seat outside the administration block in the centre of the compound. Bou Meng and Chum Mey are already at their station, waiting for the first circuit of tourists to complete.

I file the entrance ticket in the unwritten pages of my ledger to keep it pristine, and look up to see the bespectacled young lady who has been sent to deal with me. I suspect she has been given the chore due to her fluency in English. With arms folded defensively across her chest the headmistress does not look entirely happy to see me. She explains that my email enquiry received no response because although the site is online it is not functioning. A couple of months later I send a follow up email, which is either ignored, or suggests that the site is still not functioning. Disarmed by her age, beauty and stance, I shape my questions carefully. It feels like noodling for piranha at the bottom of a barrel, admittedly in the hope that I don't get a bite.

During my research I'd become increasingly cynical towards established dark sites with regards to their engagement with the public. It appeared they were only interested in providing a set narrative, with no desire or remit to engage further, especially when questions related to their role within dark tourism, although the various conferences suggested that they were more than willing to discuss the topic amongst themselves behind closed doors.

Cambodia was not the first instance of mass murder within living memory, nor the last. Dark tourism is on the rise, in part due to the prevalence of such atrocities and the subsequent packaging for tourist consumption, yet there appears to be no coalition between the various museums charged with presenting their respective testimonies.

However in conversation it transpires that there has indeed been cooperation between Tuol Sleng and another dark museum overseas, and although I am aware of this particular museum, it wasn't one I was expecting to be mentioned because it has no association with genocide. And I can't reveal which museum, because although the young lady relaxes as we talk, there is an ultimate caveat.

"If you wish to use any of my answers, you must first write to my director for his approval. I think this will take perhaps one month, maybe longer."

She smiles, "I don't think you have that long."

I smile ruefully, say I will leave it, and thank her for her time, wondering why this proviso wasn't mentioned from the outset. I don't volunteer that I'm not a real journalist, or that there's no deadline per se. My National Union of Journalists affiliate membership card has long since expired. I couldn't earn enough from writing to justify renewal, and now its sole purpose is to stiffen my wallet and to provide packing to prevent high street loyalty cards inadvertently falling out.

T HE VERY NATURE OF DARK SITES LENDS ITSELF TO QUESTION why anyone would want to visit them, and although there are a multitude of reasons covering those who do, Tuol Sleng is the perfect illustration of why it is a privilege. Not only did I choose to come here, I can afford to. For every 344 visitors from overseas, Tuol Sleng receives only one Cambodian.

Students in private education visit, however it is less accessible for those in state education. In an attempt to correct this there is a tented table in the far corner where tourists are asked for a $2 donation so the museum can provide transportation, buying two forty-five-seater buses to bring students within state education to the museum.

This goal focuses on tomorrow's students, rather than today's, and although this practice of soliciting western tourists to fund Cambodia's education of their own genocide, (in light of how the west recognised the Khmer Rouge at the United Nations), seems only fitting, perhaps raising admission by $2, so everyone donates, and hiring transportation, might provide a realistic alternative solution.

Whilst this convoluted fundraising continues, the museum conducts outreach programmes to schools. At least with this published ratio of 344–1, Tuol Sleng is not using schoolchildren to swell their attendance figures. It is however, using the *lack* of schoolchildren to encourage donations.

The independent backpacking crowd are respectfully dressed for the most part, and there is very little navel gazing or DayGlo to be seen, although I wouldn't have mentioned either if there hadn't been examples of both. Those souvenir sarongs bought in Thailand during their Southeast Asian sojourn have come in handy. It may be that Cambodia just happens to be on the gap year route to account for the numbers of beach bodies at Tuol Sleng and Choeung Ek, however there is also a sizeable genteel crowd on timed packaged tours, who consequently come, view, and go, at a quicker pace. The backpackers have more time, and may simply be using the shade of the dark sites to while away the day before indulging in serious partying at night.

Yet there appears genuine interest and engagement within this museum, which may stem from the fact that this genocide is comparatively recent, even though it comes from a time before the backpackers were born. Perhaps, unlike the Nazi Holocaust, there is no lobbying in our western societies to promote it, which may inadvertently give the Cambodian genocide a certain cache, likely to stimulate interest rather than induce fatigue.

During my time in Tuol Sleng over a period of four days, in my self-appointed role of spying on my fellow dark tourists, I never witness anyone having a souvenir 'I was there' photograph taken in the compound, or performing the selfie ritual. I believe the signs with the laughing face crossed through, predominantly displayed at the doorways of the classrooms where the abandoned dead were found, have a positive effect, and set the tone. There is a lot of signage in Tuol Sleng:

No filming/video

No photography [in certain, specified areas]

No eating [depicted by a crossed-out burger]

No smoking [I'd temporarily quit]

No smiling/laughing

No graffiti

There are also signs that states 'No Pokémon here', although whether this is pre-emptive or a response to those searching is unknown. Surprisingly there isn't one for 'No spitting', because I do witness a couple of locals clearing their throats in the grounds.

The 'No photography' signs are not universal throughout. They appear on the doorways to those rooms where the dead were discovered. Instruments of torture, and the endless photographic portraits of the condemned, are also prohibited from capture.

Visitors have also left their tags on the walls, although there is now a plasterboard installed in a nook room in an attempt to contain this. However, the desire to write is such that the scrawls spider onto the ceiling. 'Never again!', lifted from the Nazi Holocaust, appears a favourite, although in the context of a genocide museum it is somewhat thoughtless; it would be more appropriate if 'Never again!' was changed to 'Until Next Time!'

There is a subdued atmosphere within the blocks. Much of what is on display in genuinely chilling in terms of photographic evidence, the artefacts, including implements of torture and the apparatus for waterboarding, and the internal layout of the institution itself, with the cells, chains, iron beds, and barbed wire culminating in the stark collection of skulls at the end.

Yet the tourists are engaged. It is quiet within the museum, with just the shuffling of flip-flops and sandals, because everyone is reading the texts detailing the displays, or absorbed by their audio guide, which is the best I personally have experienced. It is comprehensive, with appropriate musical idents bookending each segment, narrated by a Cambodian gentleman whose pitch and timbre is in harmony with both the surroundings and their history. There are thirty-two stops on the audio tour, a supplementary nine suffixes, with a further ten optional 'listen anytime' background pieces that give a comprehensive package of the institution under the control of the Khmer Rouge.

Once done, many tourists seek shade on the metal benches outside the blocks and under the trees, and despite the lingering darkness of Tuol Sleng, inherited from its previous incarnation, evidence of which lies all around, the scented courtyard garden is a peaceful place from which malevolence has been utterly expunged.

THE KHMER ROUGE, A RAG-TAG GROUP OF MAOIST GUERRILLAS, dressed in black with a trademark red sash, came to prominence after a period of instability within Cambodia initiated by the US bombing campaign of 1969–1970. The Americans were trying to target the North Vietnamese, who were using their neighbour's territory to camouflage their supply lines during their war with the US.

Prince Norodom Sihanouk, Cambodia's 'sun king' ruler who had been deposed in a bloodless coup whilst on a visit to Paris in 1970, now called on his people from the safety of exile, to back the insurgency of the Khmer Rouge against the military that usurped him.

Despite the token resistance offered against the guerrillas, Cambodia's middle class continued to dine out as the Khmer Rouge advanced towards the capital. Initially the revolutionaries were welcomed as heroes on the streets of Phnom Penh, but within hours the mood changed as they forcibly evacuated the city's inhabitants under the pretence of an impending US aerial bombardment that never materialised. The exodus to the countryside happened over two days, and saw those too elderly, ill, or in the middle of surgery, simply left to die. Anyone who possessed a degree of education now risked exposure and death from their new masters, who had brainwashed their uneducated, predominantly peasant, followers.

In the new 'Democratic Kampuchea' everything revolved round 'Angkar Loeu', or 'Organization on High', with the stated aim of creating a new agrarian socialist Utopia. Their figurehead, Pol Pot, had ironically come from a middle-class established family, and had received his senior education in Paris. Although unsuccessful with his studies, it was during this time he became active in communism. Prior to his ascension as leader of the Khmer Rouge he taught French literature and history in a private college.

Having evacuated the capital's population, the Khmer Rouge forced the so-called 'new' people out into the countryside to join the existing 'old' or 'base' people, the peasants who worked the land, the rationale being that once cut adrift from their comfortable lifestyle they would be easier to control. Housed in makeshift communal camps, the population became forced labour fed on starvation rations. Children were made to work. There was no sentiment, schools, or religion, only 'struggle' in the pursuit of 'victory' over the land, working towards an ideal for the country to become self-sufficient. To this end the populace were worked all day, given political indoctrination by night, after which they had about four hours sleep before doing it all again, every day under the threat of being taken away to be tortured and killed.

Many starved or fell sick, and disease was rife. Former doctors hid in plain sight. Haing Ngor, who would later receive an Oscar for his portrayal of journalist Dith Pran in the 1984 film *The Killing Fields*, pretended to be a former taxi driver, and lived in constant fear of being recognised and having the educated status of his past life exposed. He was suspected and tortured on three separate occasions, but refused to confess he was a doctor, as such an admission would mean certain death.

There seemed little thought or process to the revolution, where only demoralisation and destruction of the population was effectively accomplished. The ethos of the Khmer Rouge was chillingly epitomised in their saying, "To keep you is no benefit, to destroy you is no loss."

DARA IS ALREADY HOVERING OUTSIDE THE LOBBY, EVEN THOUGH I'm early. He was due to pick me up from the airport as my complementary shuttle, but the hotel sent someone else instead, or something like that. He's taking me to the Choeung Ek Killing Fields in his blissfully air conditioned Lexus SUV. Whilst his return fare of $25 may be twice that of a tuk-tuk, it does allow me to ride shotgun, so I can listen as he talks about his wife and their three sons, how the bottom has fallen out of the price of rice, and that despite being born in 1982, after the genocide, he has family members who remain genuinely terrified that the dark days of the Khmer Rouge will return. Dara is of Chinese descent. Like most in this country, predominantly populated by the young, he lost family members to Year Zero.

Memorial stupa, Tuol Sleng

He first visited Choeung Ek, which he pronounces 'Young — Eck', with a click at the end, in 1999. He waves a reproachful hand at the development encroaching on the panorama beyond the windscreen:

"None of this was here then..."

I tell Dara I delivered the newspapers the day the story broke in the UK, back in 1979, to help discount the fact that he is wondering what's happened to his world, where the years went, and how he got to be so old. He drops me off in the car park, already filled with coaches, and we settle on three hours before a rendezvous. I appreciate he will have a long day tomorrow, driving some bloody tourist all the way to Battambang so they can see the Killing Caves.

It costs $6 on the gate for foreign visitors to enter the 'Choeung Ek Genocidal Center'. The site is dominated by the giant stupa, described on the reverse of the ticket as the 'Memorial Charnel'. It also says (in prayer book eight-point text):

'Please pay respects to the spirits of victims by offering flowers and lighting an incense and candle in front of the charnel before starting your visit at the site.'

It also says:

'Revenue from the admission fee is used for developing, conserving the Cener [sic] and sponsoring poor and talented students.'

The audio guide is included in the admission fee, and has nineteen clips, with eighteen add-ons. One of the disadvantages of Choeung Ek is that much of what was there when the site was discovered is there no longer. Buildings, such as the Khmer Rouge office, were dismantled and recycled in the aftermath, so now the tourist is self-guided to numbered audio posts to study an artist's impression of the structure with accompanying text, mounted on a board, topped with a tiled 'hat' for a roof. Reportedly eighty-six out of the 129 mass graves have been excavated, accounting for nearly 9,000 corpses. There is an exhumed grave, now penned behind bamboo fencing, decorated with the colourful string bracelets that are prolific throughout Cambodia. A

Sign at mass grave, Choeung Ek.

traditional thatch roof protects the grave, the dirt below littered with trinket offerings and bank notes.

The site was originally an orchard, part of which was sold off to a Chinese association to be used as a graveyard, and some of these graves, pre-dating the genocide, are highlighted on the tour. There are a number of signs that ask for respectful silence, and away from the hubbub of the entrance/exit, it is observed, although there is a school nearby and the excitement during break time is carried across the graves on the breeze.

The path divides, presenting a choice of walking either the external or internal perimeter of the lake, depending on your schedule, although it only takes an extra ten minutes to take the outer path. This borders the wire perimeter fence of the site, giving the opportunity for a lurking worker in the adjoining field to present his cap for a few dollar bills, although he also gratefully accepts the local currency.

This part of the tour affords the opportunity to sit on a bench in the shade and listen to testimonies from various survivors before returning towards the central memorial stupa and the remaining exhibits. At which point I encounter a group of serious American Christians being led in prayer. They've chosen to stand either side of the walkway so I pull up short, too deferential to disturb the impromptu congregation. I define their level of commitment by the man who is down on one knee in prayer. I assume he has only gone half way because he is obese, and therefore will need to brace himself on his other knee to stand when the praying is through.

The woman leading the prayers mentions 'the children', then mentions them again, and again, and again, and I assume this particular trigger is going to be squeezed until the chamber goes click, to ensure the lady weeping openly to her right gets the grief out of her system. Other tourists overtake me and gatecrash the church. Pragmatism dictates I follow suit, just in case the prayer meeting is going to run on.

The core exhibits are viewed from meandering wooden walkways, including several glass boxes containing clothing, bones, and teeth, which are still being recovered after the rains. The raised walkways have the benefit of guiding tourists around the unexcavated mass grave, where you can see clothing and bone fossilised into the compacted soil. There is a sign urging people to be careful where they tread when they step off at the end.

The route takes in two trees of note. The first is a Chankiri tree, known as 'The Killing Tree', where the children of parents accused of crimes against the Khmer Rouge were swung against the trunk and battered to death, an image depicted in one of the paintings by Vann Nath, a mother kneeling, begging for clemency in vain. In another haunting painting, a baby is tossed into the air to be impaled on another soldier's bayonet.

The idea behind killing the kids was to prevent them growing up and taking revenge for their parents' death, a policy defined by the saying, 'When pulling out weeds, remove them roots and all.' It was reported that the soldiers laughed as they killed the children, because not to do so would indicate sympathy, thereby making today's executioners tomorrow's condemned. When the true nature of Choeung Ek was revealed, brain matter and hair was found trapped in the bark. An adjacent excavated grave was filled exclusively with women and children. 'The Killing Tree' is now smothered with coloured wrist strings.

The Khmer Rouge carried out their executions at night, using a generator to light the scene, and played music to cover the screams so any locals would think it was simply a propaganda meeting. To this end a loudspeaker was hung from what was known as 'The Magic Tree', which is clearly marked on the boardwalk route.

Designed by Cambodian architect Lim Ourk, and influenced by the Royal Palace in Phnom Pehn, the giant stupa of Choeung Ek was constructed in 1988, and is sixty-two metres high. This centrepiece is a charnel house holding the remains of the dead for remembrance. Symbolism has been incorporated into the structure with 'sky tassels' decorating the gables to ward off airborne evil spirits, and giant snakes from Khmer mythology guarding the roof. The white stone used in the construction represents death and decay in Khmer Buddhism.

There are tall glass doors on each of the four faces, open to the public at the front, accessed by a flight of steps, with signage directing the removal of shoes before doing so. A stall at the side sells flowers for those wishing to leave a token. There is very little space inside the confinement to navigate the glazed core, where a pane of glass separates your nose from the neatly stacked skulls, rising above your head.

Back outside, the nineteenth and final audio stop recognises other episodes of genocide worldwide, and the realisation that it will happen again. A musical composition completes the tour. In all honesty this nineteenth and final segment fails to distract from the 'mini golf course' feel of the site. I'm not sure if it is the gentle undulating landscape of the bunker graves, the walkways between the exhibits, or that they are coincidentally numbered 1 to 18, but once the surreal impression took hold I couldn't shake it.

The central path that runs from the stupa back towards the entrance/exit

Memorial Charnel, Choeung Ek.

and Dara returns me to my hotel, I find myself walking back to Tuol Sleng for the third consecutive day.

EVEN AFTER JOHN PILGER BROKE THE NEWS OF THE TRAGEDY OVER breakfast tables in the UK, Cambodia's problems were far from over. True, the public response to Year Zero was phenomenal; £50,000 in private donations poured into the *Daily Mirror* offices. By 28th September a Cargolux DC-8 had been chartered to take relief to the stricken country. That the plane took off from Luxembourg, not the UK, illustrates that no matter how well intentioned the British public might have been, now they were informed, their elected government were not disposed to support the humanitarian effort Pilger's reporting had lit.

The problem was that the Vietnamese had liberated Cambodia, and geopolitics ensured that their presence provided the flimsiest of excuses for major western countries and relief agencies to stay any helping hand, despite Cambodia's desperate call for aid. The United Nations had recognised Pol Pot's regime, so the new interim government were denied international legitimacy, although they now controlled some 90% of the country. The only assistance from the UK government came to those who survived the gauntlet of people smugglers, bandits, and mine fields to reach refugee camps over the Thai border.

Pilger's efforts to bring the story to a wider audience were supported by the screening of his documentary *Year Zero: The Silent Death of Cambodia*, produced and directed by David Munro, which ultimately raised another £3.5m, again donated by the public. A bus driver anonymously gave his wages, a single parent sent her savings of £50, and an eighty-year-old sent her pension for two months. This selfless generosity may have been due to Pilger's final piece to camera before the credits:

"You can assume that most of the people you saw in tonight's film are now dead."

When Pilger's film was screened around the world, another $45m was donated to send medical supplies, rebuild ruined schools and clinics, and restore the water supply. Of the UK aid agencies, only Oxfam defied the government to send relief to the estimated two and a quarter million people in desperate need, including the orphaned children who'd forgotten their names and had resorted to wandering the forest, eating plants and bark off the trees.

Nearly a decade later the fundraising was still continuing with BBC's children's TV staple *Blue Peter*, which designated Cambodia as the beneficiary of their Christmas 1988 appeal. British Prime Minister Margaret Thatcher, who'd toured the Cambodian refugee camps in Thailand, gave an interview, donating a koala bear paperweight, part of her collection, for auction.

"And you will let me know how much it raises", cooed the PM, keeping a keen eye on the bottom line of the heirloom collection.

What stuck in the craw was that Thatcher had recognised and articulated a very unpalatable solution for Cambodia:

"The more reasonable ones in the Khmer Rouge will have to play some part in a future government."[2]

The truth was they were already in place. When the Vietnamese took Phnom Penh, Pol Pot himself having fled, they installed a government composed of former Khmer Rouge defectors who had deserted the sinking ship, and relocated to Vietnam. Elements of the regime had thus re-integrated themselves into the running of their country, which they themselves had brought to the brink of destruction, only now they were following an acceptable 'liberal capitalist' line.

The Vietnamese withdrew unconditionally from Cambodia in 1989.

NEWS TRAVELS FAST IN BATTAMBANG. BY THE TIME I RETURN TO hotel reception from dumping the bag in my room there's a tuk-tuk tout lying in wait to ambush me. He can take me to 'The Killing Caves' at Phnom Sampeau tomorrow, as part of a day tour. We haggle, not over price but destinations, because I've come to the city in the northwest of Cambodia specifically for this one dark site, with no interest in being fed through a succession of tourist traps.

Sure enough, the following morning he hands me off to one of his cadre, and we are off to a succession of tourist traps, each one timed so the driver can have a doze whilst the locals set about extracting money from me. Around noon my driver asks if I am hungry. I tell him no, I just want to go to Phnom Sampeau. Instead he takes me to a restaurant at the edge of a lake filled quarry-cum-building site, the idea being that here we can have lunch and 'just relax' for an hour or so.

He demonstrates by climbing into a hammock, adopting the default position that he's occupied for most of the morning, and explains that there is another cave at Phnom Sampeau filled with bats, but they don't start flying until much later, so it is too early to go. I'm aware of this, having read a review on Trip Advisor:

"I visited the mountain and I saw the monkey on the top. The monkey came closer to me and want to steal my mango. And then I came down to see the bat. It was so wonderful."

Which is why I want to go now, out of sync with the crowds who will be traipsing over Phnom Sampeau for the wildlife later this afternoon, in favour of the dead who I know will already be waiting.

"How would you like your money, a tip, and to go home early?"

Bribery does the trick, although he subsequently dons his crash helmet for

---

2) To appreciate the implication of this statement fully, imagine Germany post-WWII, and substitute the SS for the Khmer Rouge.

Hell Garden, Phnom Sampeau, Battambang.

the duration of the trip, I suspect in part so he can ignore me. Hopefully the tip will cover any kickbacks he misses out on, although I assume he's in no rush to return home to his young family who've seemingly kept him up all night, whereas a truncated tour affords me an opportunity to do some DIY laundry in the shower before heading downtown to trendy road No. 1.5 by the river for something alcoholic and spicy, whilst writing up my scribbled notes in best.[3]

'The Killing Caves' are halfway up the limestone mountain of Phnom Sampeau, although 'mountain' feels like a generous description. There's a commercial market community of some twenty stalls catering for tourists at the foot, and a ticket office for the $3 admission. My tuk-tuk driver can have a lie down, because rides up the steep cement road are monopolised by the locals, who will charge for a 'backie' to the top, although this mad dog is naturally walking. Half way to the summit there's a set of steps that fork towards a large golden Buddha mounted on a stone dais under a canopy. Beyond this, over the saddle in the hillside, the path leads down towards the 'Killing Caves' and a surprise worth swearing for. It's a Hell Garden, a small sculpture park depicting *Naraka*, the Buddhist Hell, and I had absolutely no expectation of encountering one here, as there was no mention on Trip Advisor. They are more commonly associated with neighbouring Thailand, the Wang Saen Suk

---

3) I concede conventional tourists may have more fun with 'after hours' Cambodia than their dark counterparts.

Skylight through which victims were thrown. Killing caves, Phnom Sampeau. Battambang.

Hell Garden outside Bangkok being a prime example.

Twenty figures are actively engaged in multiple practices of torture at the behest of a pair of judges, who dispense punishment from a ledger of past misdeeds. The condemned are boiled in oil, have their tongues extracted with pliers, or their heads morph to become those of chickens. The women have it worse, forced to climb a giant cactus naked as a moustachioed torturer thrusts his spear up the harlot's rectum, while another suffers the indignity of a giant black caterpillar devouring her breast. One naked lady has her neck and praying hands locked in a stock whilst a buzz-saw blade cleaves her skull. It's grotesque, graphic, fascinating and is apparently to assist parents in educating their children about the fate that befalls those who stray from a virtuous life.

Bearing to the right the path dips and the hillside reveals a cavern below, the overhang fringed with animated foliage as a Macaque monkey comes to investigate who has arrived ahead of schedule, because I have the place to myself.

A grand staircase with guardian serpentine finials, baring their teeth, descends and curves into the cool shade and a surreal setting. The cavern has a mosaic floor in red, yellow and green swirls, with prayer flags garlanding the ceiling. To the right the expanse contains a sleeping, smiling golden Buddha, and an intricately decorated gold stupa sixteen feet high, with an open glass door containing charnel, predominantly skulls. On carpets spread before the Buddha sits an elderly gentleman, the charnel custodian, surrounded by candles and incense. He smiles and offers me a *sampeah*, which I return.

The left hand side of the cave develops into a flue, illuminated by an open skylight in the roof, thirty to forty feet above a field of jagged rocks. One can only hope the victims were killed before they were thrown in. The body needs to reach a speed in excess of 100–120 mph to attain terminal velocity before it ceases to send pain signals to the brain on impact.

Some of those who died here are interned in the stupa and I respectfully make my way towards it, past beautiful models of sailing ships and drawings of animals and landscapes pegged from a low line skirting the floor, each attended by a collection bowl. I remove my shoes before walking onto the carpet, conscious of how I can capture the remains in an appropriate manner

Hell Garden, Phnom Sampeau, Battambang

whilst the sole focus of scrutiny.

However photographing the skulls is not an issue for the custodian, who uncoils himself from the floor, and ushers me enthusiastically towards the stupa. He points at something leathery and mummified amongst the jumbled remains.

"Human skin."

Then again, just in case I didn't understand the first time:

"Human skin."

We negate my lack of Khmer by sitting in comfortable silence on his carpet. In return for the donation I add to his plate he insists on tying a piece of red string around my wrist, although I'm sorely tempted to ask for one of his firecracker cigarettes instead. I leave him with a paper crane, which brings a smile, and we part with copious amounts of bowing. I recover my shoes and ascend the stairs to the strains of the first approaching tour group arriving from above.

PAPER CRANES

I T MIGHT SEEM BIZARRE, SPENDING PRECIOUS HOLIDAY TIME IN pursuit of the dead and the memorials established in their memory, but occasionally travelling to dark sites is a treat in itself. Today is one of those days. The 'Hiraki' Shinkansen glides into the platform at Tokyo station like a blade from Japanese mythology. The design has morphed during the thirty years since I last had the privilege of riding the 'bullet train', yet their styling still retains that futuristic edge. At 7:03 a.m precisely the train seamlessly pulls away, taking me south towards Kyushu, and although there will be two changes of train during the journey, the Japanese National Railway network will transport me in style to the Nagasaki terminus in seven hours and forty-seven minutes, during which time I can regress and travel as the little boy who just loved the thrill of being on a train.

Seven hours and forty-seven minutes later, sickeningly to the second, I step out onto the platform at Nagasaki, and the spell is broken. Once again I'm a middle-aged man for whom telling the time is no longer a tick-box achievement of growing up, more a pressing concern now I'm counting down.

N AGASAKI NEARLY ESCAPED ITS DARK HISTORY. THE PRIMARY target for the second atomic bomb to be dropped by the United States was to be Kokura, an arsenal town with a population of 168,000. That Kokura remains a place the world has simply never heard of is because it led a charmed life. It had initially been the designated reserve target on 6th August 1945, but the skies were clear above the primary target that morning, so Kokura was spared while Hiroshima suffered the unimaginable fate. Three days later, when Kokura was designated as the primary target, it was blanketed by a combination of cloud, drifting smoke from a firebomb raid in the vicinity from the previous day, and emissions from the chimneys of the Yawata Steel Works. So *Bockscar*, the B-29 carrying the 'Fat Man' plutonium bomb, flew on to attack Nagasaki, a seaport to the south, aiming for the Mitsubishi shipyards. For Kokura, life and history would continue in harmonious obscurity.

When *Bockscar* arrived over Nagasaki the city was also obscured by 80% cloud cover, but then a gap appeared to the north, and with the aircraft desperately short on fuel for its home run, the bomb was released anyway. It missed the Mitsubishi shipyards by a couple of kilometres, instead exploding several hundred metres from the Urakami Cathedral at 11:02 a.m. Fat Man was nearly twice as powerful as Little Boy, the uranium bomb dropped on Hiroshima, although fewer Nagasakians were killed in the plutonium blast as the surrounding hills absorbed the shockwave.

The casualty list was horrendous nonetheless. More than 30,000 people were killed instantly, some estimates put it close to 40,000, including the majority of Japanese Christians, notably the fifty Catholics waiting in line for confession. Ironically Nagasaki was the beating Christian heart of Japan, and its inhabitants believed they had been spared the extensive firebombing that had destroyed over sixty Japanese cities, because the British and the Americans recognised them as fellow Christians, when in fact their fate was sealed at the whim of the clouds.

The bomb blast not only destroyed the medical and educational facilities, but it decapitated the statue of Christ above the doors of Urakami Cathedral, symbolically repudiating the faith of all concerned on either side.

NAGASAKI EXUDES REMORSELESS CHARM ON THE WALK DOWN towards the tram stop: a clowder of cats in the tiny backstreet, shrines tucked into nooks, and a quaint row of independent shops, complete with welcoming shopkeepers, opposite the steep step-cut cemetery. From a vantage point at the top, few buildings dominate the panorama, while clusters of compact dwellings stuck to the opposite hillside appear as if sprays of *sakura*, the revered cherry blossom. The weather is mild, the patisseries a delight, and the trams are the retro icing on the cake, winding through the streets of a city quietly minding its own business, just as it was on the morning of 9th August 1945.

With a flat fare of ¥120, less than a quid, and an onboard digital map with complementary audio announcements in American-English and Chinese, I ride in serenity to alight at Matsuyama-Machi, the Christian neighbourhood of Nagasaki, spied through the clouds by the crew of *Bockscar*, and the hypocentre, the point where Fat Man exploded, 500m above the bustling community.

Across the main road lies the Memorial Park, founded in 1955, upon an elevated plateau, accessed by either a flight of steps with a glorious island flower bed, bedecked in pansies and forget-me-nots, or by the adjoining covered escalator, which features a melodic singsong greeting piped through speakers, so there's a cascading overlapping effect as you ride to the top.[1]

Stepping out into the park itself at the southern entrance the first installation encountered is the Fountain of Peace, constructed in August 1969 by Nagasaki City and the National Council for World Peace and the Abolition of Nuclear Weapons, using donations from all over Japan. That's what it says on the sign, which also informs me that the diameter of the fountain is 18m, and that the twin spray jets, which represent the beating wings of a dove of peace,

---

1) For the record there are also lifts, marked on all the tourist maps, to facilitate wheelchair access into the park.

rise and fall between 0.5 and 6m. The text notes that multiple victims of both atomic bombs who survived the initial detonation begged for water to quench their thirst, only for it to kill them.

Through the synchronised curtains of sparkling water, the giant jade green Peace Statue sits placidly in the distance. Instinctively I sense something's wrong with it. Ruefully I throw a handful of cheap change into the fountain, following the established custom by those who have come before, but mostly to assuage my critical nature for targeting a memorial like a sniper.

Past the fountain lie the foundations of what was once the Urakami Prison, the closest public building to the hypocentre, where the steel reinforced perimeter walls were obliterated by the blast, along with the staff and inmates, leaving just a forlorn chimney. Now even that's gone, the only evidence it ever stood in the black and white photograph taken in the aftermath. The accompanying text explains that there are memorials to both Chinese and Korean victims of the bomb within the park, prisoners here at the time.

There is a suspended memorial bell, recovered from the ruins of Urakami Cathedral, supported by four aerial trapeze artists, and even although it's early, and the weekend, there are already people below in respectful attendance.

Posing before the Peace Statue, Nagasaki.

Attached to the modernist frame of the bell tower, a testimony from an anonymous survivor, whose boss at the Mitsubishi Arms Plant ordered him to another factory, just as Fat Boy detonated 1.1km away. Of the thirty-two workers, only he and one other survived, protected by a pillar that shielded them from the intense heat of the blast. "The boss died on the spot." The testimony concludes: "I want to convey the fear of the Atomic bombs and importance of peace."

At the northern end of the park lies a plaza, the stage for tourists to have their group photo taken before the 10m high Statue of Peace. The figure symbolically points his finger to the sky, a warning of the bomb, the other open hand extended in a gesture of peace, one leg folded indicating meditation, with the other leg braced to stand and rescue us, presumably from the folly of our own leaders. It is set on a plinth surrounded by a rectangular pool of water, flanked by two small wooden shrines both packed with hanging chains of paper cranes in every conceivable hue.

Designed by Nagasaki artist Seibou Kitamura, unveiled in April 1955, the statue itself is a fusion of western and eastern styles, which is an admirable concept, but in reality conveys an unnatural awkwardness, which caught my

attention from a distance. The gentle eastern face, eyes closed in prayer, does not blend seamlessly with the flowing wavy hair, nor the anatomically perfect ripped torso, a physique more in keeping with Michelangelo's *David*, and consequently it appears slightly jarred in its execution. On reflection I concede that the concept should transcend any of my aesthetic niggles. Set over water, with 360° access, both the reflection and subsequent perambulation afford very flattering views.

The tourists are happy to mirror the figure's pose for their souvenir photos, although their attempts are interpretive. Because doing an impression appears contagious I despise myself for wondering if the elderly lady in the wheelchair will have a go; she can do the arms, which is what everyone else does. Thankfully she doesn't and is wheeled away as a young mum adopts an original flamingo stance, proving she does yoga.

For those larger tour groups looking for a more formal presentation, the resident professional photographer provides wooden staging. Groups follow flag-bearing uniformed guides, and none stay for long, but the plaza appears synchronised; no sooner has one group departed than another arrives, although interestingly none of the tourists are Caucasian. I assume western tour parties only go as far south as Hiroshima. One atom bomb city is probably considered enough on a conventional tourist itinerary, even if Japan has two, and arguably there's more to occupy tourists in the environs of Hiroshima, although the English audio on the Nagasaki trams indicates there are plenty of westerners coming here, and the port has been open to trade since the Portuguese arrived in the sixteenth century.

There are numerous memorials throughout the park donated from overseas, including those from China, Bulgaria, USSR, and Cuba. Mothers and their children are a recurrent theme. Retuning to the foot of the escalator and taking a sharp left, there are a series of original air raid shelters, little more than holes in the hillside. The shelters are also visible in the background of an accompanying painting by Shigenobu Tsukiji, showing piles of bodies waiting to be cremated. The depicted corpses occupied the ground where I now stand.

While there are several public WCs within the park, there appears nowhere for refreshments, however a 7/11-style

Entrance to the Nagasaki Atomic Bomb Museum

convenience store across the street provides mid-morning refuelling.

The hypocentre cenotaph in the adjacent park is an elegant black triangular monolith, set within concentric stepped grass rings, which again allows 360° access, so it is possible to view the needle without it being lost within the background treeline. There is also an original section of the distinctive red brick Urakami Cathedral, and a memorial to commemorate the fiftieth anniversary of the bomb, of a mother holding a stricken child, which, the explanatory plaque states, symbolises Japan being supported by the rest of the world in its efforts to become the peaceful country it is today. I wonder if there's another country in the world that might prostrate itself with such humility, given its previous aggression, at which point I am approached by a couple from Gondar,[2] who would like me to take a memento of them standing in front of the statue.

It is the first time I recall being asked to take such a photo at a memorial site, certainly using the camera phone they offer me, which has no strap to ensure 'Butterfingers' doesn't drop it. I have little comprehension of their *Star Trek* technology, or why they decided to ask me, because I'm shooting with a Lomo 'tank' from the Eastern Bloc, on 35mm film. I've also no idea why they would choose this particular backdrop, but they seen suitably delighted with the result. Nonetheless, I surreptitiously check over my shoulder to see if they ask anyone else to do the honours, now I've walked away.

Perhaps the most interesting exhibit within the Hypocentre Park is hidden from cursory view, down a short flight of steps at the side, to an inbuilt glass display case, presenting a substrata section of the ground as it was after the bomb dropped. Exposed to a temperature of 3,000°C, the soil is fused to rock, capturing the remnants of debris including glass, decorative ceramics, and a pair of workman's pincers. The rest of the soil composition is left to the imagination.

T HE NAGASAKI ATOMIC BOMB MUSEUM WAS OPENED IN 1996, AND the purpose built facility now houses the artefacts recovered from their Ground Zero, originally displayed in the Nagasaki International Culture Hall. It is open to the public from 8:30 a.m., until 17:30 p.m; and is closed from December 29th–31st. Admission is through a spiral ramp leading down through an atrium, illuminated from above by a glass dome, subtly mirroring the Genbaku Dome at Hiroshima, although my initial reference to the grid skylight was *Dr. No*'s tarantula room. There is an ingenious giant letterbox window just before the ramp slopes below ground level, presenting a view across the rotunda into the glass-walled cafeteria, where a couple are being served by a waitress. A veritable washing line of white paper cranes is strung around the wall on the last rotation before the ticket desk. It is a *Senbazuru*, the practice of folding 1,000 paper cranes, which the Japanese believe grants them a wish.

---

2) That's Gondar, Ethiopia, not Gondor, Middle Earth.

Entry to the museum costs ¥200, and I feel cheapened using the 50% discount voucher for admission to key Nagasaki attractions given to me by my hosts at the guest house; however I won't have time to visit the Nagasaki penguin aquarium, so cash it in here.

The audio guide is perfunctory, but there is very little scene setting and no idents to frame the dialogue, meaning there are periods of silence before you realise the next number on the control pad has to be keyed in. The lady presenting the English narrative has a North American twang and her pitch is too singsong cheerful for delivering this specific subject matter. Audio signposts are incorporated into the displays, unobtrusive to the point that occasionally they are camouflaged. However the exhibits are thoughtfully curated, with an illuminated model of Nagasaki's topography showing the extent of the fireball, blast, and radiation. There is a full-scale replica of the Fat Man device with a cut away view of the core, and an eerie reproduction of an archway from the Urakami Cathedral, flanked by sorrowful Christian figures presiding over a mound of rubble.

As always it is the personal items that carry the most weight: perforated clothing worn by those exposed to the blast, a belt, a pair of spectacles, lenses melted in their wire frames, and a schoolchild's bento lunchbox, the contents charred to a black crisp. Unusually for a museum of this dark nature, there appear to be no shoes on display, however there are a selection of rosaries, crucifixes, and crosses worn as personal adornments, reinforcing the Christian heritage of this particular dark site.

What is surprising is that there are parents taking their very young children into the exhibition, given that some of the photographic content on display is graphic, including vivid images of facial keloid scars, corpses burnt black beyond recognition with only the teeth providing definition, a dead horse, and a genuinely shocking image of a traumatised woman standing amongst the debris, a skull at her heels. The most extraordinary 'photograph' is the pre-Banksy shadow guard and his ladder, captured at an observation post over 4km away from the hypocentre, where the flash exposed the tar on the structure, leaving the negative of the man and ladder fixed with a frightening degree of definition.

Several screens with seating afford the opportunity to view video testimony of survivors, including one from an Australian POW in Nagasaki at the time. The exhibition closes with an extensive section devoted to the depressing nuclear arms race during the Cold War, the continual nuclear weapons testing, and its ensuing collateral damage, including Bikini Atoll, the US test site from 1946–1958 where, although the islanders were evacuated, they were still exposed to the subsequent fallout, and remain in exile due to the persistent high levels of radiation to this day.

The museum stresses Nagasaki's legacy, to ensure that it is the last city an atomic bomb is ever dropped upon.

Nagasaki Atomic Bomb Museum

T HE CAFÉ LOOKS OUT ONTO A SMALL STONE COURTYARD WITH A waterfall, and the curved exterior wall of the atrium. Now, looking back through the letterbox window I can see visitors spiralling down the ramp towards the museum. It's a light and tranquil space for a coffee, and seats approximately twenty at glass tables with light wooden chairs, staffed by two ladies who serve a menu of plated food, a selection of tall glass sundaes, and beverages. I order a cappuccino, take a seat, and start to fold a paper crane while the coffee cools.

A Japanese family of three, mum, dad, and grown up daughter, arrive at the next table, and I invite the ladies to join me so we can fold together. Dad just smiles and wisely leaves us to it. It's not a race, although I am soundly thrashed despite my head start, and they politely applaud my finished effort, offering me their birds as a memento. They ask me for my opinion of Nagasaki. I confess I regret not coming here sooner, because its human scale, cubbyhole shrines, tram network, cake shops, and decorative manhole covers have charmed me, although in truth I only came for the city's dark heritage. My tick-all-the-boxes answer delights them, they thank me for coming, and we part with copious bowing all round.

There is a tiny shop selling books and postcards of historical images relating to the bomb, and a small range of t-shirts and button badges advocating peace. Of particular interest is the handwritten sign in English, stuck in the window in the manner of 'two schoolchildren at a time', which says that all profits go towards a 'peace campaign'. In fairness the shop is so small you couldn't get three schoolchildren in there. The note appears to be pre-emptive, to dispel the notion of commercial gain through the sale of souvenirs at a dark site in the minds of foreign tourists.

Outside the museum is a walkway to a crow's nest gallery, which affords a panoramic view of the modern city with a corresponding photograph mounted below, taken in October 1945 to show what this landscape looked like in the aftermath of the bomb, the peak of the hill on the horizon being the obvious reference point. The devastation of the 'Hypocenter Zone' was total and utter. Through television news we are aware of war-torn cities and the aftermath of earthquakes, but this is unlike any of those images. There are no partially destroyed buildings in the scene from 1945, because the debris appears to have been pulverized repeatedly under a steamroller. In retrospect it is amazing that even the referential skyline survived.

The lady at the information desk is very helpful and supplies me with a paper map on which she highlights the route to the 'Sanno Shrine One-Legged Torii Gate' with a fluorescent marker. In truth I just needed her to point me in the general direction. Nagasaki has embraced its bomb history, and the sites are well marked with specific signposts in heritage brown with white script in Japanese, English and Chinese, including metric footfall distances from sign to site. It's easy to find 'One-Leg' inside ten minutes, most of which is spent at pedestrian crossings waiting beside empty roads for the 'crossing now' sign to illuminate, accompanied by an audio woodpecker, and the only effort involved is climbing the tiers of stone steps from street level to access it.

This stone gate was set approximately 800m from the hypocentre, and although the shrine was levelled, one of the pillars and part of the lintel survives to this day, although it has been subsequently reinforced as a precaution. The broken pieces of the missing pillar and lintel have been laid in a sectioned area to the side, under a pre-war photograph of the gate in its entirety, and although the original shrine may have gone, the pillar is still sacred, with a *shimenawa* ("enclosing rope") tied around it, indicating a sacred space in the Shinto religion to ward off evil spirits, with a *shide* ("lightning wand") attached, a zigzag paper streamer, representing purification. People have brought jarred candles, left neatly at the base of the pillar.

Around the corner to the left lies another short flight of steps, which led to the original shrine, flanked by a pair of giant Camphor trees, joined by an enormous *shimenawa* umbilical, bedecked with multiple *shides* that ripple in the breeze. The plaque informs that the two trees were 'stripped naked and split down the trunk by the blast and scorched black by the heat rays'. There's a grainy black and white photograph to prove it, the skeletal branches like brittle claws.

Although they were considered dead, the trees returned to life and are now designated natural monuments. The plaque ends with the enduring theme: 'prayer for the repose of the souls of the people who died here and to ensure that this tragedy is never repeated.'

Camphor Tree, Nagasaki

The living trees are hugely impressive. The Camphor, indigenous to southern Japan, has been known to live for over 1,000 years, and, as these magnificent examples have conclusively proved, are able to survive an atomic bomb. Naturally the presence of the Camphor trees remind me of the Callery pear, the designated 'Survivor Tree' on the Memorial Plaza at 9/11. Later research reveals the Callery pear is a species native to China, and ironically Vietnam, although I understand why its provenance might not have been mentioned either on the 9/11 walking tour or memorial website. From a dark tourism perspective, the Camphor trees here in Nagasaki, and the Callery pear in New York, highlight the role of 'trees that should have died yet lived' at dark sites.[3]

Whilst it is in no way a competition for 'best survivor tree', the Camphors of Nagasaki are the majestic originals. However in purely commercial terms, New York's Survivor Tree has swept the board: commemorative tray $16,

---

3) There's a Chinese parasol tree in Hiroshima's Peace Park, supported by a teepee of staves, which also survived, despite being only 1,300 metres from the hypocentre. It has been replanted close to the museum café. Although the tree is deciduous, and I am no arborist, in March 2017 it looked decidedly dead.

keychain $6.95, magnet $6.95, metal keepsake $24.95, and, last but not least, a mug — $18.

By my reckoning that's $72.85 for the Callery pear tree set, whilst Nagasaki doesn't appear to even offer a postcard of its surviving Camphor trees for sale. A pity, because the wide angle lens on my camera is insufficient to do them justice.

There's a sign indicating the direction of the Sakamoto International Cemetery, 300 metres away. Established in 1888, predominantly as a final resting place for foreigners, it has very little connection with the atomic bomb, although Takashi Nagai, a survivor, is now interred there. I know the graveyard will be steep, stepped, full of cats, and that I won't have long before daylight evaporates into the murk, even less before the rain arrives, but mine is an obsessive compulsion, so there's little point resisting. I sling my bag across my shoulder and dutifully tramp uphill.

I T HAS BEEN OVER THIRTY YEARS SINCE I LAST LOOKED UPON Hiroshima's Genbaku Dome. There's been some minor preservation work undertaken since, yet the years and seasons have been kinder to the ruin than to the returning tourist, and only one of us has been afforded UNESCO World Heritage status during the intervening period.[4]

The sun streams through the skullcap skeletal remains of what was once the Hiroshima Prefectural Industrial Promotion Hall, painting an evocative silhouette just as it did once before. There's nostalgia with the fun time memory of being a novelty westerner, folding paper cranes with a gaggle of Japanese schoolchildren, before the melancholy returns. This single structure, above all others, serves notice that whatever the solution to war may be, it surely cannot be this.

---

4) The Product Exhibition Hall, designed by Czech architect Jan Letzel, was completed in 1915. The site attained UNESCO World Heritage status in 1996, based on the following criteria: its survival of the atomic bomb, as the focal point of the first use of the bomb on a human population, and its subsequent representation as a peace symbol. Both China and the USA expressed reservations.

China suggested the monument could be used to discount Japan's aggressions against other countries during WWII.

The USA disassociated itself from UNESCO's decision, in the belief that granting a war site heritage status blurred historical context, in that the bomb was used to end the war. However Hiroshima is only a 'war site' because America targeted it, a city predominantly populated with civilians. The atomic bombs did not end the war. The US conducted conventional bombing post-Hiroshima and Nagasaki, including day/night raids on 14th August. That the last bombs to fall on Japan, prior to its surrender, were neither uranium nor plutonium supports this. Emperor Hirohito broadcast the intention to surrender at noon on 15th August 1945. As detailed in Paul Ham's meticulous account, Hiroshima Nagasaki, the declaration of war on Japan by Russia in the wake of Hiroshima was the tipping point, with the Japanese preferring to surrender to the US, rather than Russia.

While China's reasoning is valid, given our global reliance on nuclear deterrents, it's difficult to imagine a more appropriate monument to world peace than the Genbaku Dome.

MUCH AS I LOVE THE BEAUTY, FORM, AND SYMBOLISM OF THE twin memorial pools of 9/11, for me the design of Hiroshima's Peace Park is as good as it gets.

Kenzō Tange came to international prominence in 1949 at the age of thirty-six with the award-winning design for the Hiroshima Peace Memorial Park, by employing a linear design. Here the rectangular museum on stilts (influenced by the work of Swiss architect Le Corbusier) the saddle memorial cenotaph, and the peace flame are set in symmetry on an axis, running from the ruins of the Genbaku Dome. What sets this vision apart is that it is untroubled by the Motoyasu River that bisects the line, the river negated by the Motoyasu-bashi Bridge, which allows the visitor access between park and Dome. The Memorial Park is set at the tip of an elongated island, forked by the Motoyasu River on the eastern flank, and the Ota River on the west, the triangular cartography suspended by the iconic T-shaped Aioi Bridge.

It's early and the park is in the process of waking up, although it is not permissible to sleep within the grounds overnight. This point is included on an official notice of seven regulations at the entrance, which also includes 'Please be sure to leash and clean up after your dog', and, inevitably, 'Please do not feed the pigeons'. Our behaviour has usurped the signage, for there's an addendum, and one I've not seen before. 'Drones Banned', a black line through four circular space invaders and a radio control handset.

At the cenotaph, a team of seniors sporting bonnets and hi-vis are arranging the fresh floristry as they do every morning before 8:30 a.m. There is already a queue waiting outside the entrance to the museum, including a tour group from the UK, still gushing about yesterday's day trip to the island of Miyajima to see the great Torii floating gate and the temple of Daisho-in, a reminder that not everyone comes to Hiroshima in pursuit of dark tourism.

The uniformed guards open the doors at precisely 8:30 a.m., the public file in and are directed to the stairs to the permanent exhibition on the first floor, while I detach and cross to the information desk.

"Ohayo gozaimasu." The 'u' is silent on the end.

I throw in a bow and a smile for good measure to smooth my pronunciation. The receptionist replies in kind, says she remembers me, and picks up the phone. I'd stopped by before closing time yesterday, asking if there was anyone available to answer some questions. The receptionist made enquiries and asked if it would be possible for me to return in the morning. So here I am. In truth I'm not expecting anything, as with the exception of Tuol Sleng none of the other major sites I've approached have been willing to engage, and Tuol Sleng hardly qualified as a success. So it comes as a genuine surprise when one of the uniformed guards is directed to usher me downstairs.

Rie Nakanishi is already waiting for me at the far end of a seemingly endless corridor, standing in perfect symmetry, undoubtedly at a precise right angle to the doorway of her office. I stop in my tracks, compelled to bow by her perfect presentation, and she graciously returns the compliment, before showing me through the door, when I eventually reach it.

The Hiroshima Peace Memorial Museum opened in August 1955 and by 2005 had attracted some fifty-three million visitors. Rie tells me they now receive approximately 1.5 million visitors annually, but stresses that tourists don't just come to Hiroshima solely because of what happened in 1945; they also come to visit Miyajima.

"And Ōkunoshima?"

"Yes!"

Rie looks delighted that I know about Ōkunoshima. I tell her it's on my itinerary for tomorrow, but don't volunteer that I'm not going there for the tourist attraction most commonly associated with the island. She tells me the Hiroshima and Nagasaki museums combine to tour an exhibition overseas. In 2016 they exhibited in Chicago, and in 2017 it will be Budapest.

"Who pays for the museum?"

The government. Admission is ¥200, the same as its sister museum in Nagasaki. The exchange rate at this time was £1–¥143, so admission is about £1.50.

The sedge of paper cranes decorating Rie Nakanishi's desk take no notice as I introduce one of my own to the fold. It's made from Japanese origami paper, so hopefully there won't be any ruffled feathers with my next question, because it's a delicate one.

"They are selling paper cranes in the 9/11 Museum gift shop. Are you (the

Genbaku Dome, Hiroshima Peace Park.

Hiroshima museum) supplying them? Or are you receiving a percentage from the sales of the cranes from 9/11?"

Rie says there is one of Sadoko's cranes in the 9/11 Tribute Center. Yes, I tell her I've seen it, a miniscule piece of exquisite folding in red foil, personally gifted to the Tribute Center by Sadako's brother. She tells me Hiroshima do not supply the cranes being sold in the National September 11 Museum gift shop. They didn't know cranes were being sold there, and asks how much they cost. $16.95. I add that I've sent an email regarding the sale of cranes to the museum media contact in New York, but have yet to receive a reply.

The National September 11 Memorial and Museum says it "places utmost value on ethical conduct and integrity." However it appears the paper cranes sent in the aftermath of 9/11 by children around the world not only provided comfort, but inspiration to sell cranes as 'keepsakes'. In fairness crane earrings are sold in Hiroshima within the park, clearly marked 'Made in Hiroshima', but it is their icon to sell. Of course there is nothing to prevent the Hiroshima Peace Memorial Museum reciprocating in kind, by copying something sold from the National September 11 Museum gift shop; perhaps a rock, stamped with an inappropriate classical quotation.

I've taken up enough of Rie's time. I present her with the crane as a parting gift, and she gives me her business card in return, which informs me her job title is 'Manager'.

T HE MUSEUM IS UNDERGOING RESTORATION, SCHEDULED FOR completion in 2018, so the East Building is closed to the public.[5] Consequently the exhibition is overcrowded, although because this is Japan there is inexhaustible patience and politeness as everyone pointedly waits their turn to see the individual pieces in the collection.

Some of the exhibits I recall from my previous visit: the pocket watch with the hands stuck at 8:15, 'the time that it's always been', the solid stack of needles fused together by the intense heat, and the shadow of a person sitting on the steps of the Sumitomo bank, captured by exposure to the flash. Then there's the diorama of wax figures, a mother with her two children, stumbling through the burning ruins, arms extended like the walking dead, skin dripping, clothes shredded. As with Nagasaki, it is possible to take photographs of the exhibits, as long as it is done without the aid of a flash, and as with Nagasaki there are selected pieces you can physically touch, such as roof tiles and surreal fused bottles, exposed to the tremendous temperature.

There is a piece that wasn't here last time, known as Shin's tricycle. Shinichi Tetsutani, three-years-old, was playing outside his house riding his favourite toy. After the explosion his family recovered the little boy from the ruins of the house, badly injured. He would not survive the night. Rather than bury Shin in the cemetery, they interred him, with his tricycle, in the back garden. Forty years later, Mr. Tetsutani exhumed his son's remains, moved him to the family plot in the cemetery, and donated his son's beloved tricycle to the museum. Given that memorial museums are looking for opportunities to retell their stories, often by unearthing a lost artefact, this is one Hiroshima cannot have expected, coming literally from beyond the grave.

Sadako Sasaki, Hiroshima's most famous daughter, has her own section within the exhibition, with a pair of donated red sandals and a selection of her paper cranes. Although Sadako survived the initial explosion, at the age of two she was one of thousands of *Hibakusha*,[6] the Japanese term for 'bomb-

---

5) The section closed to the public for renovation focuses on the war and the development of the bomb, the reasons it was dropped and why Hiroshima was the designated target. It also tells the story of the postwar efforts of Hiroshima to strive for the end of nuclear weapons, again reflecting the efforts of its sister city.

6) The Hibakusha suffered terribly at the hands of their fellow Japanese. Ostracized by prejudice, they were denied compensation for years, visible reminders of Japan's shame in defeat. They struggled to gain employment, and if successful were forced to work the graveyard shift, isolated from the workforce. Marriage was rare. Hibakusha children, saddled with the physical pain of their scars, also had to endure psychological injury, stigmatized by their contemporaries when they re-entered society. Suicides amongst the Hibakusha were prevalent.

It wasn't until 1954, after Japanese fishermen were exposed to the fallout from the US Bikini tests, that public opinion forced the Japanese government to recognise the Hibakusha, and provide compensation.

affected person', was diagnosed with leukaemia a decade later, and died aged twelve.

Artefacts, Hiroshima Peace Memorial Museum

As with Nagasaki, there is a walk-around scale model of the city after its destruction, a giant red sphere suspended above the hypocentre, a tiny model of the matchstick A-Bomb Dome below.

The twin cities are not 'dark'. Although it is left unsaid today, the Americans were desperate to avoid them being seen as 'martyred cities'. The Japanese were a brutal enemy, fanatical and, as illustrated by the actions of their leaders in the immediate aftermath of the rapid double punch nuclear bombs, willing to sacrifice both cities and population to protect their Emperor. America felt justified in their use of the bomb in an attempt to end the war, and in retaliation for losses suffered at Pearl Harbor, where nearly 2,500 were killed, in addition to the Batann Death March, where American losses were estimated to be between 500 and 650 men.

After the surrender, the death toll in Hiroshima and Nagasaki rose, as radiation sickness claimed yet more victims. Censorship was introduced by the occupying forces to muzzle the press on both sides, with the US war machine suggesting that because the bombs had been airborne during detonation, there were no side-effects, because the radiation rose with the mushroom cloud to dissipate. However radiation then returned to earth in Hiroshima as 'black rain'. Despite the spin, American doctors were keen to study the effects of the radiation on the victims, although they treated the affected like guinea pigs rather than patients.

Although synonymous with the events of August 1945, the subsequent combined efforts of Hiroshima and Nagasaki are to provide testimony in the hope this will prevent anyone else suffering their fate. Both cities have successfully reinvented themselves under a banner of peace.

On the way to the exit is a display of messages left by visiting dignitaries over the years, including Pope John Paul II, from his visit on February 25th 1981, who wrote:

God's hope is "one of peace, not one of pain."

The relevance of this comment here, at Hiroshima, is beyond my theological comprehension, and I can only assume something was lost in translation.

Model of Hiroshima illustrating the hypocentre

In pride of place, within its own glass case is a handwritten note alongside one of two paper cranes folded personally by then President of the United States, Barack Obama, on his visit of 27th May 2016:

"We have known the agony of war. Let us now find the courage, together, to spread peace, and pursue a world without nuclear weapons."[7]

A book is available for the public to leave comments. Accompanying text informs visitors that each completed book contains some 600–700 entries, and over 1,000 books have already been filled. I couldn't bring myself to look through any of the previous comments in case someone had written 'Never Again!', given what happened at Nagasaki three days later. There is also a red ink seal, should you wish to print something commemorative for a souvenir, although there appears nothing provided to print on.

The ground floor corner café has a glass wall that looks out onto the plaza towards the cenotaph. It can be accessed through both the interior of the museum and the plaza itself, which gives the impression of it being an annex operating independently, while still being part of the museum building. It seats approximately forty people in a cleanly designed interior, providing drinks and plated food from a counter service. What is unusual is that it combines catering with a gift counter. I have absolutely no idea what compels women (and it is women) to buy a makeup brush in the cafeteria of a museum dedicated to the world's first atomic bombing. The items available appear generic, with no discernable connection with Hiroshima, but over a coffee the stand does attract considerable female attention.

The Hiroshima Peace Memorial Museum provides an informative and thought provoking exhibition, dedicated to the single most horrendous moment in our recorded history. The platitudes written by VIPs, who presumably saw the same exhibition as I, are merely that. Depressed, I need a cigarette.

En route to the designated smoking stand, round the back by the bins, I pass the 'Peace Watch', set behind the museum glass and visible to all passing by. It has two digital counters; one records 'Number of Days since the First Dropping of the A-Bomb' (26159), the other 'Number of Days since the Latest Nuclear Test' (192).

At some point, presumably before the year is out, that counter will be reset to zero. At some point in our collective future the counter above may become irrelevant, because we didn't learn from what happened here. I hope I'm not around to see it. For once a cigarette might help.

---

7) As President, Obama reduced the American nuclear arsenal by 5%, yet, as reported in the *Washington Times*, December 2016, "President Obama already has committed to spending as much as $20 billion a year to update the nation's ability to conduct a nuclear war."

Given some of the other comments left by dignitaries I'm relieved no British Prime Minister, former or incumbent, has visited Hiroshima to write anything.

EXIT THE PARK AT THE SOUTHERN END AND CROSS THE MAIN ROAD of Heiwa Odori, dreadfully and unnecessarily referred to as 'Peace Boulevard'. Here stands a work by the French artist Carla Halter and architect Jean-Michel Wilmotte, who created the sixtieth anniversary memorial known as the 'Gates of Peace' established in 2005. The structure consists of ten 9m high gates running parallel for 75m to the museum across the street. The steel framed gates covered with tempered glass are inscribed with the word 'peace' translated into forty-nine different languages, which are illuminated at night. The structure was donated to Hiroshima under the auspices of the French government.

The drawback, or advantage depending on your personal taste, is that the museum cannot be viewed through the gates, as the southern side is fenced in by a hospital. While the installation is impressive as a solo piece, it doesn't reflect the aesthetics of the museum across the street. In truth I wouldn't have noticed the gates had I not slipped round the back for a smoke.

The small museum gift shop is set into the rear of the museum, across the hall from the cafeteria, again feeling rather like an annex. It sells books mostly, although there are about a dozen displayed t-shirts in various designs, predominantly reflecting the peace message. There's no neckties or souvenir cookware. I content myself with a metal lapel pin of the Genbaku Dome, to add to my memorial pin collection, and a couple of packets of souvenir postcards; one pack of five paintings of scenes within the park, including the lit lanterns floating on the river for the 6th August anniversary. They're so nice I decide to buy another pack for their intended purpose. Sending postcards — it's what tourists do. The gift shop conveniently sells stamps, and there's even an adjacent postbox.

Returning to the plaza, the saddle cenotaph, technically a hyperbolic parabola, sits before a large rectangular rill, framed by low box shrubbery, bordered with parallel pedestrian paths and screened with immaculately manicured bushes. At the end of the rill the eternal flame is set in a modernist granite holder, seemingly depicting upturned cupped hands. Turning east, towards the banks of the Motoyasu River is the Memorial Hall for the Atomic Bomb Victims. This was not here thirty years ago, and it is an intriguing structure. From ground level a circular ribbed wall frames a letterbox view of the fountain behind. The centerpiece is a glass clock face. It is tilted towards the viewer, like a sliced pie, corresponding to the time of 8:15 a.m. when the bomb dropped. The circular tabletop black fountain on which it sits is fringed by rubble excavated during the memorial's construction. Counterclockwise steps lead down into the hall and admission is free.

Internally the ramp spirals down, also counterclockwise, the idea being that the visitor is going back in time, and leads into a circular 'Hall of Remembrance' divided into twelve segments with a stool at the base of each pier. The back wall is a tinted 360° panoramic photograph of the ruined city.

Souvenir key rings, Hiroshima.

The chamber is lit by the central skylight, the 8:15 clock face seen outside. Set in the floor directly below the skylight is a water feature, which also mirrors the 8:15 theme.

I sit on a stool, not so much for quiet contemplation of the dead, for which the hall was intended, rather in awe at the concept, design, and execution of the structure itself. Although designed around a specific time on a clock face, the interior feels timeless. It is the most stunning piece of interior memorial architecture I have ever experienced and, better still, I have its serenity all to myself for priceless minutes before passing that pleasure onto someone else.

There is a hi-tech archive in the basement, where visitors can search for an individual by name, and public readings of personal testimony are also held here in seminar rooms on the first floor, adjacent to a state of the art library.

On my way out I ask who designed the Memorial Hall. The receptionist informs me it was Kenzō Tange, who also designed the original museum. It must have been his final project, because Tange retired in 2002, when this memorial was established, and passed away in 2005 aged ninety-one.

The shadows are starting to lengthen, sunlight glowing on the faces of the posse of Japanese 'huggers' congregated on the Motoyasu-bashi Bridge. They hold placards announcing 'Free Hugs', and I can't resist asking one of the ladies with a twinkle in her eye if she wants one. Egged on by her friends we have an overblown hug much to everyone's amusement. Peace Park lives up to its name.

The Rest House lies just south of the Motoyasu-bashi Bridge, and retains

Diorama, Hiroshima Peace Memorial Museum.

the art deco finishing of its original 1929 construction as the Taishoya kimono shop, before it was converted into a fuel distribution station during the shortages of 1944. When Little Boy exploded, the thirty-six people inside all died, just a lone man in the basement survived. Today the first and second floor are used as offices, the ground floor as a tourist information center and souvenir shop, and, as the name Rest House suggests, you can just go inside to take the weight off your feet in the chairs provided.

I peruse the souvenirs on offer, which appear to be glittery baubles with a proliferation of colourful Bomb Dome key rings (made in China) and crane earrings (made in Hiroshima). But they have two lapel pins (both made in China) for my expanding collection. One is of the Bomb Dome with a blue crane in the foreground, and is nice enough, but the other is solid dark tourism kitsch gold. It has the Bomb Dome, with the blue crane in the background, but it's the added foreground figure of Hello Kitty that wows me: a global marketing juggernaut, worth some $7 billion a year, twinned with Hiroshima's legacy of peace. The lady at the register tells me the Hello Kitty pin is more expensive (¥540) than the other (¥380). I reciprocate her concern by pretending to wrestle with the dichotomy before handing over my money for both. Seriously, I would have happily paid double for Hello Kitty alone. It was the last one.

With my trophy safely bagged, and childishly thrilled, I make for the hypocentre memorial itself. It resides outside the park to the east, some 260 metres from the T center of the Aioi Bridge, the actual target for the bomb. Amazingly the bridge survived the explosion and, once repaired, operated until 1983 when it was replaced by a replica.

The hypocentre memorial stands, without fuss, by the wall of the Shima Surgical Clinic, a very simple plinth, less than two metres high with a mounted plaque showing an image of the destruction with perfunctory information: that the bomb was carried from Tinian Island by the B-29 'Enola Gay' and exploded some 600 metres above this point, that the city below was exposed to temperatures between 3,000–4,000°C, and that most were killed instantly by the blast. The death toll from the initial blast was set at 70,000, with a further 70,000 killed as a result of exposure to the radioactive fallout. Someone has left fresh flowers.

Back at the Dome, Yamaguchi-san is instructing three tourists how to fold paper cranes. They sit in his al fresco classroom, the ladies on the tiny folding stools provided, as he encourages them with their origami. He is what can only be described as a character, resplendent in full professional cycle wear, topped with a 'Le Jeune' cap, and it's not for show; he cycles 30km from his home in the suburbs to the Dome daily, and he looks well on it, although he must be in his mid-seventies because he was a survivor of the bomb. Placed on the kerb around Yamaguchi-san are multiple copies of a testimony entitled *That Day* by Mito Kosei in various languages. Tourists sit and read the book in this impromptu library on the banks of the river. It's twenty-five pages, complete with photographs, illustrations, and maps. No one appears to give up halfway through.

The blue sky of this morning has turned flat grey, and the lights downtown are beginning to sharpen behind the A-Bomb Dome. It will be lit tonight, and because my hotel is so close I can return later to take photographs. Right now I'm worn out. It's been a long day, but then I swear — I forgot to check the doors on the toilet stalls in the museum! My watch betrays me, because there's still time, although the museum feels miles away. However in the spirit of fair play and pedantic curiosity, I have to return, back across the bridge, now devoid of huggers although I could really use one.

It's past last admissions, so I slip in through the café door from the plaza and access the museum from there. The bathroom is superbly appointed, tank-like urinals set on the floor in gleaming white ceramic, befitting anyone in a 'Gundam' robot suit. The stalls, and in this particular bathroom there are three, have full-length doors and dividing walls, and for the record, the toilets are western style.[8]

---

8) I like to think the rollout of western toilets across much of Japan's tourist infrastructure over the past thirty years is their nod to globalization. It's a relief, because without putting too fine a point on it, I can't squat on my haunches like I used to, never knew which way to face, or indeed what to do with my trousers. So I used to visit specific establishments sympathetic to my needs; they're known as 'McDonald's'. Ironic really, because the western style toilets in Japan now all come with illustrated instructions, encouraging people not to climb onto the seat to squat, while the Japanese model remains shrouded in mystery.

This, then, is the enduring legacy of a last minute trip to the bathroom at the 9/11 Museum in September: visiting the toilets at dark sites. Yet to be fair to that institution, I'm compelled to consider the conveniences of others.

I exit through the café onto the deserted plaza and suddenly notice there's a queue at the cenotaph, which has seemingly appeared from nowhere. There's nothing specific relating to today's date, and although during the day there's been ones and twos standing before the arch, hands together in prayer, bowing their heads, now there must be at least twenty to thirty people. It's not a tour group, rather a cross section of Japanese society, young and old, parents holding their children by the hand as they patiently, silently, wait their turn. I stand and watch, humbled, my cynicism dispelled by the evidence of my own eyes. It will be 72 years in August, and they're still coming on a nondescript evening in March, bringing children too young to even understand war and its consequences.

There's a train of thought that memorials are the first step to forgetting. Hiroshima, it seems, begs to differ. And here I am, taking photographs of the queue as if to prove it. I do the only decent thing, put my camera away, and join the end of the line.

WHEN IS A DARK TOURISM SITE NOT A DARK TOURISM SITE? When it is Ōkunoshima Island. This is the most incredible piece of 'dark' camouflage that pulls in an estimated 100,000 visitors annually, and on reflection is something only Japan could have carried off with such aplomb. Take the Shinkansen from Hiroshima station to Mihara, twenty-eight minutes, and change onto a local train bound for Hiro, to enjoy a picturesque coastal route along the Inland Sea of Japan. After twenty-one minutes alight at Tadanoumi. The chances are you will not be alone.

From Tadanoumi station just follow the crowd for a ten-minute walk along the street to your right, towards Tadanoumi port. At the terminal there's an automated ticket machine for the ferry, which is not covered by the Japan rail pass. The crossing will take twelve minutes. Here you'll have the chance to pick up some food — for the rabbits you are going to see. There's a variety of mixes to choose from, presumably providing an exciting range of flavours, such as carrot and cabbage. To be honest I didn't buy any, because the two German girls in front looked as though they were buying enough to feed the entire island population.

On the ferry it's announced that we are off to see the rabbits — and that there is also the remnants of a chemical weapons facility on the island.

"Yay!"

"Yay!"

That wasn't an echo, rather someone else at the back of the boat, although it was unclear whether they were mirroring my own dark anticipation, or if it was merely sarcasm.

Rabbits are now synonymous with Okunoshima Island. In WWII the island was home to a chemical weapons factory.

The hoppity residents are waiting to greet us at the dock. There are rabbits everywhere, so it is necessary to mind where you are putting your feet, so you don't step on Bunny, or in what Bunny deposits. They have no natural predators on the island, where dogs and cats are prohibited, as are other unwanted pet rabbits, so this population is self-sustaining and effectively quarantined. There is a visitor center complete with interactivity for the kids, and me, when no one else is looking. The island even boasts a hotel, served by a shuttle bus from the dock, although it is only a fifteen-minute walk, inevitably extended as you are waylaid by feeding rabbits, taking photographs of rabbits, or just stopping to watch rabbits as they mob tourists.

A girl is employed to trundle a trolley case of water to refresh the bowls stationed around the four kilometre perimeter of the island, so they have clean water to drink. If you're here for the rabbits then you'll have a fantastic time, and although I wasn't, they are still a very amusing distraction, and the embodiment of 'kawaii', the Japanese definition of cute.

The small single storey brick-built poison gas museum is on the way to the hotel. Established in 1988[9] by the local government, with exhibits donated

9) The fact that Japan had manufactured and deployed chemical weapons was kept secret from the Japanese public until 1984.

Interior of the Peace Memorial Hall, Hiroshima.

by the families of those who worked there and suffered the after-effects as a consequence, the museum's stated intent is to "alert as many people as possible to the dreadful truths about poison gas".

It is open from 9 a.m. to 5 p.m., closed on Tuesdays, and admission costs ¥100. No photography is permitted inside the museum, which is a single room, approximately twenty five feet by fifteen. Glass cases of exhibits line two and a half sides. Ceramic containers used for storing liquefied gas complete the display. There are section titles in English, but the individual artefacts are only described in Japanese, so the personal connections and stories they tell were admittedly lost to me. There is however an A4 leaflet in English that details the categories of gas manufactured, and their effects.

Workers suffered from respiratory conditions and horrendous blisters on their skin. Those that suffered after-effects from production of Iprit gas (mustard gas), were transferred to the Lachrymatory department to manufacture tear gas, where numerous eye injuries occurred.

In 1929, the Japanese government constructed the chemical weapons facility on the island in secret, selected because it was hidden from the mainland and isolated from the population in case of an accident. Ōkunoshima was then officially removed from the map. Although the use of such weapons was banned, bizarrely their manufacture and storage was not. Japan's chemical weapon capability was subsequently deployed in China between 1937 and 1945, and the mustard gas was responsible for reportedly over 80,000 casualties and over 6,000 deaths of civilian and military personnel.

When the US occupied Japan after the surrender, they helped to dismantle the facility. Surprisingly no charges were pressed, although the Japanese who had worked at the facility were fearful of such repercussions. There are several ruins dotted around the island, chambers for storage, an air raid shelter, and former laboratory buildings, fenced off to prohibit entry, unless you have long ears, a twitchy nose, and the propensity to burrow.

In truth, although there is a hotel with public restaurant, this is essentially a day trip.

However what is of considerable interest is the juxtaposition of dark tourism and cute tourism. If the introduction of a chemical weapons factory effectively removed Ōkunoshima Island from the map, the rabbits, starring in online video clips, have stamped it back on with interest. There is a popular myth that the current population are descended from those let loose from the laboratories after the facility capitulated at the end of the war. However, the reality, according to a former director of the museum, is that the rabbits were released onto the island when it became part of the Inland Sea National Park initiative by an elementary school.

The rabbits have not been used to airbrush the island's history. There is no indication that they were deliberately introduced in order to provide a distraction, or a tourist attraction in their own right, although with 100,000 visitors every year they most certainly have. While certain sites wrestle with their unintended dark histories, Ōkunoshima, through its good fortune of having an environment conducive to rabbits, appears to have found the perfect solution. People genuinely look forward to visiting the island, albeit for the feel-good factor of the rabbits, rather than the gas museum's warning from history. I sympathized with the museum, which I had to myself, where a genuine attempt at contrition and education has been overshadowed by the happiness the rabbits spread.

Ōkunoshima made me think of the wildlife at other dark sites. Hiroshima and Nagasaki do not want people feeding the pigeons, and both have signs to this effect. Birds inhabited both the courtyard garden at Tuol Sleng and the fields of Choeung Ek, while Chernobyl is famous for the wildlife that has thrived in our absence, despite the radioactive environment we've left behind, and although it's an urban myth that neither bird nor beast ventures anywhere near Auschwitz-Birkenau, I've seen photographs of deer and bird tracks in the snow at the memorial.

Would the former concentration camps really want tourists to see a rabbit colony behind the barbed wire, either because of the physical damage they would inflict on a memorial, or the psychologically uplifting impact they unintentionally provide, as they have at Ōkunoshima? It begs the question; do dark sites implement pest control? Enquiries would likely receive no response, but it would provide respite from obsessing about the length of toilet stall doors.

'YELLOW-SAN'

IT WOULD HAVE BEEN EXPEDIENT IF WRITING A BOOK ON DARK TOURISM had led me down a progressively darker path, with the Japanese suicide forest of Aokigahara waiting, inevitably, and appropriately, at the end. Instead it was the other way round. Discovery of the forest and dark tourism led to writing the book, and the realisation that somewhere within its unwritten pages my moral compass may have lost its bearings.

Japan had been off my travel radar for thirty years. Things would have changed over time, although one thing was certain; any changes would be gift-wrapped beautifully. The fallout from the tsunami at Fukushima was a possibility now guided tours were being offered, but the Chernobyl weekender was fresh in the memory, so there was a need for something different.

Aokigahara[1] fitted that criteria: a legendary, mysterious forest where the troubled and tormented went to end their lives. Nestled at the base of Mt. Fuji, in the Yamanashi prefecture, the 'Sea of Trees', the *Jukai*, had been standing for centuries, sentinelling its dead, cultivating mythology, seemingly unknown to the outside world. The lure to enter was overwhelming, and at this point the alarm bells should have rung. Why would anyone travel to Japan in order to poke through the undergrowth of a supposedly haunted forest, synonymous with suicides and the litter of broken lives? As Friedrich Nietzsche noted:

"And if you gaze long enough into an abyss, the abyss will gaze back into you."

But the thought never occurred. I was purely focusing on when might be the optimum time to go.

Research indicated that March, the end of the Japanese financial year, was when many people, reportedly including CEOs, wandered one way through the treeline. The Japanese had adopted a pragmatic attitude towards suicide, which stemmed from their samurai culture. They saw the practice as a noble and honourable end, without the stigma attached to it in the west, where it was simplistically associated with cowardice. Such enlightenment regarding the taking of one's own life meant the Japanese had published research into which days of the week were statistically the most popular for those seeking permanent closure.

Unsurprisingly Monday was the most prevalent day of the week for suicide

---

1) It is pronounced 'Ow- (as in 'cow') -key–ga-hara', and literally translated it means 'Blue Tree Centre'. Blue, not green: bizarrely the Japanese did not have a word for green until the Heian period (794–1185 A.D.) when 'midori' was introduced into the lexicon.

in Japan, indicating that perhaps our respective cultures weren't so very different after all. The second most popular day was Sunday, third Tuesday. Therefore the three most likely days for suicide in Japan fell consecutively, at the start of the week. Now it was just a case of working out which Sunday, Monday, and Tuesday in March.

This was down to instinctive guesswork and involved the lunar cycle. Whenever I had trouble sleeping I'd invariably find myself staring at a full moon, so wondered if there was any correlation between lunar cycles and suicide. It transpired that people with suicidal tendencies were considered more vulnerable under a new moon, according to a study of 1,400 suicides carried out by the Finnish National Public Health Institute, reported by BBC online in July 2000.

The study suggested the new moons in the autumn and winter had more influence than those in the spring, where conversely a full moon had more impact. However spring tended to be a peak for suicides in Finland anyway, due to the increased levels of daylight in combination with the cold, which apparently confused the body clock into believing it was still winter. Why this should be a tipping point for Finnish suicides, the BBC article did not explain. Personally I felt full moons were just as likely to turn you into a werewolf, or a bear with a sore head through insomnia. The latter certainly applied in my case.

The idea of a lunar cycle having a bearing on when someone might chose to take their life seemed a bit thin, and the Centre for Suicide Research at the University of Oxford informed me that "in high quality studies from around the world there is no evidence for a link between any moon phase and suicide rates." Yet the Finns had at least conducted a study. Of course, transposing a study conducted in Finland onto the Japanese population wasn't scientific in any way, but I wanted to believe in something.

There were four Mondays in March. I needed to pick one. A full moon would rise over Japan on Tuesday 11th April 2017. That felt too late. However a new moon would rise over Japan on Tuesday 28th March. It was a guess, nothing more, but I wondered if there could at least be the possibility of some activity at Aokigahara on Sunday 26th March and Monday 27th March 2017, the eve of the new moon.

Naturally if I'd been able to 'calculate' a likely set of dates, so could anyone else with an interest in the suicides associated with the forest. One of the snippets gleaned from online research suggested that the *Yakuza*, Japan's notorious gangsters, would send subordinates into the forest to retrieve any valuables from the corpses. Had this been a story circulated about a suicide forest in the UK, I would have immediately dismissed it as spin, nothing more than a clumsy attempt to keep inquisitive ghouls at bay, or crude, lowest common denominator click-bait. But this was Japan. They had pet cafés with cats, rabbits and owls, and zoo bars where the hostesses dressed as animals. It was an utterly bonkers country where even the vending machines worked, so anything was possible. As a westerner I was not prepared to take anything for granted.

The idea of wandering into the depths of a forest famed for suicides, voluntarily contributing myself and my valuables to a corpse stripper in the pay of the *Yakuza*, was downright stupid. As was getting lost. Wandering alone off the trail would place a lone tourist within an environment that looked the same in every direction. There were reports that the minerals in the undulating lava field the forest grew upon affected instrumentation, although there were counter-reports that everything worked fine. Placing faith in technology, even a compass, is great, until it fails amongst the trees, with the light failing, when those reports that everything works aren't much use at all. Who would you blame other than yourself?

Sounds were reportedly muffled, the light poor, disorientation likely, the lava knolls underfoot treacherous, with holes, crevices, and exposed roots to trap and turn an ankle. There was reportedly no cell phone reception within its depths, and even if there were, who would you call for help, and how could they practically assist? You've fallen over, immobilised, no idea where you are, totally surrounded by anonymous forest, and can't speak the language of the emergency services.

Then there was the prospect of meeting someone else inside, with no indication as to their motives for being there, as they in turn would have no idea of yours. Were they a person on the edge, or were you? Even without the likely language barrier, communication would be fraught.

Many entering the forest laid a tape trail as if navigating a labyrinth, so they could retrace their steps if they subsequently decided life was worth living, in the same manner as divers lay a line when penetrating a wreck. Clearly getting lost was a distinct possibility, so this was a sensible precaution. However thinking outside the box it also carried a potential risk. Hopefully no one would decide to follow your quivering lifeline, bringing them right up behind you, or alternatively sever your umbilical at its source for a practical joke.

Whilst this train of thought seemed paranoid and melodramatic, the notoriety of the location compelled me to give personal safety rational consideration. Aokigahara was a black site. People went there to take their lives in order to abandon their responsibility to themselves and to those who loved them. Would you really want to get in their way, given their precarious state of mind? While the annual body count was no longer made public, suicides continued, and the last set of figures released from 2003 indicated that there had been, on average, two suicides every week.

Choosing to explore the forest might be ghoulish, but that wasn't an excuse to abdicate personal responsibility. Someone might see you, a solitary figure, walking off the trail, naturally assume the worst, and call the police, like the last time I'd been caught 'just looking' over a black site in County Durham, and although I couldn't understand Geordie then, and couldn't understand

Japanese now, I'd learned my lesson. I wouldn't be venturing off the path on my own, inviting concern.

Never mind. This was next year's holiday itinerary, so there was plenty of time to find a reputable guide to explore with. There was just one thing left to do before turning in for the night. The term encountered during the surf of Aokigahara: 'Dark Tourism'. What was that, exactly?

I entered a new search enquiry, and my years of travelling to dark destinations began to unravel.

Talk about not being able to see the wood for the trees.

A TRIP TO AOKIGAHARA IS, IN ITSELF, NOT GHOULISH. THE AREA is renowned for its natural beauty, presenting stunning views of Fuji-san,[2] Japan's iconic natural landmark, the Fuji Five Lakes, and is categorized as a UNESCO World Heritage site. The evergreen forest presents a dramatic panorama, hence its Sea of Trees moniker. Walking tours are available, including exploration of a Wind Cave and Ice Cave. There's a hiking trail through the forest, close to the northern perimeter, between parking lots and a tourist centre, where it is possible to view the *Jukai* from within, where lush moss and exposed roots create a Tolkienesque landscape. This trail is available on Google Street View, allowing a virtual desktop 'walk thru', during which you can see the signed rope barriers, prohibiting further progress.

The controversy surrounding exploration begins once you step off the path to the south, crossing over the rope barriers. During my online research I discovered a basic, uncredited map, where the shaded area south of the car park was marked 'Dead Bodies (Hopefully)'. The use of the word 'hopefully' provided focus. Exactly why was I going, and what did I really expect to see and do once I got there? I'd seen the photographs and videos online. The images were sad and unpleasant. If I encountered the body of a poor individual who had taken their own life, what would I learn? In truth I was more interested in the personal minutiae the suicides left behind. The forest was in essence, an evolving memorial, where, in conjunction with the trinkets and floral tributes offered in memory of the bereaved, the dead themselves would leave their last significant traces behind in an impromptu display.

The 'why' I would go to Aokigahara could now be conveniently discounted. I had the justification, admittedly tenuous, of needing a black site for this book. There seemed little point in taking a Ripper Walk at the lighter end of the dark tourism spectrum, only to baulk when exploration of the phenomena led to the darkest band at the end. In truth if I needed a black site, a suicide spot, it would only be a few hours drive to the south coast of England, to the UK's own notorious jumping off point at Beachy Head. However it was unlikely that any of the souls casting themselves onto the rocks below would

2) The suffix 'san' is used as an honorific term in Japan.

Barrier rope, Aokigahara.

build a camp on the headland while contemplating their decision, or that any of their last items would be left undisturbed on display. They would jump, leaving no tangible evidence for anyone walking above that they had done so. Once the body had been recovered the only trace left would be on paper in the coroner's report, or perhaps a floral tribute from someone who cared.

Yet Aokigahara is unique, even within black sites, due to its woodland setting. All the other global suicide sites of note offer self-defenestration, a jump from height.

However I chose to spin the trip, once I stepped over the barrier ropes bearing the 'No Entry' sign into the forest I was looking for a corpse, or the detritus one had left behind, or for others, like myself, who were also searching. There would likely be ribbons of tape, winding through the trees, which, for the most part appears to be what the DIY corpse hunters actually find. Some clearly got a buzz out of this. There are numerous amateur video explorations of Aokigahara uploaded on YouTube, some with an introductory piece to camera, taking pains to claim they're going not seeking sensationalism, but merely in order to 'document', only for the mask to slip the moment something is found. Far more interesting were those who had honestly considered their reasons for entry in the first place, and had subsequently discovered in light of their finds, a degree of retrospection, or a pang of guilt for having entered. As one German explorer on YouTube eloquently subtitles:

"This is not just an overstepping of legal borders but we pass a line so we enter the privacy of the people who decided to kill themselves."

Indeed this particular video, made by Christian Driese, Niko Olsen, David Nolte, and Malte Hesse, *Aokigahara — Inside The Suicide Forest*, published in September 2016, is by far and away the most credible, because they have thought about what they are doing there, and what the place represents for those who chose not to leave. As one of the quartet saliently asks:

"But does one really need to see this with your own eyes?"

That is indeed a question. For me, it was *the* question. The answer was that I did, if only to see what happened when I was within the trees, and to discover what I felt as a result, even if that might admittedly be self-revulsion.

As Friedrich Nietzsche also noted, "The doer alone learneth."

Yet my biggest concern remained another idiom, one that might yet reveal truer, darker intentions for crossing the line in Aokigahara.

"Be careful what you wish for. You might just get it."

THE SEA OF TREES CULTIVATED ITSELF ON THE LAVA FIELD IN THE aftermath of the eruption of Mt. Fuji in 864 A.D. The forest now covers approximately twelve square miles. Folklore suggests that in times of famine, families carried the elderly and infirm deep into its bowels to abandon them there, lost and left to starve, giving the collective one less mouth to feed, a practice known as *'obasute'*. Mythology associates the forest with ghosts, possession, insanity, and the belief that the disturbed spirits or *'yūrei'* created as a result of a traumatic end such as suicide, roam the woods, committed to prevent anyone who enters from ever leaving. It is reported that since 1950 some 500 people have taken their own lives within, with many more attempts. In 1998 there were seventy-three known suicides, rising to 105 in 2003, after which figures were no longer released in an attempt to stem the tide.

I discovered Aokigahara's suicide forest through the Vice documentary. Uploaded on YouTube in 2012, it has been viewed over sixteen million times. The film followed geologist Azusa Hayano, bespectacled with a soothing voice, who estimated that he'd discovered over 100 suicides during his fieldwork over the past twenty years. The video is unsettling, with stills of the victims in situ in the forest, their faces pixelated.

Mr Hayano leads the camera to an abandoned car, leaf litter trapped by the windscreen wipers, the inevitable conclusion being that the driver walked into the forest, never to return. A discarded road map on the passenger seat suggests they came from a distance in order to do so. Some troubled souls travel to Aokigahara yet never find the specific forest, and take their lives in adjacent woodlands. Locals, Mr Hayano informs us, were raised believing the forest was a scary place, and didn't enter. He theorises that people today are taking their lives in part due to their detachment from reality, with the reliance of interacting through screens, rather than face-to-face.

There are signs posted at the head of the trails. Translated they say 'your life is a precious gift from your parents — please think about them, your siblings and children — don't keep your troubles to yourself — talk about them' — then the contact details for the suicide prevention association.

As Mr Hayano leads the camera through the undergrowth, he finds streams of barrier tape, which he suggests if followed to their conclusion invariably lead to evidence that someone was there, or in extreme cases a body. He discovers a doll, inverted and nailed into a tree, which he suggests showed anger towards society by whoever hammered it there. The image is a powerful one, and was later referenced in a comic *Tales From the Suicide Forest*. Looking up into the branches, there are the remnants of a noose. The majority take their lives by hanging, or use pills.

There is a surreal encounter with a man in a tent. Mr Hayano tactfully abandons the cameraman and goes to speak to the hidden occupant. The interaction is typically Japanese, very polite and apologetic, and we are left with the hope that, as a result of this meeting, the camper will pack up and go home.

There's the detritus of lives; he finds a woman's compact and umbrella, some flowers and confectionery, presumably left by the bereaved, and finally a skeleton, still clothed, which Mr Hayano estimates has lain there for a couple of years. He is clearly empathetic for the loss, but says he does not think quietus in the forest is a heroic way to end one's life.

THE YAMANASHI AUTHORITIES HAVE RESPONDED TO THE increasing number of suicides in their forest by installing CCTV at the main entrances and staging patrols. Vigilant local shopkeepers also assist with subtle preventative measures, speaking to lone travellers whom they feel are potentially at risk in the belief that just a friendly conversation can deter an ultimate action. The forest is reportedly swept in preparation for the holiday season by the emergency services, and any bodies are removed. Japanese tradition stipulates that the corpse is taken to a room where a volunteer, selected through a *jan-ken* game (rock, paper, scissors), will spend the night with the deceased to placate the spirit and prevent it from becoming a *yūrei*. Those deceased individuals who remain unidentified are interred in the local cemetery.

Aokigahara's contemporary surge in popularity as a suitable final stage may be due to the 1960 novel by Seicho Matsumoto, *Nami no Tou*, or 'Tower of Wave', where two doomed lovers take their lives among the trees. Matsumoto didn't imply that any of his suicidal readers should choose Aokigahara as the location for their own end, however Wataru Tsurami did. His nonfiction book, *The Complete Manual of Suicide*, was published in 1993. Tsurami not only detailed the relevant pros and cons of the various methods of suicide, hanging, jumping, overdose etc., but cited the *Jukai* as the perfect setting, somewhere those who chose to commit suicide would be left in peace to do so, and not be found. Tsurami's book has sold over one million copies in Japan, although some prefectures prohibited its sale to minors.

The Complete Manual of Suicide has not been published in English, although there's a rudimentary translation of the foreword online, in which Tsurami describes life as ordinary and pre-ordained, nothing more than a meat grinder. Education will be at a local school, there might be the possibility of further education, culminating in a few years of partying before starting work, marriage and a child, climbing the corporate ladder, until retirement, hobbies, and death. The translation continues:

"And depressingly, this is the ideal life in many people's minds. If this is the case, living an ordinary life is meaningless."

Tsurami portrays committing suicide as a positive act, and tells the tale of a friend who wears a phial of angel dust around their neck, their theory being that if the urge to end it all strikes, they can take the drug then blissfully jump into oblivion in the belief that they can fly. In conclusion, Tsurami trusts the reader will consider his manual as their very own phial of angel dust.

The foreword is as nihilistic and depressing as I found it worryingly seductive, because although Tsurami's reasoning comes across as condescending towards an ordinary life, if one is searching in vain for something more, then it does not seem illogical. On the contrary, he makes a rational case without ever delving into the multifarious reasons that lead people to commit suicide.

It is likely that the National Health Service here in the UK will spend significant money on me as I enter my natural end-of-life phase, be it days, weeks, months, or even years. I will be a drain on its resources, and I know this because the media runs crisis stories about the lack of funding in the NHS on an almost daily basis. Surely the selfless thing to do would be to end it, before I too add to the burden on the already cash-strapped service, thus leaving more funding available to those who need to live for the sake of their dependents, of which I have none. Whilst I continue to earn, pay tax and consume, I contribute to society, but all too soon I will physically deteriorate, my ability to work will diminish, my disposable income will wane, age and frailty will isolate me from society, which will in turn have to pay for my uneconomical and counterproductive keep.

The drift into what is portrayed as a metaphorical 'sunset' is simply life taking its natural course, and the reality of ordinary lives within the system is what Tsurami has had the courage to address.

However his work needs to be taken in context, so whatever you might now be thinking about the ultimate meaningless of life pause and consider the following: at the time of writing Wataru Tsurami has not killed himself. Indeed he followed up his bestseller with a second book, *Our Opinion About the Complete Manual of Suicide*, which contained both fan and hate mail regarding his original work, in addition to highlighting the reasons why people committed suicide, simultaneously placating the controversy and illustrating that he cared enough about his work and reputation in order to do so. Arguably he was rehashing his first idea for a second, easier book, but I'll do likewise given the chance.

Writers famously suffer from self-loathing, which might go some way to explaining Tsurami's nihilistic slant, if not mine, but there was also a clue to his mood in the foreword, where he referenced *The Wall* by Pink Floyd, released in 1979. For those younger readers this is a seminal piece of existentialist 'rock opera'. It's interesting that Tsurami set the tone of *The Complete Manual of Suicide* to *The Wall*, as to paraphrase him:

"And depressingly, Pink Floyd's *The Wall* is the ideal dark album to reference in many author's minds. If this is the case their work requires re-evaluation."

Tsurami should have referenced Joy Division's *Closer* if he wanted a truly dark album...

H OW DO YOU DEFEND THE INDEFENSIBLE? BECAUSE WALKING into a suicide forest on the grounds of voyeurism is surely that. Dark tourism might discount their practices by providing education, whereas I would discount mine by writing a book, but the *Jukai* is a black site and has not been packaged in any way for the dark tourism industry. Indeed the Yamanashi Tourist Organization are engaged in actively trying to counter the association between the forest and its notorious tag, while still bringing tourism to the area which depends upon it. Before heading to Japan I contacted the Yamanashi Tourist Organization to enquire if I could organise a guide through them, specifically for the purpose of writing about Aokigahara's dark association. They considered my request "deeply" and politely declined, stating:

"Yamanashi Prefecture is now working on countermeasures for the prevention of suicide, and we do not support any kind of data collection that links Aokigahara with suicide."

That was completely understandable, and I thanked them for their courtesy, consideration, and honesty. Unfortunately after two Hollywood movies based on Aokigahara released in 2016, *The Forest* and *The Sea of Trees*, and the plethora of DIY documentary films on YouTube, the Yamanashi authorities face an unenviable task. People are still entering the forest every year to die, and dark tourism is on the increase, including those individuals looking for something different from the pre-packaged experiences on offer, or, as with the vloggers, promoting themselves, their 'cool', and their daring do.

Pragmatically the only thing I was likely to find within the trees, judging from the videos posted by those who had already been, would be miles of abandoned tape, some of which could have been laid by those searching for bodies, yet who'd only discovered more tape. There appeared little to be gained from that, or from loitering round the car park looking for abandoned vehicles. Any photojournalist tagging along with an official search party would have the benefit of multiple pairs of eyes, and the experience of the recovery teams, who would have a sense of which areas were favoured by the suicidal.

Regardless of when I went, the chances were that I would find very little if anything at all. I wouldn't understand why people took their lives, nor was it likely that I would be able to gain any additional insight into why people specifically took their lives in Aokigahara, beyond what I already knew. It was mysteriously beautiful, quiet, private, and recommended.

However I was interested to see if the forest did exert any influence on one's state of mind, and if there were other dark tourists there at what is considered the optimum time for suicides. It would be illuminating to meet others in a location unequivocally black and ghoulish, where we could see the whites of each other's eyes, although I suspected that they too would be there for the purpose of 'writing a book', or, more likely, 'making a film' to upload to YouTube.

I T'S SO QUIET YOU CAN HEAR A DRIP FALL FROM THE ROOF. THERE'S something alien about the exterior ambience surrounding the cabin in the woods. It's too quiet. Snug under the futon I stretch a hand up out into the cold to push back the curtain. There's so much blinding whiteness through the window that I don't need glasses to reach my conclusion. No one is committing suicide in this.

A terribly British reaction, given half an inch of snow renders the UK immobile. There has been a good four inches since we turned in just after midnight. Adam's wife Haruka had said snow was forecast for the Aokigahara region before we left Tokyo around 7 p.m., and Japan appears to be as precise with its weather forecasts as with its railway timetables.

Adam, rather heroically I feel, leaves the warmth of his bunk to start the heater. Our cabin at 'Sun Lake' is not the rudimentary shed I'd anticipated, but rather a 'glamping' wooden two-tier affair that could sleep four, with a bathroom including a welcome heated toilet seat, fridge freezer, microwave, and a television set we both studiously ignore.

The highlight of our wilderness dwelling is the kotatsu, a low table with valance that conceals a heater, allowing those seated to stick their legs beneath for toasty comfort. It's the greatest Japanese invention since dependable vending machines, shinkansen, telescopic straws, and possibly even the okonomiyaki pancake. Given the chill in the air I am now going to add the heated toilet seat to that list. Adam gets the kettle on for our pot noodle breakfast that he had the presence of mind to purchase at the motorway service station late last night.

I had only met my guide the previous afternoon, at his home in Saitama, in the southeastern quadrant of Tokyo, after a month of online correspondence. He was a friend of a friend of a friend of a friend, so, ironically, I really did not know him from Adam. However, as my friend, and the first link in the chain, was someone I knew through London's Torture Garden fetish community, I knew I'd ultimately be in capable hands and had nothing to worry about, wandering into a suicide forest with someone I'd never met before.

Adam has followed his dreams since learning the martial art of *Akido* aged thirteen. He sold his possessions and came to Japan from Albuquerque, New Mexico in 2013, and married the beautiful Haruka the following year. He works in translation and linguistics, as well as being an unofficial tour guide and fixer in his spare time. He plans to open a martial arts themed bar, and has the requisite skills; as a black belt he can throw me to the floor with the little finger of his left hand, whilst keeping his right behind his back, and his home brew is so moreish I would happily drink it until I slide under a low table. He's a big fan of black metal, which he informs me originated in Norway, and makes my favourite krautrockers Rammstein sound like Philip Glass.

Once fed and thermally insulated we tramp outside to find Adam's Dinky Toy Suzuki Wagon under a thick blanket of snow, but it only takes us seconds to sweep off, and this being magical Japan, the roads are blissfully black tarmac clear, so we're soon underway, snaking around Lake Saiko, heading for civilisation, post breakfast sustenance, and gloves, which we neglected to pack. After a pit stop at a 7-Eleven we find a sportswear and hiking outfitters in a small retail park with absolutely everything to protect us from whatever the wilderness can throw at us, although we only need gloves. To be fair it doesn't feel that cold, but Adam has been here three times previously and says we're going to need them, and there's little point in seeking local knowledge only to ignore it. He shows me a photo from his trip in February where the forest floor was covered with sheet ice. Keeping his feet was a major headache.

Adam is the first person I've encountered who has been to Aokigahara. It surprised me to hear that on his previous explorations he hadn't found any evidence of the suicides; not a corpse, or the traces left by one. I suspected this might be because he hadn't strayed from the established hiking trails or used 'Blue Sky Thinking' to predict the timing of his trips, but he tells me the reality is he was drawn to the area by its natural beauty and mythology, rather than actively searching for evidence of suicides.

We arrive at the main car park by the Wind Cave, and to my satisfaction that wishful thinking regarding the timing of the trip can now be described as rational theorising. It's busy. Most of the bays are occupied, and a coachload of tourists have disembarked. True, they are silver rather than dark and are exclusively Japanese. The sprightly seniors, resplendent in all weather apparel, fan out in the car park and collectively mirror their instructor in a gentle aerobics work out, limbering up for their hike. I imagine they're looking at the pair of us in our dark clothing, cameras strung round our necks, the only westerners in sight, patently not hikers, thinking, "Shingetsu... Dāku Kanko Kyaku!...Tsk!" (New moon... Dark Tourists!... Tsk!)

We tramp inside the souvenir shop, which Adam says will be devoted to 'Fuji-san', and sure enough it is, although the iconic volcano outside is stubbornly cloaked in cloud and I haven't caught so much as a glimpse. Clearly I wasn't expecting any souvenirs related to the suicides, but wondered if there might be something reflecting the forest itself, and find one postcard of fungi growing on a fallen tree. I'll buy it on our return from walking in the woods, where I will inevitably photograph any fungi I see.

The senior citizens and their aerobics instructor have disappeared, probably to explore one of the caves, which are proving welcome distractions, drawing everyone away from the forest itself, so we are alone as we embark on the recognised trail and take in our surroundings. It is utterly beautiful, and although I've spent time online in the forest, looking at the vlogger clips and photographs, I've never seen it with added snow. Occasionally a dusting will fall from the upper branches, like cascading icing sugar, the pervading silence then punctuated by heavier salvos impacting around us. Umbrellas offer protection, allowing us to photograph both the panorama and the eye-catching details of gnarled branches and exposed roots beneath the snow-coated canopy, some thirty feet above the rocky terrain.

Three hikers approach from the opposite direction, an elderly lady with her two grandchildren. Gran informs us they are from Texas; we assure them that the tourist centre they're seeking isn't that far. The boy has been living in Japan for a year and gran says that her granddaughter now want to join him here. As we bid farewell I wonder if grandma knows why she's walking through the woods at Aokigahara, because her grandson looks a little sheepish and has recognised Adam and I for the typical hikers we patently aren't.

We come to a junction. Two trails are signposted, leaving the third invitingly anonymous. Adam hasn't explored the unknown trail previously, so we head off in that direction without a recognised destination, over virgin snow, ducking under the bowed saplings, laced with fall and hanging so low we traverse them by looping off the path. The barrier rope still takes us by surprise, although in truth it feels somewhat anticlimactic as it droops forlorn, devoid of its 'No Entry' sign.

"Shall we?"

We shall. In fairness this is just a piece of low slung rope. It doesn't actually say 'No Entry', although the intention to bar progress is evident. Rather than step over into the pristine trail ahead, we skirt round through the undergrowth and emerge back on the trail, although our twin tracks leading up to the rope are clearly visible, and anyone who makes it this way today will be able to work out where we've gone. I had not anticipated snow when picking the sequential dates just over a year ago, and it is proving fortuitous.

Not only does it provide a unique perspective, seeing the *Jukai* masquerading as Narnia, but because we can see our footprints, and anyone else's. No one has come this way since the snow fell in the early hours. Perhaps someone arrived after dark beforehand, and made their way beyond this point by torch. The car park was busy when we arrived, many of the bays filled. Yet none of the vehicles were blanketed with snow, which would be an indication that they had been parked there overnight, and, as there are no tracks ahead of us, we could be the first to find someone who came here before the snow arrived. It would have been a hike from the nearest railway station if they had made their way on foot, yet only a meaningless distance for someone who no longer cared.

I haven't said anything to Adam because there's no need. He'll already know. The snow changes everything. It tells tales. Discovering a solitary set of footprints on the wrong side of the rope barrier would have injected real urgency and purpose to our search. When we'd arrived at the cabin I'd commented that as we'd driven through the night to reach Aokigahara, others could have done likewise, but for an entirely different reason. It needed to be considered. They would stop for petrol and food at the service stations, and pay the tolls on the expressway, just as we had. In turn we would have had to follow in their footsteps if they'd crossed the rope before us, in the possibility and hope of prevention with the dread of arriving too late.

I've wrestled with the dichotomy for years. Whose life is it anyway, and who has the right to intervene, given the chance? Some years ago, the woman who lived alone next door took pills for Christmas. She lay, silently separated from me by a brick wall, until her brother became concerned. I sat at my desk the whole time, writing, even as her 'workmen' started hammering away round the back. It transpired they were the police, breaking the door down to recover her body. She'd never said a word to raise concern.

Now standing in the silence of the forest I can't shake the feeling that my choice of picking these particular dates betrays me. Are we here today because I came in the hope of finding live people, rather than dead bodies? If the new moon has an influence, then encountering the dead would be more likely if we had come here next weekend, rather than this, on the eve.

I suspected my discovery of dark tourism might have made me feel guilty about my pursuit of the dead, or perhaps the numbers of victims I'd encountered during research over the past year were starting to prey on my conscience, bringing a cumulative, mawkish weight to bear. In truth trying to predict the optimum dates for suicide in a Japanese forest is like trying to predict snowfall there, and that was completely down to chance.

It is silent beyond the rope, not only because the habitat is cloaked and muffled by snow, but because we are now solely focused searching either side of the trail, scanning the interior for any sign of human presence, both on the ground and hanging against the tree trunks. Adam finds our first piece of faded red tape, tied round a tree. We scan the inner gloom and randomness, searching for the next piece of the jigsaw, but there's only forest. We move on and make our first tangible discovery.

Cable noose, Aokigahara.

Partially covered and frozen by snow there appears a contorted snake of rope on the ground. It looks like a noose, and on closer inspection is a wire cable, half an inch in diameter, perhaps used in engineering. A few feet away something lies buried under the snow. Clothing.

Our find is a pair of men's trousers. Bland, once beige, discarded by the owner, the pockets already turned inside out by whoever found them first, searching for an identity or valuables. There's a distinct change in our mood. The wire noose looks grotesque. It's not an exhibit, labelled, sanitised, and displayed in a crime museum. It resides within its very own gallery, one with ever-changing snapshots of lives lived and ended. Without an explanatory card to go with this piece, the outcome for whosoever fashioned the coiled cable, is unknown. The location leads, depressingly, to favour only one conclusion.

We follow the trail until we reach a dark junction. There are signs either side of the path, leading into the forest. To our left a seemingly unbroken orange line of tape, and to the right a path of yellow tapes tied around the trunks, leading to the interior. We now have a choice. Adam leans towards exploring the yellow signatures to the right, theorising that we have plenty of time to retrace our steps and follow the orange route, or alternatively we can follow it tomorrow. In a timeless forest I'm conscious of my watch, although the snow provides additional illumination, and it is only 11 a.m. At some point it will get dark, or more likely the cold and hunger will eventually get the better of us.

Abandoning our cumbersome umbrellas at the side of the path, we weave our way into the interior in a zigzagging south — east — south — east

'Yellow-San' tape trail, Aokigahara forest. Photo: Adam Tuck

pattern, following the individual I christen 'Yellow-san', in keeping with the yellow-tied trail. Progress is careful, as we pick our way over the clumped lava topography, reaching out for sapling hand holds to descend into the hollows to check our slipping feet. Occasionally these slender trees with their perched roots give way, or crack in complaint. There is tape of various faded, dirty hues underfoot, partially buried by the snow, but we concentrate on searching for yellow bands tied by 'Yellow-san' around the trunks at eye level. They're consistently set at regular intervals, not haphazardly placed. I voice my confidence to Adam that we're going towards a final destination, rather than following an exit route.

"How can you tell?"

"Put yourself in a suicide's shoes. You'd loop the tape behind the trunk and tie it off in front, facing your direction of travel. You wouldn't turn to tie behind you. Every knot is facing the same way."

Adam nods in consent and moves on. I have a caveat. Just because I believe that doesn't necessarily make it so. My reasoning has already suffered a chastening experience this morning, with the arrival of a coachload of silver tourists, when I was predicting a posse with an altogether different agenda.

I've little sense of direction as to where we are in the context of the forest, and although Adam has no signal on his mobile, his GPS runs independently, and my cheap compass clipped to my belt is still working, and both are in alignment. So is our bushcraft. Moss growing on the northern face of a tree trunk is not necessarily reliable, but in Aokigahara it appears to hold true, and is plentiful and prevalent. In addition we have 'Yellow-san's' signposted route back to the trail, as well as our own footsteps in the snow. There's now a steady drip-drip thaw, but it's not going to be sufficient to melt away our tracks.

Although sounds are muffled in the forest, we are able to communicate easily, even when we don't have a direct line of sight with each another, simply by whistling to illicit a response and indicate our direction. Adam informs me that whistling is a skill the Japanese don't naturally possess.

There's a few finds as we follow 'Yellow-san's' markers; a piece of plastic sheeting partially buried under the snow, brought in to keep off the rain, and a few large water bottles buried in the snow. Raking them clear brings a small passerine into view, clearly looking to take advantage of our ground clearance once we move off. There's what was once a makeshift larder, now just a collection of empty food packaging, a last convenience store take-away for one. Under normal circumstances this would simply be ugly litter, but in this forest it's elevated to something more meaningful. This perhaps was someone's last meal. Judging by the dirty packaging it looks as if it has been here for a while.

Adam is up ahead, out of sight when he calls.

"You need to see this..."

I pick my way over the lava castle I'm traversing, wary that the snow has hidden the foothold battlements. The abandoned umbrella would have come in useful as a probe for firm ground, and we've both had moments where our boots have found crevasses. Adam is standing below me, fixed on something beneath my feet. There's a slim fallen tree running horizontally between us, approximately eighteen feet long. I'm unsure what I'm supposed to be looking for, but without giving anything away he advises me to climb down.

From the safety of the forest floor I can see the tree running parallel at eyelevel, and there, tied round the slim trunk is a noose made from half a dozen knotted neckties. Neither of us is willing to break the silence. It's one of the saddest sights I've ever seen. Unlike the cable noose we found on the ground at the edge of the trail, this one has held fast in situ, and was undoubtedly someone's exit route. If these ties once belonged to 'Yellow-san' then he saw it through.

Adam, as the linguist, does the decent thing and articulates something suitably appropriate, speaking for both of us, hoping that the individual is now at peace. There's a smattering of snow on the ties, but also moss growing from the knots, so it is difficult to estimate how long the noose has been there, unoccupied. Adam finds a red spray marking, reminiscent of a Jesus nail used in the crucifixion, on a tree to the side and surmises that it was marked by the recovery team, who subsequently physically pushed the tree over to get the body down. Unless you were prepared to carry a lightweight ladder several miles over the tricky terrain from the car park, how else would you access the ligature to lower the body to the ground? Alternatively the tree had already fallen, and provided 'Yellow-san' with his gallows.

"Who would bring half a dozen ties into the woods if he wasn't intent on ending it?"

I answer my own question; 'Yellow-san' was a company man, someone who owned at least half a dozen ties in the first place, perhaps one for every working day of the week, given to him by a female relative, or bought by his wife so their child could give daddy a gift to celebrate completion of a project, or a birthday. The ties portray a conservative character; checked designs and stripes. Nothing distinctive or quirky — nothing flash. This was a conformist who blended in with the conservative wallpaper of life. In Japanese business, where the collective takes precedence over the individual, that's hardly surprising.

This isn't like a marker in a cemetery, where 'Yellow-san' has now been laid to rest. His method and means are there before us. We're standing in his choice of final setting, seeing the trees and terrain he would have seen before his end. We don't know him, not his name, his age, or whether he even left a wife and child frantically waiting for news when he didn't return. There could have been a divorce, perhaps a custody battle, terminal illness, insurmountable debt, or dishonour from a perceived failure at work. We will never know if there was an explanatory note. All we know is he packed up his tie collection and came to Aokigahara to escape. There would have been other opportunities in his daily life: a jump from a high building, stepping off the platform in front of a train, pills, or perhaps running a rubber hose from a car exhaust. Yet something compelled him to make the effort to come here to the forest for a seemingly ritualistic, romantic end, undeterred by the efforts of the Yamanashi Prefecture to dissuade him from his action. He could have been motivated to come here out of consideration for his family; suicide in the forest guarantees he would be found by a stranger.

The noose hangs there, frozen and immobilised by the cold. I own one tie, from the gift shop at 9/11, that remains unworn. There they sell neckties to commemorate or fund, depending on your viewpoint. Here, in the depths of the *Jukai*, they use them for an entirely different purpose. Maybe it is an ironic parting; his tie collection, symbolic of the career that may have contributed to his self-destruction, strung together to fashion his exit.

We collect our thoughts and check our bearings. Adam and I only met twenty-four hours ago, but we've just shared something that neither of us is ever going to forget, so we're now inexorably linked together through this moment. Whoever 'Yellow-san' was, without intention, he's left a legacy for us. Despite the distance between London and Tokyo I hope Adam and I will be firm friends for years to come.

We decide we are not going to retrace our steps and retrieve the abandoned umbrellas now, but will pick them up tomorrow, before we follow the orange tape on the opposite side of the trail. Adam says we've now travelled west, so we need to go north in order to return to a point somewhere on the road

Necktie noose, Aokigahara.

that skirts the forest. Compass and GPS remain in agreement and before long there's the sound of traffic in the distance. As the forest opens a convenient mouth to disgorge us back onto the road, Adam steps over a boundary log and I discover a palm-held camcorder in its pouch, squarely placed upon it, kindly retrieved from where it had fallen to the ground.

Closer inspection reveals the innards of the camcorder gutted and corroding, both batteries and memory card removed. There's nothing to see and no story here.

I TAKE MY TURN TO FIRE UP THE HEATER BEFORE STEPPING OUT onto the porch to assess the weather. Snow came again overnight, but the sky is clear this morning, and the view across the lake to the backdrop of mountains is as monochromatic as it is spectacular, trees etched as if with a needle, the water below still and black, framed with a lush white ribbon shore. The inspiration for all those remarkable Japanese winter landscape prints is right there, before my eyes.

Inside Adam has his feet under the *kotatsu*, swotting up on nuclear fission on YouTube, and I join him to give a brief weather report, to enthuse about the view outside, but mostly because toasting my toes under the table is irresistible. We agree to return to the trail and recover our umbrellas, before someone else discovers them and assumes we were a pair of stereotypical Japanese lovers, doomed by our respective family's disapproval, retreating into the woods in a final pact of defiance. If we'd found a pair of umbrellas, left at the edge of the trail, we too would have started looking for a couple.

There's a brief pit stop at the local '7-Eleven' for breakfast and my seemingly habitual egg sandwich, Snickers bar, and cold latte combo, before returning to the sparsely populated car park. It's Monday. Most are back at work. A cursory scan doesn't reveal any vehicles that appear to have been abandoned overnight; again there is nothing completely covered with fresh snow.

We follow our route from yesterday to retrieve our umbrellas, but find only one. The track beyond the roped barrier was undisturbed, our footprints from yesterday eradicated under virgin snow. No one has come this way. We scuff our feet through the snow like sullen adolescents, convinced the brolly must be buried, but our search is fruitless. Perhaps a *yūrei* has taken a fancy to it, which would explain the lack of footprints.

Adam has elaborated on the Japanese ghosts, describing them as monochromatic women with long hair, covering the face, exactly like the character depicted in cult horror film *The Ring*. She'll be perfectly camouflaged in our current environment, especially now she has a white umbrella to hide behind. I'm vexed, convinced they were left together, and yet the brolly is simply nowhere to be found.

"Just a thought, Adam. Next time snow's forecast, bring a red umbrella, eh?"

Abandoning our search we follow the orange tape leading into the forest on the opposite side of the trail. It's a strong unbroken taut line, well above ground. It goes on and on, until the roll is exhausted, when it is spliced into another roll. When this too runs out, another clear unbroken yellow line of tape continues from the next sapling. Whoever laid this line wasn't taking any chances, but already it feels like too much tape, with no discernable end in sight. Adam, who possesses an uncanny sense of direction, regardless of the GPS in his pocket, realises we are following a loop, and thinks this is a searched area mapped by recovery volunteers, and as it eventually funnels us back towards the outgoing run I'm inclined to agree with him. So far the odd rusting beer can and a solitary metal fork stuck in a niche in a lava knoll are our only discoveries.

Then Adam finds a solitary white sandal at the base of a tree. The encroaching green on the uppers suggests it has been there for some time. There's a discarded bottle that once contained alcohol; 'Mild' stands out amongst the kanji script. There's no way of knowing if the whole bottle was drunk for fortification, or to wash down the pills. We debate the sex of the shoe's owner. Adam is in favour of it having belonged to a woman.

"It looks too large for a woman's shoe. She would have been very tall."

Adam suggests that maybe that was her reason for being there in the first place. With the average height of Japanese women being five feet two inches, the men at five feet seven, very tall girls might have limited opportunities for matrimony. Again, our knowledge of 'Sandal-san' is speculation and nothing more.

The bottle is admittedly a tempting souvenir. Cleaned up it would be a macabre conversation piece in its own right, but its significance is no different from the personal effects and artefacts I've previously encountered diving a shipwreck, so there is no way I'm taking anything other than photographs.

Japan is universally spotless and this *doufukushi*, or litter, hidden away in the forest is an abnormality verging on obscenity. But it is a reminder of what happens here. If the authorities were actively trying to deter sightseers within the forest, they could remove all evidence of humanity, then it would simply be a walk in the woods with the prospect of finding even less. The trappings the dead abandon fill our memorial museums. In Aokigahara they have more impact because, like the shipwrecks, the rotting bric-a-brac lies in situ.

I can only assume that the litter is left in the hope that anyone following in the footsteps of the suicides sees it for what it is, incredibly sad final traces, and that these might act as a deterrent. It's either that, or the authorities leave them for the bereaved, or the *yūrei*. We find so little that someone must clear the detritus over time, even if it is macabre souvenir hunters.

As we depart Aokigahara and head towards Tokyo's rush hour Adam throws me a question: "How do I feel now I've seen what we have inside the forest?"

I'm glad I've been to see for myself, especially as we didn't find any suicides. If we'd found a body I would have had to write that, and for those who are thinking of going it might only reinforce the sense that every time someone went looking, they were guaranteed to find. If we had found anyone we would have needed to cordon off the area and inform the authorities, go through the pockets looking for identification, simply because it would be the decent thing to do. Someone would be receiving a dreadful call, but it must be worse not knowing. I took a roll of red and white barrier tape with me, just in case. The necktie noose is likely to remain one of the saddest things I will ever see.

Dying alone to decompose in a forest is not how most would choose to go. However the location is, without question, beautiful, especially in the snow. Although my rationale regarding the time of my visit did not culminate in finding a body, or even anticipated hordes of dark tourists searching for them, it did afford me the opportunity to see Aokigahara as a winter wonderland. It is an area of outstanding natural beauty, and those who visit predominantly come for that, despite its dark association, and therefore tourism to the area is assured. The forest did focus my thoughts towards those who leave the path, seeking peace and isolation in order to end their lives. It is the definitive lonely place. Yet so was the world beyond the trees they chose to leave behind.

I turn the question back to Adam; how does he feel?

He says it's sobering, having seen the evidence of what happens in the forest with his own eyes. It does change things for him, but he'll be back. His love of the outdoors inherited in New Mexico is part of who he is, and he would happily settle in Aokigahara. I'm relieved the weirdo from London who wanted to enter

Abandoned sandal, Aokigahara.

the woods on the trail of suicides hasn't ruined it for him.

The two of us spent approximately seven and a half hours inside the restricted area of the *Jukai* over a Sunday and Monday, statistically the most likely days for suicide, in March, statistically the most likely month. During our time with two pairs of eyes we found:

- One sandal
- An empty bottle of alcohol
- One length of twisted metal cable, which may or
    may not have been fashioned as a noose
- One pair of trousers
- Tape tied to tree trunks in various colours
- Tape lines on the ground leading to nowhere in particular
- An old luminous wrist band on an overhanging branch on the trail
- Several rusty drink cans
- Several old water bottles bought from a convenience store
- Old food packaging bought from a convenience store
- Two pieces of plastic sheeting (found separately)
- A fork stuck in a lava niche
- Several sprayed red markings on tree trunks at the edge of the
    trail, presumably made by search and recovery teams
- A necktie noose

We did not find any human remains, and while the snow may have covered the ground, we were still able to locate plastic sheeting that had been buried.

We did not encounter any other individuals walking off the official trails.

We lost one white umbrella.

From the gift shop we bought one postcard of fungi, two pairs of socks as gifts for Adam's wife and sister-in-law, and one model train, a Shinkansen Series E5 Hayabusa 1/189 scale. I wanted to buy something other than a postcard of fungi, and didn't fancy a 'Fuji-san' t-shirt. OK, I admit, buying stuff is not *solely* the preserve of women, just mostly — but it's a model of a Shinkansen bullet train, what's more it's boxed, and it's staying that way. Who wouldn't want that?

The day after the new moon rose over Tokyo, Wednesday 29th March, the morning commute was disrupted. There were substantial delays on the Takasaki line, Metro Hanzōmon line, Shōnan–Shinjuku line, and Tokyu Den-en-toshi Line. In all four cases the cause for the delays was given as 'passenger injury'. I doubted that all those unfortunates had got their fingers caught in the sliding doors. Inevitably my thoughts returned to Aokigahara, and what might be found today, below the waves in the Sea of Trees.

FOR THE TOURIST, NOT JUST THE DARK TOURIST, JAPAN IS ABOUT AS GOOD *as it gets. The public transport is second to none, as is the customer service, given that so much of Southeast Asian hospitality verges on subservience, whereas the Japanese have courtesy and deference ingrained in their collective psyche. This promotes mutual respect with every single interaction.*

It is amazing they even have a word for litter, as the country is immaculate, and you won't go hungry or thirsty anywhere. Tourists are more than adequately catered for, with English and Chinese widely used on screens throughout the transportation networks, and if you're lost on the street someone will happily walk with you to find your required destination, be it stunning temple, underground restaurant, or secondhand record store. They did this for me thirty years ago and the practice continues today, which is my definition of progress.

The Japanese have retained their national identity, culture, and areas of natural beauty, whilst embracing both the surreal and the cute, and spend an inordinate amount of time smiling. As a Brit I reluctantly concede they are even more accomplished in the art of queuing, because they do so without rolling their eyes, audible sighing, or witty banter. This is the face Japan presents to its visitors, not the suicides in the Jukai.

The suicide rate in Japan is falling, but reportedly remains the most common cause of death for men between the ages of twenty and forty-four. Over 25,000 Japanese took their own lives in 2014, a rate of seventy per day from a population of 127.3 million. In comparison there were 6,122 suicides in the UK in 2014, a rate of sixteen per day from a population of 64.5 million.

Japan's birth rate is also in decline, and in 2016 dropped below one million, the lowest recorded for over a century. Nearly 40% of respondents to a government survey conducted in 2015–2016 described romantic relationships as 'bothersome', with singles preferring to focus on hobbies or work instead. So despite my rave review, something isn't working. Whatever that may be, it is not the fault of the Japanese public; they are literally working themselves to death.

Adam made the observation that while Japan was a great place if you worked for yourself, it wasn't so good if you worked for someone else, and highlighted the case of Matsuri Takahashi, a twenty-four-year-old female employee of Dentsu, the international advertising and PR company, who jumped from the roof of the company dormitory building in December 2015, citing exhaustion from her workload. The Japanese call this, 'karoshi', death from overwork. It is not uncommon, which is why they have a word for it.

Ms Takahashi had competed 105 hours of overtime in a month. Dentsu's president, Tadashi Ishii, resigned in the aftermath of the scandal, and Prime Minister Shinzo Abe campaigned for reforms to employment laws, aimed at restricting the number of hours employees would be expected to work in future.

In March 2017 the Prime Minister, the nation's biggest business lobby, Keidanren, and Rengo, the trade union confederation, met for talks. They agreed to cap monthly overtime at 100 hours per month, during busy periods.

UK: The Samaritans (116 123)
USA: National Suicide Prevention Lifeline (800-273-TALK/8255)
AUS: The Samaritans (135 247)

THE VILLAGE

I SPY DOWN UPON THE FLORIST, CURTAIN TWITCHING FROM MY HOTEL room across the street, as she dresses the pavement with plastic pots of cut flowers. Blue skies this early suggests a glorious day, although my insides don't feel like celebrating. Nothing to do with the cooked breakfast, rather that my appetite struggled with the reality. I re-arranged it and bit lumps out of the toast to make the abandoned plate look better.

The knots inside have been progressively tightening. This destination is the one I least wish to visit, which inevitably means it's the one I have to take first. Any investigation of the dark tourism phenomena needs a 'control': a place devastated by tragedy where tourism was never cultivated, a destination without guided tours, bereft of souvenir shops, where education had never been used as justification for welcoming tourists and the inherent theatricality and revenue that they bring.

That there is no tourist infrastructure means there's none of that comforting sanitisation which allows dark tourism to function and thrive. This will be raw. I am going to feel it, hence the stomach churning. This is how dark tourism *should* feel. Yet if it did, if it weren't surreptitiously sterilised for the masses by adding 'education', 'poignancy', 'keepsakes' and coffeeshops, then those attendance figures dark sites boast might not be quite so impressive.

In forty years of traipsing cemeteries I've never felt this apprehensive, because part of me knows I should not be going to this one, not for just a look or even for writing a book, and that I should stay away. Six weeks ago I could never have dreamt of coming here, because the last time I was 'here' was in an indelible childhood nightmare. I pick my jacket from the unmade bed, and shrug it on. It feels too heavy for the day ahead, like it's lead-lined with guilt.

The florist tells me she's off on holiday tomorrow, barely able to contain her excitement — a cruise... The Mediterranean? No! The Caribbean! I share in her sense of expectation, which avoids declaring that I too am on holiday and what's on today's itinerary, which starts with me buying her white carnations. She wraps the flowers, chattering about the gorgeous weather she is leaving behind, trying to discount the fact that she is off to the Caribbean.

So I wish her *bon voyage*, and clutching the slim bouquet head for the bus terminal. Today is going to be unforgettable, just like that one in 1966, for those old enough to remember. Nothing to do with Bobby Moore hoisted aloft, clutching the Jules Rimet trophy, but the other one. Even now, nearly fifty years on, everyone, from the Queen on down remembers what happened four miles down the road.

The Heolgerrig Social Club of Merthyr said, in memoriam, that a garden had been destroyed in a village, because God needed flowers. I don't believe in God, and yet I too have gone for the white carnations.

I JOIN THE QUEUE FOR THE BUS, MAKING SURE I'M THE LAST TO BOARD, self-conscious of my destination, thereby minimising it from earshot. The bus driver is wearing sunglasses. So am I. It is going to be a glorious day. I clear my throat.

"LLANFAIRPWLLGWYNGYLLGOGERYCHWYRNDROBWLLLLAN-TYSILI-OGOGOGOCH."

If only. No, it's the other Welsh village, the one with the far more pronounceable name, yet the one every senior in the UK struggles with to this day.

The Stagecoach bus takes a circuitous route round the retail and trading park on the outskirts of Merthyr Tydfil, then heads out to cater for the villages, threading down narrow streets past yesteryear shops with time capsule windows. Mothers with prams board and alight. I scan passing road signs for my destination, but there's no mention. Then the landscape opens like a pop-up book, and straight ahead looms the imposing brick red wall of 'The Mack', the former Mackintosh Hotel, boarded up, defunct, with just CCTV keeping a beady eye on its lifeless doorways.

The bus continues into Bronheulog Terrace, and the narrow row of terraced houses closes off the view. My fellow passengers remain stoically seated, and worse still there's no one waiting for the bus at the next stop to bail me out. Reluctantly I pull myself to my feet, ting the bell, avoid all eye contact, thank the driver, and step out at the Wye Fish Bar.

The bus pulls away and I'm alone. The stone clad public house up ahead won't open its doors until 3 p.m. In the house next door there's a printed note stuck in the window, tight to the pavement, inviting anyone to just drop in for a chat and a cup of tea in the afternoon. No pressure. That the note is here, in this particular village, adds a resonance beyond traditional Welsh hospitality, and although I'm sure they wouldn't turn me away, the invitation is not meant for me.

Still early and nothing stirs other than the birds. Looking at the terrace houses, neat and tidy, the front gardens in readiness for summer, it seems inconceivable that such darkness literally descended to envelop everything. There's no need for a map, as the route has been committed to pictorial memory, using Google Street View in advance. I didn't want to pull a map out here. That would be just like a bloody tourist, and that's the last thing I want, although my presence alone makes it unavoidable. I remove my sunglasses, as if that will help.

WHEN DAWN BROKE ON 21ST OCTOBER 1966, OVER THE HIGH ridge of Mynydd Merthyr, the Welsh mining village of Aberfan was at peace, nestled and shrouded in the archetypal autumnal mist 500 feet below.

On the way to school that morning, visibility was down to ten yards at most. It would not have been possible to see the dominant landscape rising above; a monster baring seven gigantic teeth, the tips of mining spoil, some 100 feet high. But everyone knew they were there. The schoolchildren drew them in their pictures of daily life. The mining industry and the village were locked in a symbiotic relationship, the geology underground reflected in the topography above.

That morning, the relationship was about to change, and the world would know of it, because Aberfan was going to be transformed from a little village unknown beyond the valleys of South Wales, into something synonymous with the worst kind of disaster imaginable. The children of the Pantglas Junior School sang the hymn All Things Bright And Beautiful in assembly, before returning to their classrooms to wish away the day for the bell that would signal the start of the half term holidays.

At 9:10 a. m., the tipping gang employed to dump the mining spoil watched helplessly as waste tip No. 7 subsided, and 150,000 tonnes of liquefied slurry slid away down the hillside, to be swallowed by the mist. The black mass moved so fast there was no time for a warning. It outran crane driver David Jones, who gave chase in vain, and swept away Hafod-Tanglwys-Uchaf farm, claiming its first victims, Mrs Probert and her two grandchildren. Loaded with debris including trucks and trees, it swamped a disused canal, overran an embankment and ploughed into the school and twenty houses below.

Four schoolboys in the street, late for class, saw the wall of slurry pounding towards them. They split and ran. Two survived, two died. Those pulled from the wreckage of what had once been their classrooms recalled the sound of a jet engine coming inexorably closer, before the avalanche engulfed them through the walls, windows, and ceilings. It buried the school alive. The classes at the rear facing the oncoming tide stood no chance at all. After that there was just the silence.

In total 144 villagers lost their lives, of which 116 were children between the ages of seven and ten. Some of their teachers and the headmistress were among the dead.

Trapped inside the remnants of their school, those children who'd miraculously survived were now confronted by their classmates who had not. One pupil recalled coming round as rescuers broke in through the windows, then seeing their friend, blood running from his nose, and knowing instantly that they were gone.

Melvyn Walker was eight-years-old, and in one of the classes that bore the brunt of the impact. It took him fifty years to be able to speak publicly to the

Aberfan archive photo.

Western Mail about what had happened, describing how the teacher went to the window to investigate the thundering roar and was killed in front of him. Melvyn sat at a desk in the middle of the classroom, but was pushed to one side by the force of the slurry. He heard a girl shouting for help, pulled her from the sludge, and the pair made their escape by climbing through a hole in the roof.

Melvyn didn't return to schooling for two years.

"Nobody knew. I used to go out and then head up to the mountainside in my uniform and sit there on my own all day."

The Pantglas Junior School lay under an avalanche of debris, thirty feet deep. Houses in Moy Road and Pantglas Road had also been demolished or lay submerged under the liquid mud. From the hillside, where cattle had been buried, only the apexes of the school roof stuck out, like stovepipe hats cast onto the black slurry. One rescuer commented to Sam Knight, the first journalist on the scene from the *Merthyr Express*:

"It's like a blitz — as though a bomb had been dropped on the whole school."

Villagers rushed to the scene and dug frantically with their bare hands, men clambered in through windows in their desperate efforts to reach the innards of the ruin.

Local miners abandoned their shift when the news broke. The entire colliery was out, soon joined by their colleagues from neighbouring pits. Some were digging for their own children, including the local Baptist minister. Many were in tears as they dug. Chain gangs of volunteers removed buckets of sludge. Women passed chunks of broken masonry down the line. Periodically the work fell silent as rescuers listened for sounds of life. Witnesses said it was so quiet you couldn't hear a bird. Then the digging started again.

The BBC reported that the deputy head teacher, Mr Benyon, was found dead. "He was clutching five children in his arms as if he had been protecting them", said a rescuer. A pregnant woman went into labour when told the news that her son had been killed.

Rescuers dug all day, but no one was brought out alive from the ruins after 11 a.m. that morning, at which time the slurry was still creeping, diluted by a broken water main, crushing sheds and garages like a tank, making further inroads into the village, the map of which would now have to be redrawn.

A makeshift mortuary was set up in the nearby Bethania Chapel. That night the bodies of those who had been recovered were laid out on the pews. Parents, having waited patiently for news all day long, now queued to identify their children. BBC reporter Cliff Michelmore visibly fought back tears as he broadcast from the scene that night.

"Never in my life have I ever seen anything like this... I hope that I shall never ever see anything like it again."

In the past there had been roll calls after mining disasters. This time it was taken from the school register.

That evening, the Mayor of Merthyr Vale issued an appeal for help.

Aberfan was the UK's first televised disaster and instantly became a shared national tragedy that reached out and touched far beyond the borders of Wales. The Aberfan Disaster Fund would reach £1.75m, the equivalent of £30m today.

People worked through the Friday evening, both rescuers and their volunteer support staff, making tea and sandwiches to sustain the effort. By Saturday there were some 2,000 volunteers at the site, accompanied by mechanical diggers, which had problems accessing the site, as it was located in a cul-de-sac. People abandoned their vehicles miles away and walked in to dig, but even with all the manpower and machinery it took nearly a week before the last body was recovered.

CONDOLENCES CAME IN FROM WORLD LEADERS, FROM THE POPE down. Dignitaries arrived. Prime Minister Harold Wilson visited on the Friday evening. The Duke of Edinburgh and Lord Snowdon came on the Saturday, then Lord Robens, Chairman of the National Coal Board. He arrived already convinced that the disaster had nothing to do with the NCB, without any idea as to what had actually caused the collapse. The Queen came to Aberfan nine days after the disaster. Commentators reflected she was there in her capacity as a mother, rather than a monarch. She received a posy, presented by a little girl with an accompanying card, 'From the remaining children of Aberfan.' It struck a chord. In the black and white British Pathé news footage that recorded her visit, the Queen looked close to tears.

In school assemblies throughout the country, prayers were said for Aberfan. It brought the reality of mortality to a generation of schoolchildren overnight. They prayed in their assembly halls, heads bowed, eyes too tightly shut, watched over by their Welsh teachers: Miss Ungoed, Mrs Williams, Miss Cavanagh, Mrs Davies, Jonesy...

On Monday 24th October, the inquest of thirty children took place, in a charged atmosphere. The *Merthyr Express* reported a ruckus when one child's name was read out, the cause of death given as asphyxia and multiple injuries. The father of the child objected, "No, sir, buried alive by the National Coal Board." The coroner appealed for order, but the father refused to back down: "I want it recorded — Buried alive by the National Coal Board. That is what I want to see on the record. That is the feeling of those present. Those are the words we want to go on the certificate."

On Thursday 27th October, Aberfan shut for the mass funeral and burials at the local cemetery, with 3,000 mourners in attendance. Floral tributes were laid on the hillside in the shape of a cross, 150 feet long, above the trench that had been cut for the graves.

The following day the Secretary of State for Wales appointed a Tribunal of Inquiry into the causes and circumstances of the disaster under the supervision of Lord Justice Edmund Davies. The Attorney General, Sir Elwyn Jones, Q.C., imposed reporting restrictions into the probable causes, a move the press were far from happy with.

The tribunal lasted for seventy-six days. In its final throes, Lord Robens arrived to deliver testimony, and eventually conceded that the NCB had been at fault. In a move that would be echoed nearly fifty years later with Hillsborough, the NCB maintained a stonewall defence for nearly eleven weeks, all at the taxpayer's expense, when it could have admitted liability at the very beginning. Desmond Acker, QC, representing the prosecution, described Lord Robens as an incompetent, unhelpful, and contradictory witness, and dismissed his evidence as "inconsistent".

The tip had been waterlogged with rain in the days prior to the slip, and its footings had been sited on a spring. Robens and the NCB said they had no knowledge of a spring under the tip, although the villagers contradicted this, and incontrovertible proof came with an Ordnance Survey map of 1919, with the spring clearly marked. Tipping began in 1958.

Tip slides were not unknown. There had been minor slides at tip No.7 itself, in 1944 and again in 1963. Sagging in the spoil had been noted on the morning of the disaster and tipping had ceased, but by then it was too late. Nobody in authority thought a slip would reach the village, or that it would be of such magnitude.

The tribunal published its damning report on 3rd August 1967. "Bungling ineptitude", "failure", "total lack of direction from above", and memorably described NCB witnesses as, "like moles being asked about the habits of birds."

The NCB dug relentlessly with no concern about what they threw away over their shoulder, where it landed, or any potential consequences. Spoil heaps grew and multiplied across the region as a result. Where there was a mine, there was a tiny dependent community sitting in the shadow of an ominous man-made mountain.

The tribunal found the NCB responsible, although no one was prosecuted, demoted or dismissed, and there were no criminal proceedings. The NCB paid compensation of £500 for each child killed, and covered the damage to property. Lord Robens offered to resign, but this was rejected. He retained the support of the majority of both Labour MPs and members within the National Union of Mineworkers.

The remaining tips continued to overlook Aberfan. The NCB claimed they posed no danger, quantified by adding that it was not possible to remove them unless someone else was willing to pay, and dismissed the villagers fear of further tip slides as 'irrational'.

Incensed villagers formed the Aberfan Tip Removal Committee, and marched on the offices of George Thomas, the Secretary of State for Wales, where they dumped spoil over his floor. Further slurry was washed down into Aberfan during a storm in 1968, after which they were finally removed.

So Aberfan's first two years of bereavement were overshadowed with the constant reminder on their skyline. The cost for the removal of the spoil mountains was £850,000; the NCB contributed £350,000, the Aberfan Disaster Fund £150,000, and the Exchequer paid the rest.

Taking money from the Aberfan Disaster Fund to contribute to the removal of the tips was controversial, but the NCB was already in debt, so funds had to come from elsewhere to remove their spoil. Beyond the community what happened was seen as an accident. The verdict at the inquest was of accidental death in all 144 cases, hence no one was prosecuted, no one was found guilty, and no one said sorry.

Aberfan was an isolated working-class community, contending with grief, anger, bitterness, and guilt in the glare of the media spotlight. There were no heart attacks or suicides, although a local doctor later stated he believed many residents died prematurely, due to the effects of the disaster. The birth rate rose, as did alcoholism. The tragedy had severe psychological consequences that exist to this day. There was the understandable friction between those who had lost children and those who had not, those who had lost their homes and those who had not. Parents had to contend with the guilt of sending their children to school on the last day of term, when many wanted to stay home.

Those children who survived no longer played in the street. They understood the effect it would have on the families who no longer had any children left to play with them. Children blamed themselves for their lives when their siblings had lost theirs, and wished they could swap places, between bed and grave. People in the village had sleeping disorders, many were on sedatives, but they didn't take them when it rained, because it had rained persistently in the days before the slip. Some children were now too scared to even close their bedroom doors.[1]

And so many within this one small community were bereaved in the worst possible manner. Miners were strong, brave, and didn't discuss their feelings. Many men headed for the solidarity and sanctuary of the pub in the evenings, because they could not face going home. A bereaved father's group didn't last, yet the women's group, the Aberfan Young Wives Club, met every week, and continues to this day. They organised outings, although for years when they were asked where they were from, they always said 'Merthyr Tydfil', the name of their village now indelibly associated with the tragedy.

There was an appreciation that there would be psychological difficulties for the surviving children, as well as the adults. However in 1966 mental health problems were stigmatized. One child, Gaynor Madgwick, who had been pulled from the wreckage of the school with physical injuries, later wrote an autobiographical account of the disaster, *Aberfan: Struggling Out of the Darkness*, where she expressed horror at the prospect of being taken to see a "shrink", because of what others might think.

Today any disaster would be accompanied with telephone helplines, leaflets and counselling services. Evidence of our understanding regarding mental health issues is reflected in today's television, where the credits contain phone lines open twenty-four hours a day, if we have been affected by any of the issues raised.

The romantic notion of a Welsh mining village is of a snug, close-knit community, where everyone knows everyone else. Life revolved around the church, pub, pit, school, and rugby field, accompanied by the soundtrack of the male voice choir that makes the hairs on your arm stand to attention. Many see the community spirit, the very 'Welshness' in the village, as being fundamental to recovery. The churches united and provided support. For some their faith was strengthened, some non-religious residents even found faith, whilst inevitably others lost theirs, and although the village struggled in isolation, the receipt of tens of thousands of letters of condolence were gratefully appreciated. The *Merthyr Express* of 4th November 1966 published letters of condolence from the USA, Canada, Australia, and even one from Zambia.

There was insensitivity too. Journalists filed divisive reports, painting a community at war with itself, exacerbating the friction that existed. The media wanted answers. Those in the community who could bring themselves

---

1) PTSD was not fully understood at the time. The sudden unexpected loss, inherent with a disaster, is harder to reconcile than an expected loss such as long-term illness. The loss of one's child, where the natural order is reversed, is harder still. A 'man-made' disaster, where fault and blame are attached, is harder to accept than a natural disaster, such as a tsunami. The UK is not prone to such calamities.

to speak wore their hearts on their sleeves, and now the inquiry was over there were no reporting restrictions to keep journalists in check. Indeed there had been little restraint during the digging for rescue and recovery. An anonymous rescue worker was quoted in the *Times*:

"I was helping to dig the children out when I heard a photographer tell a kiddie to cry for her dead friends, so that he could get a good picture."

Despite the detrimental reporting, some good came as a result. When the Mayor of Merthyr Vale appealed for help under the arc lights on the evening of the disaster, he could have had no inkling of the tremendous response from every conceivable source; from showbusiness to sport, trade unions to business, money was sent from prisoners in jail, even the journalists covering the story made a collection. The Kray twins, notorious gangsters of London's East End, gave £100. One donation came in an envelope from a child in Wimbledon, simply addressed:

"Dear postman, please send this to the school disaster man in Wales."

Along with the donations there were some 50,000 letters of condolence. They were subsequently given to the Merthyr Tydfil library on the proviso that they were to remain sealed for 100 years.

The £1.75m donated is remarkable because in 1966 there were no credit card hotlines, no text donation service, no twenty-four hour rolling news coverage, and no celebrities fronting campaigns.

The Charity Commission administered the fund, and paid bereaved families £500 for each child lost. They agreed the proposed memorial, at a cost of £40,000, would enhance the beauty of the cemetery, so taking that from the fund was not an issue, nor, ironically, was the £150,000 towards the tip removal.

While today it would be inconceivable for any benevolent fund to be raided in order to rectify the cause of the catastrophe, it did enable the tips to be removed. The village needed money for the maintenance of the memorial garden, built on the site of the demolished school, and the upkeep of the graves. As one bereaved parent speaking thirty years after the disaster noted:

"Where is it going to come from in later years when we're gone?"

In 1997 when Labour returned to power, the £150,000 taken from the disaster fund was repaid, but without any interest that it would have accrued over thirty years. The Secretary of State for Wales, Ron Davies, said the money should never have been taken in the first place. In February 2007, the Welsh Assembly donated £2m to the Aberfan Disaster Memorial Fund to compensate for the money and lost interest that had been drawn from the fund to remove the tips.

In 1987 the NCB was renamed the British Coal Corporation, and its assets privatised. On the twenty-fifth anniversary of the disaster it donated £10,000 to the fund. It also provides a wreath to the annual memorial service, which takes place in Aberfan at 9:15 a.m. every 21st October.

Of the survivors, many stayed and grew up in the village and are still there. Some of those who moved away subsequently returned, the draw of home too strong. A former pupil of Pantglas Junior School commented:

"What happened in Aberfan that day was the dark little secret when we were young and it still is."

They kept quiet for the sake of others and didn't even discuss it amongst themselves.

"Most of us live in the same small village and have grown up together, yet we all kept everything locked away inside ourselves."

WHEN I LOOKED IN THE MIRROR AND FIRST ACKNOWLEDGED myself as a dark tourist, the first destination I thought of was Aberfan. Although I'd been unwittingly ticking off dark sites for forty years, travelling far and wide to experience various degrees of darkness, I'd never considered visiting the Welsh mining village. Perhaps the thought of going there felt like a trespass beyond the pale.

Aberfan wasn't mentioned in the publications I'd read on dark tourism, although the authors were from the UK. This was curious, because there was a memorial there, it had been the UK's first televised disaster, it remains the country's worst postwar disaster, and the very name is part of the nation's psyche. Why travel to New York for 9/11, or to Krakow for Auschwitz-Birkenau when there had been a globally recognised tragedy here in the UK? It wasn't as if there was no tourism in Wales, and the disaster had occurred well within living memory. That the majority of the victims had been children did not seem a sufficient reason for omission, as children had died at other dark sites that had been referenced.

True, there were no package tours, no gift shops, and the community had made it plain that they did not welcome casual sightseers. However it was curious that Aberfan did not warrant a mention, if only in the context that here was a place where tourism had clearly been rejected, and never encouraged. Surely Aberfan was an example, arguably *the example*, of how death and disaster does not have to be automatically exploited for the sake of tourism.

The community depended on mining. When the colliery closed there was no other resource readily available to ensure the village's survival, and yet despite this, they still hadn't resorted to tourism. Inadvertently the village shamed the dark tourism industry. They had managed their grief without the need to sell souvenirs, set up a Facebook page, or employ education as a *raison d'être*.

However my own reaction to the prospect of visiting indicated why others writing about dark tourism might have avoided the village. The thought of going to Aberfan affected me in ways other sites had not. I had no tangible connections to any of the sites I'd explored, or intended to visit, and no connection with Aberfan. Yet in the weeks before the trip my trepidation grew.

I doubted the legitimacy of going, regardless of my intent to write about the tragedy. Aberfan exerted an emotional influence on me personally, unlike any other site. I felt guilt about intruding on an insular community, amplified by there being no tourist infrastructure to validate my presence.

There would be no tour group, so no escorting minibus in which to retreat once the requisite photo opportunity had been captured, as there was in Chernobyl. When the bus pulled away in Aberfan you'd be on your own, and there would be no anonymity as there was amongst the masses at Auschwitz-Birkenau. There was no promotion, or active encouragement to visit and learn, as there'd been at the National September 11 Memorial and Museum in New York, where you could 'take in' the memorial, then hail a cab and escape to another district for lunch before ticking off Central Park or the Guggenheim to restore equilibrium in the afternoon.

Venturing in alone was not the problem. I'd wandered around plenty of cemeteries on my own, conscious of the potential pitfalls they present, such as Peru's magnificent *Presbitero Maestro*. As the guard unlocked the gates, the local guide I'd employed explained how the cemetery had been closed for years because it was "very dangerous"; there were deep excavations to fall into and he would show me the dried blood where the bereaved had performed ritual sacrifices with chickens. Not this one. I'd moved like greased lightning that day. Unbeknown to my guide, I'd visited the *Maestro* seventeen years ago, before it was placed under lock and key. Wandering its avenues of high-rise tombs I'd been confronted by two individuals brandishing a cutthroat razor and ran for my life.

In Aberfan, however, the risk was exposure, although not from a higher dose of background radiation. There was no reason for me to be in the village other than the disaster. So it wouldn't be your choice of clothes, the colour of your skin, your camera, or even your accent when you opened your mouth that would give you away.

This was the same close-knit community. They would know why you were there simply because they didn't know who you were, who your Mam was, or your auntie for that matter. The people you passed on the street, queued behind in the post office, or who saw you from their windows, would instinctively know why you were there. Effectively you'd be walking the streets of Aberfan under a spotlight.

Whereas in Cambodia, at Tuol Sleng, you might meet a survivor with the tacit understanding of the symbiotic commercial relationship between dark tourism site and dark tourist, where they'd impart their experience in return for the revenue you'd bring, in Aberfan you'd likely meet a survivor, or the bereaved, or both, in the street just minding their own business. There would be no language barrier, local guide, or interpreter to act as a buffer. The residents were bilingual, and could speak their mind to your face if they chose to do so.

Aberfan has no interest in encouraging tourists, underlined by the fact that there's nothing there for them to spend their money on. The pub is not open until 3 p.m; the Chinese take-away looks as if it hasn't lifted its shutters this century, which just leaves a café, a chippy, a post office-cum-store, and a pharmacy, the essentials for village life.

I felt I could only justify going if I had an invitation, and contacted Professor Iain McLean, Professor of Politics at the University of Oxford, who together with Martin Johnes, Research Fellow in Contemporary Welsh History at the University of Wales, Cardiff, had written *Aberfan: Government & Disasters*, an extensive account of the tragedy and the aftermath. Professor McLean advised me to contact the library in Merthyr Tydfil, and reiterated the sensitivity required in carrying out my research.

My enquiries led to the community library in Aberfan, who discreetly released my contact details to any survivors of the disaster who wished to talk. In due course I received one acknowledgement, but then the individual decided not to correspond. I didn't blame them in the slightest. I was upset researching the tragedy from a distance over a few weeks, not living with it for fifty years. The disaster itself was just the beginning for Aberfan.

AWAY FROM THE TRAIN STATION AND SHOPPING CENTRE, MERTHYR Tydfil's high street appears much like my own: tanning, tattoos, takeaways, Turkish barbers, boozers, and bookies. The hotel has a touch of The Overlook about it, and I appear to be their only guest. It hasn't been redecorated since the late 1980s judging by the wallpaper and decorative border.

I leaf through the flyers for local attractions in the foyer, looking for anything on Aberfan, but there's not even a mention. Local tourism is geared towards experiencing the great outdoors with a horse, a bike, or a hike. The receptionist informs me the Merthyr Tydfil Tourist Information bureau closed some years ago. The town itself no longer has any postcards. I bought the last two from a shop on the corner that printed their own, of the Cefn Coed viaduct. Even the art deco Castle cinema, there in '66, has been razed to the ground and turfed over.

However what Merthyr Tydfil does have, and what I've come for, is the most beautifully appointed library, with a wooden revolving door and a semicircular 'books in/books out' reception desk. Alan Bennett would love it. I make my request, *sotto voce*, offering my printed email invitation to conduct research. The lady with the cherubic face telephones her supervisor to inform of my arrival, a trifle too loudly. Now everyone knows why I'm here.

Five minutes later, ensconced in a reading room, two librarians enter, each carrying a stack of what are referred to as 'The Black Boxes'. They tell me, "this is the tip of the iceberg", which makes me wonder what they say in the libraries that carry *Titanic* archives.

Closing time is four hours away. I begin reading the aged, thinning copy, recognising source material from Professor McLean's book. It's only when reading the initial press reports filed at the time that I fully comprehend his seemingly superfluous warning about the need for sensitivity. Some of the reporting beggars belief, with sections of the press seemingly hell-bent on goading the village into a civil war. The ladies light up the photocopier until the paper is exhausted. I pay for them to post me the rest, which they do. When I'm finished I rearrange the clippings, so the gutter journalism is buried deeper than where I found it, then wash my hands and go for a stiff drink.

THE ROAD FORKS AND I START THE PLOD UP RHIWR ORSAF, SEMI-detached houses and front gardens above my head. I exchange "Morning" with a man cutting his grass before the heat of the day, hoping he's seen my spray of white carnations, although he knows where I'm going, even if he hasn't. In truth I've still no idea who they're for.

The switch back turns me towards the cemetery, the gabled chapel set between the firs. Up ahead the polished pearl white granite colonnade stands out against the hillside, your eyes inevitably drawn towards it. The saddest sight in the British Isles is also one of its most beautiful. Fully restored in 2007–2008, the twin rows of arches and walkways are intersected by a stub row of seven arches at the mouth, the grass banking between the graves artificial evergreen. Most of the graves are adorned with floral tributes, even now, fifty years on. Very few of them are plastic.

Slowly I make my way along the rows. There's the grave of Sidney Russell and his son Graham, names I now recognise. They ran the tuck shop in Moy Road, and must have served so many children that Friday morning, before the slurry struck. That which flowed past the school destroyed their shop and claimed both their lives. Pat and Tommy, brother and sister, now reunited with their parents, William and Betty, whom died within a year of each other after living twenty-plus years without their children.

The silence is suddenly broken. Over my shoulder there's the sound of a motorcycle. The rider climbs through the haze towards the memorial, and for a paranoid moment I think he is responding to my presence, because there's no one else here. I pointedly walk away along the length of the memorial, but of course it's a Friday, the day of the disaster. He parks, dismounts, and walks a few yards into the colonnade to address a grave, hands clasped in front, head bowed. He keeps his crash helmet on. I feel guilty for even being there to witness him pay his respects, to a brother or sister perhaps, and walk on further still to the small walled garden, with a bas-relief of Jesus, arms outstretched above the legend, 'Children, Come Unto Me'.

I take a seat on the bench and take in the view, in front of an inscription that reads:

This place of peace and reflection.

Memorial graves, Aberfan cemetery.

Commemorates with our heartfelt thanks
The thoughts and prayers and assistance
Received in our time of need
From all our friends both near and far

It's too hot. I seek shade from where I can look along the memorial without appearing I'm actually looking at the man in the motorcycle helmet, and shamefully experience a sense of relief that he's gone. No idea if he'd have preferred to be alone with his thoughts, or whether he's consoled that outsiders haven't forgotten, and still come to pay their respects. Regardless, I imagine he'll be back the same time next week. I won't.

Sharon Lewis was nine. Her grave is towards the end of the row, and I wonder if those who visit the memorial find it an emotional struggle to walk the whole length. Reading the inscriptions, one by one, the tangible grief in the tributes, and the ages of so many of the children, is almost too much. Then there are the addresses on the stones; kids who sat next to each other in class, lived next door to each other, or next door but one. They played together, died together, and were laid to rest together.

Sharon is 'missed by her parents', although her father has since joined her, his passing marked on her grave. I trust that if Mrs Lewis comes, perhaps later today or tomorrow, she'll forgive me for the liberty I'm about to take. Flowers, as someone once said, are the last things you can give.

Drizzle is all that is left in the vase. There's a beautiful standpipe

incorporated into a black surround, set in the middle of the walkway, a far cry from the functional cemetery standpipe I'm accustomed to. Ironically, for a Virgo, I've nothing to carry the water with. Away from the memorial I fish an old milk carton from a waste bin, top up the vase, and fuss over Sharon's floristry until I'm satisfied with the arrangement, then bin the rubbish and take the steps cut into the hillside to sit high above the memorial. I dig out a notebook and pen and try to find the words.

Unobserved in my crow's nest, appreciating the panorama, I watch a couple wander along the memorial to sit at a bench. Five minutes later they retrace their steps. Whoever they were, they didn't make it as far as Sharon today. I take some time to wander through the graveyard, under the trees, looking at the markers that aren't associated with the disaster, either before or since, but the bright white rows are hypnotic, and it's hard to look away for long.

Back down in the village I stop at the post office-cum-store for a bottle of water. The beautiful day has become the proverbial scorcher. The kid at the counter is also thirsty, and buying a bottle of fizzy pop, but the lady behind the counter is telling him its £1.09. He thought it was a pound, and he's only got a pound.

"I'll put it back, shall I?" she says.

I'm conspicuous enough, just standing there, so decide to intervene.

"I've got that..."

The little lad looks up at me, eyes like flying saucers, like I'm some kind of hero.

Overlooking Aberfan cemetery.

"Thank! You!"

He's welcome. Children, especially in Aberfan today, rule. The lady says something about if she'd had any money on her she'd have given it to him, then goes to give me the penny change, receives my best practised pained look in return, and deposits it in the charity box.

The fryer at the Wye Fish Bar is sitting on his step in the sun reading a newspaper. Too hot to be bothered with batter, I take a seat shy of the window in the Megabytes café next door. There are no computers, but fortunately there's a blackboard menu boasting a chicken mayo baguette. Past the decorative bunting and ornamental birdcages, a cluster of villagers chat away on the pavement waiting for the bus to town at what appears to be an impromptu stop. And everybody *does* know everybody, both out on the street, and when they enter the café. It's all first name terms and everyday chitchat and no one other than the waitress pays me a blind bit of attention.

I walk off lunch by heading to the Memorial Garden, just before the playground in Moy Road, situated on what was once the site of the Pantglas Junior School. The school is still there in garden form. The original exterior walls have been incorporated into the perimeter, and the internal shrub boarders map the classrooms. It's immaculately maintained, and very peaceful on a bench under the dappled shade from the birch and maple. There's a delicate white blossom cherry tree, planted by the Queen on 9th May 1997. After her initial visit in the dark days of '66, she promised to return and has made three subsequent trips.

A grandfather enters and promenades his granddaughter back and forth in her stroller. We exchange pleasantries, and I feel pathetically grateful for that. Sitting there, writing my notes, I notice that the first floor windows of the houses opposite the garden allow the residents of Moy Road to keep a watchful eye over their memorial, and when they can't there's always the ever present CCTV.

The houses destroyed where Moy Road curves down towards 'The Mack' were cleared to build the Aberfan and Merthyr Vale Community Centre, which officially opened in 1973. There's a swimming pool and fitness centre. The adjacent library is my next stop. A man, late twenties to early thirties, follows his child to the swings in the playground. He doesn't say anything or check his stride, just pins me with a discernable frown that unmistakably conveys, "Who are you and what do you think are you doing here?" Children born here after the disaster are all taught their local history. It might be fifty years ago, but the events are still raw, and have been passed down to the next generation. The thirtysomethings of Aberfan have experienced growing up with a missing generation, while surrounded by mass bereavement within their tight streets.

Inside the community library it's quiet. Library Assistant Carron Williams is expecting me and leads the way to a discreet table with an armful of reference books on Aberfan, then provides a welcome cup of tea. Coming from a neighbouring village, Carron provides a perfect liaison between the visitor and the local community. She is not there in any tourist capacity whatsoever, but will direct people to the cemetery or the memorial garden. She recalls a couple from South Africa and an elderly gentleman from Hull who'd wanted to visit Aberfan for years. And especially the lady she directed to the cemetery, only for her to return in real distress:

"I thought — Oh, God! Someone's said something to her! But it wasn't that at all. She said she just felt she was intruding. She said she wished that she'd never come."

I empathise, knowing exactly how that woman felt. Then there was the man who came in, asking for a leaflet. Carron genuinely didn't know what he wanted. Apparently he was after something that you would find at the 'Big Pit' National Coal Museum, a printed guide to the village. She told him there was absolutely nothing like that. Not even a postcard. He left disappointed.

"The whole village is a living memorial", Carron says.

Aberfan would not allow tourism to develop; the very idea seems incomprehensible to them now, as it has always been, and it's not just words. The Mackintosh Hotel, open at the time of the disaster, has been closed, the locals think, for about twenty years or more.

There was talk of it being turned into flats, but nothing has come of it. From the photographs taken at the time of the disaster, and those that predate it, there were many more shops and businesses in Aberfan than there are today.

The pit closed in August 1989, followed by the Hoover factory in Merthyr Tydfil in March 2009, leaving little in the way of an alternative source of jobs to support the local economy. Those people looking for employment now enter the service, retail, or care sectors.

Carron remembers a time when if you lived in the valley and didn't like a job you could leave on the Friday, and have a new one by Monday. It's not like that now. There's a job club in the library where she assists those seeking work. Although Cardiff developed with regeneration in the 1990s, after a period of decline in the 1970s and 1980s the valleys of South Wales, including Aberfan, remain geographically and economically isolated. Housing is much cheaper here, but there's been little sign of a commuter exodus for homes in the valleys.

"And how do people who move here integrate into the community?"

"Fine. No problems. Would you like another cup of tea?"

Carron brings out a black box file containing yet more photographs. Fixed inside the lid is a hand written note:

'Please note that people involved in this dreadful time still live in Aberfan.'

After the photos I need the bathroom off the corridor outside. Then, while reading Gaynor Madgwick's autobiographical account of the tragedy, I excuse myself on the pretence of having a cigarette, but the reality is I need the sanctuary of the bathroom again. I'm sure Carron has noted I'm flitting in and out with increasing regularity, although I'm shutting the bathroom door carefully so it doesn't draw attention to the fact that I'm washing my face again.

"It's tough, isn't it?"

She has.

There is a book of black and white photographs of Aberfan in the aftermath, pictures of the miners returning to work, the church congregation, a Christmas wedding with a solitary bridesmaid, and a mother stood in the mud at the graveside, weeping. In so many of the photographs there are solitary children; a boy draped over the roundabout in a playground he has all to himself. This is the work of Bronx-born freelancer, I.C. Rapoport, himself a young father, he portrayed the community with both perspective and a sympathetic eye.

Even in the midst of their grief, when Aberfan could be excused from thinking that nothing outside their valley mattered anymore, they responded to a subsequent disaster that befell another community, and sent their children's clothes to Florence, Italy, where in November 1966 there had been catastrophic flooding, where over 100 people had lost their lives.

The Italians were so touched by the gesture they sent a marble plaque from the Fine Arts Academy in Rome: 'To The Mothers Of The Little Children Of Aberfan Who's Deepest Grief Inspired The Sublime Poetry Of Heartfelt Solidarity.' The plaque hangs upstairs in the community centre.

Turning the page of another book, there's a poem entitled 'A Cry From "The Heart" of Aberfan', written at Christmas 1966 by one of the mothers who lost her child, about how, despite her grief, she'll forgive the NCB. It's beautifully worded through the pain, from Sharon Lewis' mother, Sheila; of all the children's graves I passed today, I laid flowers at her daughter's.

T HE FIFTIETH ANNIVERSARY HERALDS ABERFAN'S RETURN TO the national conscience, although Carron told me that many of the residents were dreading it. Some take their annual holidays over the anniversary so they are not at home, although one villager never leaves, living as a recluse. Others continue to suffer from the effects of PTSD. The BBC reports on a conference organised by the Cardiff University School of Journalism, 'Remembering, Forgetting and Moving On.' Some are compelled to stand and speak about the disaster and its subsequent effects for the first time, including Yvonne Price, a former WPC who finally sought treatment forty-five years after the events. The Welsh football team visit the memorial gardens to pay their respects, as do the Welsh rugby team. Articles appear in national newspapers as the media revisits the disaster.

Then on 21st October 2016, Wales falls silent in memory at 9:15 a.m. Prince Charles attends the memorial service, plants a tree in the garden and reads a message on behalf of the Queen, in which she recalls the posy she received on her first visit, "From the remaining children of Aberfan." The story leads the national news broadcasts.

There are four documentaries: ITV screen *The Aberfan Young Wives Club*, about the women who bonded together in the wake of the disaster, and *Aberfan: The Day Our Lives Changed*, which features Phil Thomas, a schoolboy rescued from under a collapsed wall by firemen, with whom he is reunited with for the first time in fifty years. He meets them again 'for the first time', albeit in a different location, in the BBC documentary *Surviving Aberfan*.

Huw Edwards presents *Aberfan: The Fight for Justice*, which includes a dramatization of the tribunal, and the BBC also screens highlights of a memorial concert in Cardiff. To round it off, BBC online reports on 25th October that the card accompanying the wreath laid by Prince Charles at the cemetery has been stolen.

C ARRON THINKS THE DISASTER HAD, AND CONTINUES TO HAVE, such an effect beyond the community because it is simple; the tip fell on the school with the children inside, and that's true. But the disaster had a profound and personal effect on me, although as a three-year-old it is unlikely the events would have fully registered at the time. It was different a year later, with an item remembering Aberfan on children's TV staple *Blue Peter*. The children who'd lost their lives in Pantglas Junior School were, to my mind, not so much older than myself as to make any difference. I was an only child, and when the realisation dawned that I too could die at any time, even at school, I was hysterical.

My mum was one of a great many I suspect, miles from Aberfan, who had to deal with the protracted aftermath of the disaster, with no copy of *Good Parenting* to tell them how to pacify their child who has suddenly recognised death for the reality it is, beyond the fairground goldfish that magically disappears, flushed down the U-bend after bedtime.

Mum did what mums do. She didn't tell me I wasn't going to die, or that the angels would take me up to heaven when I did, but hugged me to bits and told me she hoped I would have a very long and happy life, with lots of wonderful adventures, and that, over time, I would come to understand.

"Now let's dry your eyes, blow your nose, and then you can have beans on toast for tea."

Something like that, I suspect.

We didn't mention my death again, and I certainly never considered hers, until she died suddenly two years later. I've lived life with death ever since. But it was Aberfan where I first noticed its omnipresent shadow.

AS SO OFTEN HAPPENS THE LESSONS OF WHAT HAPPENED AT Aberfan were not learned. As a direct result of the disaster in Wales, the dams of mining spoil overlooking the town of Buffalo Creek, West Virginia, USA, were inspected. They were inspected again, and passed, just four days before they were breached.

After persistent heavy rains, on 26th February 1972 the three dams constructed of coarse mining refuse and built on slurry sediment collapsed like dominoes, and 132,000,000 gallons of black waste water subsequently flooded the coal towns along the hollow, killing 125 including children, injuring 1,121, and leaving over 4,000 people homeless. I have not visited Buffalo Creek, but there appears to be a simple stone marker bearing the names of those who died, and a memorial library.

As with Aberfan, Buffalo Creek has resisted the lure of dark tourism. I don't think this is a coincidence. The initial thought would be that this is due to these particular sites being physically isolated, yet so are many dark sites, including the crash site of Flight 93. That has a tourist centre. If you wish to discount this you could argue Flight 93 epitomises patriotism for Americans, while Buffalo Creek does not.

However the underlining factor is that both Aberfan and Buffalo Creek were mining communities, ingrained into the landscape which ultimately consumed them, and although both were devastated, those who survived drew strength from the inherent characteristics that defined them. And tellingly they had a choice regarding the development of dark tourism in their close-knit communities. Both rejected it.

Aberfan did receive funding to build a beautiful memorial and garden to those they lost, and a community centre that has catered for the living. Its use has adapted as times and habits have changed. Carron said there used to be concerts held there, but not these days. Of course there's effectively a generation missing who would have attended such shows, and we now live in the age of the sofa and the DVD box set. While I was researching a lady came into the library to order the second series of *The Walking Dead*.

There used to be a community newspaper in Aberfan, founded in the wake of the disaster and distributed free to all the residents, called *Headway*, the philosophy being that 'everyone should get the same story at the same time', a counter to the popular press and their occasionally skewed reporting. It published into the 1990s. There were a plethora of community groups set up in the wake of the tragedy: judo, rugby, youth and senior choirs of some repute, a canoeing club, even a chrysanthemum club. Somehow the survivors and the bereaved carried on as best they could.

However there is one outstanding legacy from Aberfan that has never been recognised, and one that flies in the face of today's seemingly insatiable appetite to capitalise on disaster through dark tourism.

It is that those who survived, together with those who were bereaved, and the generation born to those who remember the events of 1966, have acted with one unified purpose, and protected the dignity of their dead and their memory for the past fifty years. That legacy will continue. As survivor and resident Gaynor Madgwick observed in the media spotlight cast by the fiftieth anniversary, the villagers were there for the forty-ninth anniversary, and they would be there again for the fifty-first.

There's been no pragmatism, no moving with the grief bandwagon times, no exhibition displaying a lost child's shoe, or gift shop selling teddy bears or apparel, no leaflet or postcard, and no guided walking tour. Education has not been employed as a means to justify the ends, or even a museum. There's no press office or media contact to promote their 'agenda', or solicit a donation. There's not even a Facebook page to 'like'.[2]

Aberfan has achieved this, despite the loss of its livelihood. The continued protection of the dead from any form of exploitation allows the community to hold a mirror up to reflect any visitor's true motives for being there in the first place.

If you are going to walk in their cemetery, memorial garden, and streets, you are going to do so in order to pay your respects. They've ensured there's nothing else to distract from that.

T HE TWO-CARRIAGE TRAIN GRUDGINGLY PULLS OUT OF MERTHYR Tydfil, taking me on the first leg of the journey home. Four miles south it rounds the bend and the trees give way to a view across the valley. The horizon is crowned with pylons, the hillside dotted with graves, and there is the unmistakable colonnade of white memorial arches, a zip running across the vista, seemingly without end, until the trees rush past the window, drawing their curtain to hide it from sight, and the outside world.

---

2) Buffalo Creek has a Facebook page, primarily to reconnect with people who have moved away since the disaster.

SKELETONS

DARK TOURISM IS A COMPETITIVE BUSINESS, IRONICALLY DEFINED by the number of live bodies a site can attract through its doors.

To this end the two undisputed heavyweights, Auschwitz-Birkenau from the twentieth century, and the National September 11 Memorial Museum from the twenty first, are now locked in perpetual struggle for the ongoing blessing of the most coveted dark tourist of all. The Pope.

In July 2016, Pope Francis became the third consecutive pontiff to visit Auschwitz-Birkenau, following in the footsteps of Pope Benedict XVI, who visited in May 2006, and Pope John Paul II, who made the inaugural visit by a sitting pontiff in June 1979.

Pope John Paul II went to the camp as a show of reconciliation between Catholics and Jews. In doing so he started a papal trend of pilgrimage to the world's most notorious destination. John Paul II was Polish, came from the diocese in which Auschwitz-Birkenau was situated, and had previously visited on numerous occasions. By returning as pontiff the media duly took note.

Pope Benedict XVI had also been to Auschwitz-Birkenau before his official visit. He first went as part of the entourage for his predecessor, then again the following year with a bench of German bishops, whilst holding the office of Archbishop of Munich. There were no rainbows during his previous trips, and I only mention this in light of the gem served up by America's NBC when reporting on Pope Benedict's official trip:

"Scattered rain fell over Auschwitz until the main ceremony when the skies cleared and a rainbow appeared."

Papal visits to Auschwitz-Birkenau are now polished media affairs, where even the prevailing meteorological conditions appear stage-managed. There was reportedly an awkward moment when Benedict XVI was about to be driven through the 'Arbeit Macht Frei' gate, until it was explained this was a privilege reserved for the *Schutzstaffel*, the SS, so he walked instead. The ensuing photo opportunity contributed to the gate's iconic status and ensured that every successive pontiff must do a 'walk thru'.

The current incumbent, Pope Francis, visited Auschwitz-Birkenau in July 2016. Captured by a remote overhead camera, he lit a candle at the 'Wall of Death' where prisoners had been summarily executed by firing squad, although the *Daily Mail* dutifully noted there were no visible bullet holes, as the original wall had been replaced. His Holiness prayed in the cell of Maximilian Kolbe, the priest canonized for giving his life to save another, signed the guestbook and met survivors and those who assisted them. The *Daily Mail* again dutifully noted these were in fact the children of the families who'd offered assistance, the wartime heroes themselves having passed away. Everything was suitably window dressed, and naturally Pope Francis did his obligatory 'walk thru'.

The *Daily Mail* commented that Pope Francis had not lived in Europe during the time of the atrocities, therefore his visit underlined the significance of the site "that in recent years has drawn ever more visitors from around the world".

9/11 New York has also courted the papal seal of approval. Pope Francis conducted a multifaith service in the Foundation Hall at the National September 11 Memorial and Museum in September 2015. He spoke with bereaved relatives, lit a candle, and touched the names on the plates surrounding the memorial pools. His predecessor also graced 'Ground Zero' in April 2008, where he too lit a candle, blessed the ground with Holy water, and spoke with rescuers and the bereaved. Pope Benedict was only there for half-an-hour, but in fairness it was just a very big hole in the ground at the time.

The Pope is invited to make visits worldwide. Attending memorials is integral to any papal tour itinerary, although they do not all receive the same coverage as the two dark staples. It should be noted that Pope John Paul II visited Hiroshima in February 1981. At the time of writing, Pope Francis is slated to tour Japan in the summer of 2018. According to the *Japan Times*, the Japanese government is exploring the possibility of adding Hiroshima to his schedule.

Clearly the papacy is going to continue to visit both Auschwitz-Birkenau and the National September 11 Memorial and Museum. Both church and dark site benefit from extensive media coverage, and there is a compelling narrative with the humble Pope, solitary and splendid in white, walking on ground where evil was perpetrated upon the innocent. The Vatican has now set a precedent, and Hiroshima won't want to be left out of the loop, regardless of the fact that Japan's Catholic contingent accounts for less than one half of a per cent of its population.

Papal approval transforms dark tourism sites from killing ground to sacred ground. His presence provides global media coverage and the long-term benefit of disassociating the site from any suggestion that it could be exploiting the dead or their memory; if the Pope is willing to visit, who could have any reservations about following in his footsteps?[1]

The competition between dark sites to attract numbers in order to remain relevant will continue, even though the march of time is against them. Already

---

1) Not all dark sites can command the Pope. However other experienced clergy are available. The current Archbishop of Canterbury, Justin Welby, has visited Auschwitz-Birkenau on four occasions, as recently as January 2017. His predecessor, Rowan Williams, also went. The endorsement of sites appears arbitrary. According to Lambeth Palace, no Archbishop of Canterbury has visited Aberfan. This is strange, because although Oświęcim is a fraction under 1,000 miles from London, Aberfan is less than 170.

one fifth of Americans have no recollection of 9/11, being born after the event. Fortunately there's plenty of colour TV footage to show future generations what happened.

Auschwitz-Birkenau and associated Holocaust sites have to contend with a rapidly dwindling pool of survivors, and grainy monochromatic footage that itself relegates the event to a bygone age. So present day survivors have been immortalized in virtual reality to provide Q&A sessions from a flat screen, artefacts from Auschwitz-Birkenau are now on tour, and shiny new memorials and learning centres continue to be established to resuscitate the Holocaust's relevance in contemporary times.

THE MEDIA PROMOTES DARK TOURISM EXTENSIVELY. WHILE THE *Daily Mail* is not the only UK newspaper to feature dark sites, it does carry the most comprehensive coverage amongst the popular dailies. The paper has run articles on every major site covered in this book.

It has also included the Japanese suicide spots of Aokigahara, and the rather more obscure Tōjinbō Cliffs. Neither site courts publicity. Beachy Head, the UK's own suicide black spot, and a household name, also regularly features within the paper's pages. Whilst the media is interested in anything relating to *Titanic*, I was convinced the *Daily Mail* would miss the wreck of the *Salem Express*; those lost were Muslim pilgrims returning from Mecca, while the wreck lies out of sight and out of mind. I was proved wrong.

Although the *Daily Mail* hadn't reported the original tragedy in 1991 (very few western media outlets did), they extensively covered dives to the interior of the wreck in a lavishly illustrated article published in 2015. That the paper covered this tomb wreck in such depth, to at least thirty metres, showed a hard-core devotion to dark tourism.

The *Daily Mail* attracts criticism for its reporting on racism, homophobia, medical and scientific issues, coverage of celebrities and their children, and property prices. Yet its obsession with dark tourism has escaped attention, and if the paper is reporting on sites as obscure and diverse as the Tōjinbō Cliffs, and the wreck of the *Salem Express*, that could be considered obsessive. Combine the *Daily Mail*'s fascination with darkness and property prices, and you get this fantastical headline from 7th June 2015:

"House of Horrors where serial killer Dennis Nilsen slaughtered rent boys and cooked them in the kitchen is sold for £300,000"

That the *Daily Mail*'s readership may be riven with armchair ghouls is perhaps not entirely a surprise, although the paper is successful because it produces articles people want to read.

Media reporting of these sites may explain the desire of the independent dark tourist, myself included, in seeking alternative experiences off the beaten track before they become legitimized, and full-blown tourism infrastructure follows.

While much of the early criticism directed at the National September 11 Memorial and Museum came from relatives of the deceased, commentators were also quick to find fault. Inevitably the museum weathered the storm, and has become an accepted tourist destination. Controversy was then stirred by focusing on the behaviour of the tourists. Again, courtesy of the *Daily Mail* (who ran a story originally published in the *New York Daily News*, of Sunday 24th June 2012), I know about the kids on a school trip who threw baseballs and soda bottles into the memorial pools. No brand names were mentioned. Both the Coca-Cola and PepsiCo Foundations had contributed to the project with donations in the '$1m — $1.9m level', as have both the New York Mets and the New York Yankees.

"Tourists visiting the site Saturday said they were disgusted by the students filthy acts".

Someone must have prompted the weekend tourists to illicit a suitable soundbite, because the school trip took place on the Thursday. In this instance media reporting painted the museum in a sympathetic light at the expense of the schoolkids, including those litterbugs who didn't ask to be there in the first place.[2]

The role of the press is to report fact, or 'alternate fact' as it's now known in the US. However, during research I discovered dark tourism reporting that can best be described as a self-fulfilling prophecy, centered on the Austrian town of Braunau am Inn, birthplace of Adolf Hitler. The BBC online published eight separate articles between 9th April 2016 and 13th February 2017.

I beg your indulgence to illustrate obsessive dark tourism reporting.

9th April 2016, under the headline 'Austria plans to seize house where Hitler was born', a video clip of the house, which was visited by reporter Bethany Bell. The accompanying text informs us:

"The Austrian government says it plans to seize the house where Adolf Hitler was born to stop it being a focal point for Nazi sympathizers."

12th July 2016, headline 'Hitler house: Austria moves to stop neo-Nazi "cult site"', then under a photograph of the house:

"Austria's government is to seize the house where Adolf Hitler was born in

---

2) This observation from a student who was present is worth noting:

"No one was disrespecting. It wasn't nothing like that. No one was being serious. Everyone was kind of bored and it was just something to do."

Whilst one might question what constitutes disrespect, the kids by their own admission were 'kind of bored'. Yet education is cited as a principal function of dark sites. That their captive audience is 'bored' throws this into question. The attendance figures being trumpeted should be tempered by accepting that some of those taken to dark sites have no wish to be there, or would prefer a shorter experience. As recipients of the education offered, their judgement is particularly valid. Naturally the National September 11 Memorial and Museum stresses the positive aspects of its educational purpose, with enthusiastic comments from teachers, photos of attentive students, and how, in 2016, more than 36,000 students "from around the world" participated in educational programs at the museum.

1889 to prevent it becoming a site of pilgrimage for neo-Nazis.”

The video is republished with a link to an archived article, 'Hitler's old house gives Austria a headache' from 29th December 2014, which again features the video and explains that:

“For years the building in the Austrian town of Braunau am Inn has been rented by the Austrian interior ministry to prevent misuse by neo-Nazis.”

17th October 2016, headline 'Hitler house in Austria to be demolished after long row', text under photograph of the house:

“The house in Austria where Adolf Hitler was born is set to be demolished to stop it becoming a focal point for neo-Nazis.”

Bethany Bell's video accompanies the piece.

The very next day, *18th October 2016*, headline 'Hitler birthplace: Austrian minister retreats on demolition', with a photograph of the house, and within the text: “Local people say the building still attracts some neo-Nazi sympathizers.”

Bethany Bell's video accompanies the piece once more

21st October 2016, and BBC heavyweight Mark Mardell files a story under the headline 'Does Hitler's legacy still cast shadow over the world?' There's a photograph of the house, and a line within the text: “The Austrian government has said it will either be torn down or restructured to stop neo-Nazis turning it into a shrine.”

No video, but bizarrely a photo of Vladimir Putin stripped to the waist astride a horse. The caption states both Hillary Clinton and David Cameron have compared some of Putin's actions to Hitler.

15th December 2016, headline 'Austrian MPs vote to seize Hitler's birthplace house', with the last line of the article, “Locals say it still attracts neo-Nazi sympathizers to Braunau am Inn, despite the efforts of local authorities to prevent this.”

At which point you wonder how hard the local authorities are trying, and whether the BBC are deliberately trying to stymie their efforts, or are simply promoting the link between Braunau am Inn and neo-Nazis. These rehashed stories could be clickbait, but if so, who are they aimed at if not dark tourists or neo-Nazis?

Incredibly, *a second story was filed on the same day*, *15th December 2016*, headline 'Hitler's Austrian birthplace will be home for disability charity'. In the penultimate line of text:

“Locals say it still attracts neo-Nazi sympathizers to Braunau am Inn, despite the efforts of local authorities to prevent this.”

Both articles feature Bethany Bell's video.

Finally, on *13th February 2017*, the headline we've all been waiting for: 'Hitler lookalike arrested in Austria.'

A twenty-five-year-old man, Harald Zenz, who'd visited the town on several occasions in military uniform, had been seen having his photograph, "taken outside the house in Braunau am Inn in which Adolf Hitler was born."

There's a pixelated photo of Harald, and a photograph of the house, which is not. He was arrested because glorifying the Nazi era is a crime in Austria. Included in the article "Last October, the Austrian authorities decided to demolish Hitler's birthplace house to stop it becoming a focal point for neo-Nazis."

The story of Zenz's arrest was carried in India, America, and Australia, and the BBC's reporting was credited, although not their extensive preparatory groundwork. I can't help wondering whether Zenz was following Hitler, or the BBC online.

I submitted the relevant form to ask the BBC Media Centre about their repetitive reporting of Braunau am Inn as a destination for neo-Nazis, and received no response. The BBC ran another story on the Hitler House on 30th June 2017, referencing that it could become a neo-Nazi shrine, accompanied by Bethany Bell's video. Again.

THERE IS NO SUCH AMBIGUITY FOR THOSE DARK SITES WITH THEIR own media departments. Their job is to project their desired narrative through chosen outlets.

The National September 11 Memorial and Museum's media department was one of several I contacted to ask if they would be willing to answer questions. They wanted to know which other sites had participated, and to what degree. I explained that while some had ignored me, others had provided tea and coffee, but suggested that they themselves should take responsibility for deciding whether or not to engage. If you are 'honoring and remembering', you shouldn't require a media strategy based on the response of others. They subsequently invited me to submit my questions. Having received no response I followed up a month later. They apologised for the delay, adding:

"Thank you for sending these questions but yes, you are correct there will be no further reply."

So what was I asking?

There had been various reports in the media regarding their annual budget and I was seeking clarification. Was it US$60m or US$72m?

Were they intending to tour exhibitions overseas (as Hiroshima, Nagasaki and Auschwitz-Birkenau do), or to open museums in other, unrelated countries, as illustrated with the Nazi Holocaust?

Had they consulted dark tourism academia, and if so why?

Did the paper cranes sold in the gift shop come from Japan and was a percentage from the sales returned there?

It transpired that the Hiroshima museum had no knowledge paper cranes were being sold in the New York gift shop.

Was there a provision for bereaved relatives to be interred in the memorial with those they lost on 9/11, and has this happened?

As mentioned in a previous chapter, former crew of the USS Arizona *can be interred in the wreck.*

Then, the key question: Was there any provision for the next of kin to have the name or image of the deceased *removed* from the memorial and/or museum?

Seriously, who owns the rights to the dead for memorialization? For me this is the pertinent issue for dark tourism. In his inaugural address of January 1961, John F. Kennedy famously said:

"And so, my fellow Americans: ask not what your country can do for you; ask what you can do for your country."

It doesn't matter if you are dead. Under certain circumstances, you can still be useful. To be fair, President Kennedy has led by example; both Arlington cemetery and Dealey Plaza illustrate his legacy to dark tourism.

I hope that the bereaved take great comfort from seeing their loved ones honored and remembered, because they may have no choice. 9/11 is inescapable, ingrained in the date. In New York, the Freedom Tower is a needling reminder. America conducts itself with great dignity on the anniversary, however if you were a bereaved child on 9/11,[3] you will have to live with the nation's memorialization of your personal loss for the rest of your life. This is in part because revenue is going to be continually required to maintain the legacy.

Media departments are not there to engage with critical thinking. Their job is simple: promote and deflect. They do both admirably.

The four email requests I sent to the media department at Auschwitz-Birkenau were all ignored, as were those sent to Tuol Sleng.

What highlighted the resistance of these recognised sites was the assistance offered by their less celebrated contemporaries. Sites with no media spokesperson or Facebook page were incredibly candid, painstakingly helpful, and welcoming. This would include Aberfan, which has no tourist infrastructure whatsoever.

IT WAS NOT JUST SOME OF THE SITES THAT WERE UNWILLING TO engage, but also the travel agency that took me to them in the first place. For this book I made two overseas field trips; one to New York, and one to Cambodia and Japan. For these I used a Flight Centre store in London. The company, founded in Australia in 1982, opened its first office in the UK in 1995, where it now boasts over eighty stores, with another 2,500 strung across Australia, New Zealand, South Africa, the USA, and Canada, making them one of the largest and most successful independent travel retailers 'in the world' according to their website. They've won awards, support charity, and have

---

3) Professor of psychiatry Dr. Cynthia Pfeffer worked with a group of the victims' children for the first two years after 9/11. She noted: "Some of them didn't want to come any more for research, they didn't want to be different. Children think being different is not good."

teamed up with Climate Care, should you wish to offset the emissions from your plane seat. They are my go-to flight provider.

New York was £500. The Tokyo dogleg, via Phnom Penh, and a Japan rail pass just over £1,700. The booker knew I was writing about dark tourism, and offered me a tour of The Killing Fields at Choeung Ek. I declined, preferring to make my own arrangements, but wondered what other dark tours Flight Centre offered. These included a Vietnam Wartime Memories package, the Bridge over the River Kwai, a Top End War History tour of Darwin, the USS *Arizona* Memorial at Pearl Harbor, Sachsenhausen concentration camp, and Gallipoli.

I emailed Fight Centre to enquire how many tours to the Sachsenhausen concentration camp they had sold over the past year, and if they would contribute a statement towards the book regarding their provision of dark tours. They deferred me to their media handlers, Rooster PR, award-winning 'Global Brand Communicators'. Rooster came back, telling me:

"Unfortunately this isn't something that Flight Centre will be able to help with on this occasion."

Dark tourism isn't something the travel industry wishes to publicly discuss, even with those customers such products are aimed at, which, in the case of Choeung Ek, Flight Centre staff were actively trying to sell me.

D ARK SITES HAVE EMBRACED THE VIRTUAL WORLD BEYOND THEIR walls. They now have outreach facilities. The 9/11 Tribute Museum (previously the 9/11 Tribute Center) can "provide an interactive distance learning experience for your school."

You can even tour Auschwitz online, without setting foot in Poland. In 2016 they hosted 164,000 'virtual visitors' from 181 countries. Real life tourists can now book their entry tickets to the camp through Facebook.

There are daily posts from the Auschwitz Memorial, the National September 11 Memorial and Museum, and the 9/11 Tribute Museum, promoting their respective sites to Like, Share, and Donate. Birthdays of the victims are also utilised by the National September 11 Memorial and Museum, who stick a flower in the name on the memorial pool, photograph it, and recycle it as a post for everyone to see. This tribute can now be virtually shown to the bereaved if they are out of state or live abroad.

In this instance social media allows the Memorial Museum, in its capacity as professional mourner, to take over the role of the bereaved[4] and when they in turn pass away, the memory of the victim will be solely owned by

---

4) It was extremely telling that the Hillsborough Family Support Group decided to end their annual Anfield memorial service after twenty-seven years, having received justice for their dead that they'd fought so long and hard for. Margaret Aspinal, who lost her son in the disaster, told the *Liverpool Echo*, "I think now they [the families] need peace." Margaret Aspinal and the Hillsborough families had a choice. They made the decision.

the memorial, acquired seamlessly.

Dark site social media isn't always about Like, Share, and Donate. On New Years Day 2017, the Auschwitz Memorial Facebook page posted a mug shot of Erich Muhsfeldt, under the caption:

"72 years ago... 72 years ago..."

Muhsfeldt, a crematorium chief at Auschwitz-Birkenau, shot tens of prisoners, a practice he continued on those unable to walk when the Flossenbürg camp was evacuated. He was tried, convicted, and hanged in January 1948.

There were 370 shares and over 250 comments in response to this post, many of which expressed sentiments such as, 'hanging was too good for him', and 'Hope he is rotting in hell'. Interestingly one lady commented:

"Good I'm glad. He is disgusting like the rest of the animals that had any part in killing millions of innocent people."

The same lady later returned to the thread to add:

"Should have made him suffer like he did to all those innocent people. Hanging was too good for him. 😡 "

While the original post is arguably educative, it is captioned in a manner

likely to provoke an emotive response. Those replying were not seeking education, rather an opportunity to express anger.[5]

PHOTOGRAPHY AT DARK SITES IS AN EMOTIVE ISSUE, BUT ALONG with buying mementoes and sending postcards, taking photos is what tourists do.

While photographing the cut-through where 25 Cromwell Street[6] once stood provokes comments of 'sick' from both media and local residents, there's not the same moral judgement levied at photographing the 'Arbeit Macht Frei' sign over the gate to Auschwitz I, which is arguably worse.

I'm not entirely sure why tourists, including myself, need to take photographs at dark sites. In Aberfan I was self-conscious about taking a photo, whereas at Auschwitz, among other tourists, it felt encouraged and the

---

5) The Facebook pages for National September 11 Memorial and Museum and the 9/11 Tribute Museum have not carried any posts I'm aware of relating to the hijackers, Islam, or 'Inside Job' conspiracy theories over the eighteen month period I've been receiving their updates.

6) Gloucestershire home of serial killer couple Fred and Rosemary West, who interred their victims in the garden and cellar.

Tourists, Genbaku Dome, Hiroshima Peace Park

camera provided a camouflage of uniformity, confirming my presence as a tourist. After all, a man dressed in black at Auschwitz *not* taking photos might suggest something else.

It is 'selfie' culture that has drawn most criticism, linked to self-promotion and social media. Yet when TV reports from a dark site, talking heads deliver their piece to camera, the site set over their shoulder. In an age where most people report the minutiae of their lives as a matter of course, it's hardly surprising they mirror professional presentation.

In the wake of the Grenfell Tower fire in North Kensington, reporters adopted their trademark pall, the gutted high-rise as backdrop. The local *Metro* newspaper ran an article featuring a resident asking people to desist from taking selfies with the tower.

"This is not the time or place to be taking selfies — in front of a tower block where my friends passed away. I understand people have come to pay their respects... But there are some people who just keep taking photographs and filming all the time like tourists, it's disrespectful."

Grenfell Tower became a dark site. People travelled to make themselves pictorially part of the story, the tower in proportion to their camera phone screens.[7]

There's a way to raise awareness regarding inappropriate behaviour. The seemingly ludicrous signage of the crossed out 'Laughing Man' at Tuol Sleng prison in Phnom Penh set the tone. Tuol Sleng doesn't prohibit people from taking photographs within the grounds, only in selected areas, but I never saw the selfie ritual performed there. The signs are prominently placed, eye-catching, thought-provoking, and people modified their behaviour accordingly.

I personally feel this is preferable to exercises in public shaming, as seen with Yolocaust, covered in a previous chapter, which clearly does not work. Taking photos of people taking selfies at dark sites provides an interesting image and social commentary. However we are approaching a time where we will be taking photographs of people taking photographs of people taking selfies at dark sites, as if it were a sport.

T OURISTS TRAVEL TO ACCESS DARK SITES, WHILE LOCALS LIVE with them. Consequently when a dark site is manufactured on their doorstep there are objections.

In July 2015, the Jack the Ripper museum opened in Cable Street in the East End of London. The owners originally applied for permission to open "the only dedicated resource in the East End to women's history", but then converted the house and basement into the Ripper Museum.

---

7) A poster displayed in the ticket hall at Latimer Road Underground station requested that visitors respect the site where so many lives had been lost, and to refrain from taking photos.

The Laughing Man signage, Tuol Sleng S21 prison.

Jack the Ripper Museum in London's East End.

Understandably there were on-site protests from locals, who felt duped. The controversy attracted considerable media interest, including Fox News, ITV, Sky News, BBC, and Canal+, all of which are now cited on the official Jack the Ripper museum website. The *Guardian* ran an article in which the founder, Mark Palmer-Edgecumbe, vowed to keep the attraction open, despite receiving death threats. For the record, the *Daily Mail* ran three articles in 2016, highlighting both the opposition and the defence.

Protesters paid for a billboard in Cable Street, championing suffragettes over serial killers, held a candlelit vigil, decapitated a 'blood soaked' effigy, and had support from both the Bishop of Stepney[8] and the Mayor of Tower Hamlets. Police were stationed outside the museum as a precaution.

According to historian Fern Riddell, writing in the *Daily Telegraph* of 12th October 2015 under the headline, "Jack the Ripper Museum: This shock attraction left me sick to my stomach", Mark Palmer-Edgecumbe recruited "a seven strong female advisory board" to assuage local opposition, and made it known that the museum employed both a female curator and interior designer, and that four out of seven employees were local working mothers.

Despite the emotive headline, the accompanying online poll, 'Should the Jack the Ripper museum be closed down?', showed 56% *opposed* the motion. The Ripper, and latterly The Krays, are East End crosses, part of the manor's culture, borne in an attempt to compete against the glitzy West End.[9]

Once the stand off between museum and protesters had dissipated, I went to see what all the fuss was about.

Finishing a fag across the street the signs of the protest are still visible. The plaque depicting the stereotypical 'Ripper', a silhouette in top hat, cane, coat and surgical bag, is splattered with pink paint. Hopefully the vandal splash will be left in situ. It makes a statement of how much ill will the attraction provoked.

The lady at the desk is lovely. She says the museum focuses on the 'educational aspect' and asks me what I know about the 'Ripper'? I mention the walking tour, tempted to add that we went to see where the prostitutes were "MURRR — DAAARRRDDD!", but decide that's inappropriate, even if on reflection I believe it to be true. It is the scenes of the murders that have become ingrained, to the point I now take detours through the area to include them. She hands me a paper guide, 'Jack the Ripper Museum and the history

---

8) While the Pope can be used to support selected dark sites, other clergy can be utilised to oppose them.

9) The West End has its own dark history. The Tyburn gallows stood at the junction of Oxford Street, Bayswater Road and Edgware Road. A plaque in a traffic island now marks the spot. Between 40,000–60,000 executions were conducted there over a period of 600 years, until November 1783. Executions were treated as public holidays and attracted large crowds. The rich paid for preferential seating with unobstructed views.

of women in the East End', in return for the £12 admission.

The first floor is a reconstruction of Police Constable Watkins discovering the body of Catherine Eddowes in Mitre Square, complete with sound effects, straw on the floor, and suitable 'horsey' aroma. The second floor is a Victorian sitting room, suggesting how the Ripper's abode *may* have looked, complete with 'Cluedo' exhibits for DIY sleuthing: medical paraphernalia, knives, and a drawing by artistic suspect, Walter Sickert. There are capes for those wishing to adopt period costume.

Floor three is a police station, with the prize exhibits of P. C. Watkins's notebook, handcuffs and truncheon in a glass case, and a waxwork of Chief Inspector Abberline, the detective in charge of the manhunt. The fourth floor is perhaps the most illuminating, showing a typical bed-for-the-night lodging for the poor women of London's East End, set to a scratchy old-time music hall lament. The mildew on the ceiling is a nice touch, although the diorama feels too freshly painted, and to a higher standard than one might expect of a Victorian lodging house for those on their uppers.

The basement 'morgue' displays autopsy photos of the victims, framed and arranged in a cross style format. The paper guide asks for them to be viewed with discretion and respect. I exit through the gift shop. Souvenirs range from pocket money skull key fobs to top hats at £45. Even by London standards the £12 admission feels too rich for a museum that takes less than twenty minutes to view.

However the Jack the Ripper museum is a prime example of *actual* demonstrative opposition towards dark tourism, while most other objections appear tenuous, inflated by commentators to justify writing about the subject.

I wrote to Mark Palmer-Edgecumbe to ask if he'd discuss the controversy surrounding his museum, and what might be the bestsellers from his souvenir range, and received no reply.

THERE IS NO DEFINITIVE ANSWER AS TO WHY PEOPLE VISIT DARK sites. Discounting schoolkids, forced to go, there are still too many dark tourists for a one-size-fits-all answer.

But having researched Aokigahara, and seen the overall picture of what I'd unwittingly been doing for the past forty years, I knew my pursuit of dark tourism inevitably stemmed from childhood. I could even put a date to it. 9th December 1969. The day mum died.

This year the 9th falls on a Friday. Next year will be worse. Saturdays are busy at the cemetery. *And here lies my utter hypocrisy.* Because I take my feet and fins globetrotting to visit the dead, as if a camera and tourist status gives me the justification. At the final resting place of those we've lost is where we are most vulnerable. Anonymity from the gaze of others is everything.

The wardrobe today is easy. Full solid black, head to toe, boots polished the night before. It's only a mile or so from home and I walk through the mizzle. The gates hang open. No need to look over my shoulder here on home soil. To the right the annex is already filled with graves, mostly fashionable black with laser cut gold script, portrait snapshots inlaid, plastic bouquets, and tinkling wind chimes.

Picking a path through the stones I take a graveyard rabbit by surprise. It bolts for cover, deaf to my apology. Surveying the panorama confirms several hundred yards of privacy, even from the wildlife. I crouch down over my grandmother's sparrow-like skeleton, lying below my heels, and brush the leaf detritus from the plinth.

The stone has darkened over time, but the text is still legible. Eventually it will become uniform black, and the brambles I periodically cut back will envelope it. The list will exacerbate, and the cemetery will fit a band with a yellow warning triangle for health and safety. It will become just another old, abandoned gravestone, its resonance and practical usefulness lost once I too am gone.

I don't talk to the stone anymore — I used to, and the tears that ran for years are gone with the realisation that by now life would have taken its natural course. I unwrap twin red roses, aware that they're for no one's benefit other than the cemetery workers, who'll remove them once they've withered to a husk. It's a pact forged with an anonymous gardener to show I haven't forgotten. Since writing about dark tourism I'm relieved my dead died anonymously, and not part of some disaster greater than my own. They're still mine, and mine alone. No institution has hijacked their memory to package and flog to people just like me.

Mum's not here. She's interred in a lawn in the adjacent crematorium. There's no plaque, so she's remembered here, with her mother. When gran died, I couldn't face the funeral. My father took me to the mud-caked grave at the weekend. My floral tribute lay with the others, bedraggled and disappointing.

"Where's mum?"

He pointed to the woman standing indifferently by the car. Difficult to have to remind him that his second wife was not mum, but I did so anyway. When pressed he confessed he didn't know. So the first piece of independent research I conducted was three days later, bunking off school in the pouring rain to return to the crematorium office to make enquiries. They dug out maps and records as my shoes squelched and apologised they could only narrow it down to a numbered lawn. It was a quiet corner, dappled shade when the sun shone, but it wasn't enough.

So when gran passed away my uncle arranged a stone for his mother and her daughter, then retired to Christchurch and bequeathed the visitations to me. It was surreal, seeing the permanence freshly recorded, especially with my name at the bottom after 'Sadly missed by her son'. A part of them stays with you it's true, but a part of you also dies along with them.

Mum died aged thirty-four, during a routine operation. It was decided that it was best if I didn't attend the funeral, and I wonder if my obsession with dark tourism is linked to that, only arriving after it's all over. There was never a suggestion of bereavement counselling. Even if it existed mum wasn't coming back, so ultimately I'd just have to work it out for myself over time. Not that there'd be any, because my father remarried before Christmas 1970, barely a year after being made a widower. Surviving abuse was going to preoccupy my foreseeable future.

IN THEORY A CUT-AND-SHUT FAMILY SHOULD FOLLOW THE MODEL established by the US sitcom of the day, *The Brady Bunch*. The reality was nothing like it. Ruled by an archetypal stepmother who favoured her own elder son, my father averted his eyes, found solace in a bottle, and let me deal with the fallout of his marriage of convenience. The abuse was sexual, physical, and psychological. The perversity lay in concealing the sexual abuse within an already abusive environment, while projecting an air of normality beyond the walls, especially for my grandmother and school, effectively incarcerating myself in a panopticon of my own design.

At least while I was being targeted, they didn't take their frustrations out on each other. It was like living in a NSPCC Christmas advert everyday.[10]

And it was Christmas when I took my first steps into dark tourism, during a contrived family gathering in Loughton. Oppressive central heating and simmering sincerity sent me off in a teenage strop, downhill, feet running away with no thought of direction. The cemetery appeared from nowhere. It matched my mood but once inside the prevailing calm diffused everything.

Cemeteries are peaceful places for contemplation in the face of an inevitable end. Your pace slows to reflect respect. There are names, ages and eulogies to read, so you slow even more.

Eventually you find the child graves, which pose the question: how much time do you have left, and what are you going to do with it? I spent hours inside, with hell to pay on my return, but I didn't feel sorry for myself anymore, and knew where to go if I did.

By the time I left school the storm on the home front had mostly ridden itself out. Subjugation must be equally exhausting for the enforcer, year upon year. I'd started labouring and stayed out as much as possible. With hindsight I should have packed my bags and abandoned my self-respect. It wasn't

---

10) The NSPCC (National Society for the Prevention of Cruelty to Children) estimates that one in seven children live with domestic violence at some point in their childhood, and that one in twenty children are sexually abused. The figure for sexual abuse is likely higher, as most cases go unreported and undetected.

planned, but it happened the other way around.

The cherry blossom in the street was falling. I snapped, struck first, second, and last. It was all over inside three minutes. I left without my vinyl collection, but recovered self-respect. As the black sheep I never returned, never took another beating, or thankfully administered one, and slept soundly in a bedsit flat with a clear conscience, the bedroom door wide open.

I DON'T PARTICIPATE IN DARK TOURISM TO FEEL REUNITED WITH my dead, because I know where they are. Visits to the grave have changed over time. It used to be that other than the 9th I'd only go when there was a need. Trips are far more frequent now I'm not motivated by self-interest.

Everyone struggles with bereavement, even if they have support, be it friends, family, or therapy. But dark sites have given me perspective. It is those places where there has been sudden and unexpected loss of life, intrinsically linked to a loss of love, where I've found empathy and solace. It's no coincidence that the firefighters' memorial on the wall of Ten House struck such a chord in recognising "those who carry on".

There would be no compulsion to visit sites if it was distressing to do so. It would be disingenuous to claim I take nothing positive from the experience, and am there solely out of respect. Some dark sites, such as Auschwitz-Birkenau and 9/11, have been intentionally developed, becoming legitimate tourist destinations for millions in the process, in turn negating the need for any individual to justify their visit.

I wondered if I'd engaged unknowingly in dark tourism as a means of self-help bereavement counselling, and contacted several professional bodies to enquire if they'd encountered this practice previously. None had, but the National Counseling Society offered to ask members through its monthly newsletter. When the responses were forwarded my question seemingly hadn't been read through, or understood. I received a handful of links to articles on dark tourism, none that related to my enquiry, most of which I'd previously seen.

Imagine for a moment that not every dark tourist visits sites in a ghoulish capacity as if attending a freakshow, but that some have come for peace, reassurance, and motivation. What if instead of branding tourists as 'messengers of remembrance' for self-aggrandizement, there was an awareness that they may have come because of their own continuing story, or as part of someone else's, rather than for the narrative the site is there to project? What if, like the 9/11 Tribute Museum, and Ten House, sites realised they could be there to help?

Dark sites have kept me going ever since I walked into Loughton cemetery. After all, no thirteen-year-old should be reading Émile Durkheim's *Suicide: A Study in Sociology*. Thankfully, ironically, I never finished it.

SETTING ASIDE THE WRECKS, WHICH OVER TIME WILL DISINTEGRATE and be supplanted by others, the five major dark tourism sites visited in this book have an interesting timeline and relevance.

Auschwitz-Birkenau records a specific event in time that is receding. Although soon to lose its connection to living memory, it will remain the cornerstone of the Holocaust by re-creating survivors in a virtual reality format. Testimony will continue to be delivered through screens, to schools, and to the general public with an artefact tour. Anti-Semitism and Holocaust denial will continue to be highlighted to ensure what happened at Auschwitz-Birkenau and elsewhere remains relevant in contemporary times.

Whilst Tuol Sleng and Choeung Ek both relate back to a specific event, they have not been exported or virtually packaged in the manner of Auschwitz-Birkenau. The memorial in Seattle apart, you have to go to Cambodia to experience their genocide. Cambodia has also taken the step of warning visitors to their sites that genocide can happen to anyone, anywhere.

9/11 is a chronological watershed. We now live in a 'post 9/11' world. As the most recent of the five sites it will be interesting to see how both the National September 11 Memorial and Museum and the 9/11 Tribute Museum develop, with the latter now positioning itself with an emphasis on promoting volunteering. I did ask the 9/11 Tribute Museum if this move was a way of attracting additional funding, but received no reply.

Highgate Cemetery tour, London.

Chernobyl has no concerns about its relevance in the modern world. It's exiled us for 20,000 years, and will comfortably see us out, even after its testimonial buildings have perished to decay, the ruins choked by weeds.

Which leaves Hiroshima and Nagasaki. Cannily they are the only sites that have risen from the ashes and subsequently reinvented themselves under the promotion of world peace, which none of the others advocate. They are looking forward. This ensures both cities and their memorials remain relevant and necessary.

The two other sites, Aberfan and Aokigahara, stand out. Although physically and historically very different, they share something in common. There is an adjudication that can be posed to any destination to discern whether it is a dark site, or a dark tourist site:

Have we been invited to come and stare?

THE PHOTOGRAPHS CAME TO ME IN BOXES AND AN OLD CADBURY'S chocolate biscuit tin in the summer of 2015. I had no idea that so many existed, and that even those I suspected had once existed, had survived. Up to that point I only had three photographs of mum: one from her wedding day, the portrait that complemented her CV, and one of her as a teenager, walking a seaside promenade with her parents. Now I had everything, her whole life before I was born, one I'd been oblivious to. It took

I AM THE DARK TOURIST

H. E. Sawyer. Photo: Paul Soso. Stylist: Florence Druart

time to go through them and it was emotionally draining, especially the ones where I was only a few months old, cradled in her arms. The grieving process that had been suspended by life getting in the way began again, and I grizzled like a six-year-old, trapped in the body of a middle aged man. John Lewis did good business with the subsequent photo frames.

It is an unconventional pursuit, visiting the places death has touched on the map. Some sites have engaged in promotion to encourage us to come. Others have tried to distance themselves, and would prefer that we didn't come at all. The dead cannot stand in the way of the living. That fate befalls the bereaved. Dark tourism will be an ongoing concern for those whose loss culminates in a memorial-cum-attraction. For others it presents an opportunity.

There is a delicate balance between remembrance and taking advantage. The memorialized dead are perfect employees: no union, toilet breaks, holidays or fatigue, and unless they can be removed from a wall they adorn in perpetuity, no alternative. We, as dark tourists, are far from perfect, which is why I suspect there is collaboration between some academics and certain providers with the intent to transform us into the compliant 'messengers of remembrance' they'd prefer us to be.

The tag is just that; a tag, and one I can live with, which is just as well after forty years. It has, however, changed the way I approach sites, looking beyond the memorial and exhibits at the infrastructure, the education, and the integrity with which the dead are packaged and presented for public consumption and consideration.

At the outset I considered whether there was a valid reason for writing this book, conscious that it was a self-indulgent pursuit. Yet research revealed a resistance within much of dark tourism to engage, and this itself provided justification. There's little value writing about a subject unless there is someone who would prefer it if you did not.

Reflecting on my personal loss, I realised that had been the real reason (and the best possible reason) all along.

The paradox is, following death to the four corners and the depths has enabled me to carry on.

This is the reason I am the dark tourist.

I suspect I'm not the only one.

Torschlusspanik

ACKNOWLEDGEMENTS

I N A BOOK OFTEN CHARACTERISED BY THOSE UNWILLING OR UNABLE to engage, it's gratifying that there are so many people to thank. Due to the static I encountered, my thanks are truly heartfelt.

Ripperologist Phillip Hutchinson, who set the tone with his honesty.

Christopher Collins, who gave invaluable feedback. Although I didn't always agree, I always listened.

Linda Masat for her understanding and encouragement to order my thoughts. That I subsequently structured this book on a napkin in Manhattan was, for me, the perfect cliché.

Rie Nakanishi of the Hiroshima Peace Memorial Museum.

Mike Parrish of the Kelvedon Hatch Secret Nuclear Bunker.

Peggy Reeve for being a wonderful sounding board.

Jeremy Scott of Swan Books for his insight and advice.

Debi Zornes for introducing me to Sissy, and all the great times we shared with her, and Helen Stoddart for the logistics and vodka tasting in Krakow.

Dylan Harris of Lupine Travel for the foreword to this book, and who together with Igor Bodnarchuk supplied all the logistics for Chernobyl.

Professor Iain McLean and Martin Johnes for their invaluable advice.

The Laxton National Holocaust Centre and Museum in Nottingham.

The Weiner Library and Auschwitz-Birkenau, for assisting with my research into Sissy's testimony.

The ladies at Merthyr Tydfil Library.

Carron Williams at the Aberfan Community Library.

David Davies JP, Chairman, Aberfan Memorial Charity.

Florence Druart for realising my imagination with the front cover concept, and for being the first link in an improbable chain.

Lukas Zpira for being the second link in the chain.

Mikeke Tre for being the third link in the chain.

Adam Tuck, who provided the logistics, unfailing hospitality, and insight into Japanese culture from Saitama to Aokigahara. I didn't get lost amongst the trees, but found a friend instead.

Garth Marenghi for the advice — hitting the keys in the right order *is* indeed the trick.

David Kerekes of Headpress. There was only ever going to be one publisher for this book, and I am indebted for the confidence you have invested in me to write it.

SOURCES

Bibliography

Dark Tourism: The Attraction of Death and Disaster. John Lennon and Malcolm Foley. CENGAGE Learning (2010)

The Darker Side of Travel: The Theory and Practice of Dark Tourism. Edited by Richard Sharpley and Philip R. Stone. Channel View Publications (2009)

The Dark Tourist. Dom Joly. Simon & Schuster (2010)

Inside 9-11: What Really Happened. The reporters, writers and editors of *Der Spiegel* magazine. St. Martin's Press (2002)

The Holocaust Industry (Second Edition). Norman G. Finkelstein. Verso (2003)

S.S. Yongala Townsville's Titanic. Max Gleeson. M. Gleeson (2000)

The Complete Maus. Art Spiegelman. Penguin Books (2003)

Hiroshima Nagasaki. Paul Ham. Black Swan (2013)

Hiroshima. John Hersey. Penguin Classics (2001)

Cliffs of Despair: A Journey to the Edge. Tom Hunt. Random House (2006)

London's Cemeteries. Darren Beach. Metro Publications (2006)

Survival in the Killing Fields. Haing Ngor with Roger Warner. Constable & Robinson (2003)

Aberfan: Government & Disasters. Iain McLean and Martin Johnes. Welsh Academic Press (2000)

Aberfan, Struggling Out of the Darkness: A Survivor's Story. Gaynor Madgwick. Valley & Vale Community Arts Ltd (1996)

When the Wind Blows. Raymond Briggs. Penguin (1982)

Tales From the Suicide Forest. El Torres. Amigo Comics (2016)

Filmography

The Battle of Chernobyl. Thomas Johnson. Play Film (2006)

Auschwitz: The Nazis & 'The Final Solution'. Laurence Rees. BBC Worldwide Ltd (2005)

Austerlitz. Sergey Loznitsa. Imperativ Film/Beauftragter der Bundesregierung für Angelegenheiten der Kultur und der Medien (BKM)/German Federal Film Board (2016)

Year Zero: The Silent Death of Cambodia. David Munro & John Pilger. Associated Television (1979)

S21: The Khmer Rouge Killing Machine. Rithy Panh. Arte France Cinema/Institut National del'Audiovisuel (2003)

The Bridge. Eric Steel. Easy There Tiger Productions/First Stripe Productions/RCA (2006)

Threads. Mick Jackson. BBC/Nine Network/Western-World Television Inc. (1984)

Let's Be Evil. Martin Owen. Ghost House Pictures/Posterity Pictures (2016)

The Forest. Jason Zada. Gramercy Pictures (2016)

The Sea of Trees. Gus Van Sant. Bloom/Gil Netter Productions (2015)

Dr. No. Terence Young. Eon Productions/United Artists (1962)

Discography

Holidays In The Sun. The Sex Pistols. Virgin Records/VS 191 (1977)

Russians. Sting. A&M Records/390 063-7 (1985)

Enola Gay. Orchestral Manoeuvres in the Dark. Dindisc/DIN 22 (1980)

Hiroshima Mon Amour. Ultravox. Island Records WIP 6691 (1981)

Dancing With Tears In My Eyes. Ultravox. Chrysalis UV 1 (1984)

Let's All Make A Bomb (from the album *Penthouse and Pavement*). Heaven 17. Virgin Records V2208 (1981)

Let's Dance. David Bowie. EMI EA 152 (1983)

Two Tribes. Frankie Goes to Hollywood. ZTT ZTAS 3 (1984)

Ceremony. New Order. Factory Records/FAC 33/12 (1981)

The Wall. Pink Floyd. Harvest/SHDW 411 (1979)

Closer. Joy Division. Factory Records/FACT 25 (1980)

Author biography

H. E. Sawyer has been traveling to dark sites for forty years, although he's only recently become aware of this. When he's not writing he's painting, or hiding in plain sight behind a mask at Torture Garden.

INDEX

A HEADPRESS BOOK
First published by Headpress in 2018

{e} headoffice@headpress.com

I AM THE DARK TOURIST
Travels to the Darkest Sites on Earth

The publisher would like to thank Jen Wallis and Ganymede Foley.

A CIP catalogue record for this book is available from the British Library

ISBN 978-1-909394-58-2 (paperback)
ISBN 978-1-909394-59-9 (ebook)
NO-ISBN (hardback)

10 9 8 7 6 5 3 2 1

Headpress. B**k publisher. Pop and Unpop Culture.
Exclusive NO-ISBN special edition hardbacks and other items
of interest are available at HEADPRESS.COM